ACCOMMODATING DIFFERENCE

Evaluating supported housing for vulnerable people

David Clapham

D1549381

P

First published in Great Britain in 2017 by

Policy Press
University of Bristol
1-9 Old Park Hill
Bristol
BS2 8BB
UK
t: +44 (0)117 954 5940
pp-info@bristol.ac.uk
www.policypress.co.uk

North America office:
Policy Press
c/o The University of Chicago Press
1427 East 60th Street
Chicago, IL 60637, USA
t: +1 773 702 7700
f: +1 773 702 9756
sales@press.uchicago.edu
www.press.uchicago.edu

© Policy Press 2017

British Library Cataloguing in Publication Data
A catalogue record for this book is available from the British Library

Library of Congress Cataloging-in-Publication Data
A catalog record for this book has been requested

ISBN 978-1-4473-0635-1 paperback
ISBN 978-1-4473-0634-4 hardcover
ISBN 978-1-4473-2108-8 ePub
ISBN 978-1-4473-2109-5 Mobi
ISBN ISBN 978-1-4473-0636-8 ePdf

The right of David Clapham to be identified as author of this work has been asserted by him
in accordance with the Copyright, Designs and Patents Act 1988.

Cover design by DoubleDagger
Front cover image: istock
Printed and bound in Great Britain by CPI Group (UK) Ltd,
Croydon, CR0 4YY
Policy Press uses environmentally responsible print partners

This book is dedicated to
Ravi, Lizzie and Hannah,
without whom I would never have had the
dedication and motivation to complete it

Contents

Acknowledgements

I am indebted to many people who have helped in the production of this book. The ideas have been formulated over 30 years of teaching about supported housing to students on Master's housing courses at the universities of Glasgow and Cardiff. The debates with these students (some of whom worked in the supported housing sector) have been invaluable. The title of the book *Accommodating difference* was first coined by Bridget Franklin, who was a colleague at Cardiff University, and this was the title of the module I taught at Cardiff for many years. My ideas on supported housing were also formulated through research on the topic undertaken with Bridget Franklin and Chris Allen at Cardiff, as well as Moira Munro in Glasgow, and Delia Lomax and Gina Netto at Heriot Watt University.

During the writing of the book I have visited supported housing schemes in both Britain and Sweden and I am grateful to the many people who made these visits possible. I was able to make the visits in Sweden because of my position as Visiting Professor at IBF at Uppsala University and I would like to thank Terry Hartig, Bo Bengtsson and Irena Molena as well as other colleagues for their support during my time there. A number of colleagues have read and made important comments on all or part of the book, including Marianne Abrahamson, Ingrid Sahlin, Marie Nordfeldt, Janet Smith, Hannu Ruonavaara, Marcus Knutagard, Bo Bengtsson, Terry Hartig and an anonymous referee. I am immensely grateful for their time and patience, in particular in helping me to understand the situation in Sweden. Any remaining mistakes and misunderstandings are of course my responsibility.

Finally I am grateful to Emily Watt and Laura Vickers at Policy Press for their support throughout the long gestation period of the book.

Some parts of Chapter Two have been reproduced from my 2010 article 'Happiness, well-being and housing policy', *Policy and Politics* 38(2), 253–67 and I am grateful for the permission from Policy Press for this. Also some parts of Chapter Three have been reproduced from my 2011 article 'The embodied use of the material home: An affordance approach', *Housing, Theory and Society* 28(4), 360–76 and I am grateful for the permission from Taylor & Francis to do this.

Introduction

The overarching aim of this book is to explore the objectives, philosophies and outcomes of supported housing in different contexts. The exploration is intended to further our understanding of an often-neglected topic in housing research and to stimulate further research in this area. But the book is also intended to share what is known about supported housing in a way that helps the planning and running of supported housing in the future and so improves the well-being of vulnerable people. The focus of the book is on the impact that supported housing makes on the well-being of those who live in it and whether some forms of supported housing are better at doing this than others.

Here, supported housing is defined very generally as accommodation with support provided, whether specifically linked to the accommodation or to the person living there. Support encompasses help with everyday tasks and can include practical help with cleaning and food preparation as well as social work, health care and other forms of support such as training or occupational therapy. The settings included in this wide definition range from institutions such as nursing homes for older people to people living in their own homes and receiving support provided to them. In between is a variety of different forms of supported housing that include sheltered housing for older people, hostels, group homes and so on. A fuller discussion of the different types of supported housing and the care and support provided is given in Chapter One.

In the US a distinction is sometimes made between 'supportive housing' and 'supported housing' (see Lipton et al, 2000; Henwood et al, 2013). The bases of the distinction vary according to different commentators, but include factors such as the permanency of the housing and the philosophy of the provision, including the emphasis on training and empowerment. The result of the debate seems to be a confusing and not particularly useful distinction. Why use a difficult binary distinction when there are other more useful ways of indicating difference between forms of provision? We return to this in Chapter One. Suffice it to say here that the definition in this book includes both of these forms.

The second important definitional issue that must be confronted at this stage is the definition of support. The different elements of support will be considered in more detail in Chapter One. Throughout the book the term 'support' will be used to denote a wide variety of functions, including those provided by social services agencies, health agencies, as well as voluntary organisations and families and friends. Sometimes the term 'care' may be used to denote the formal provision by health and social services that is defined here as being a part of the overall support provided to people. There is a literature on the differences between the terms 'care' and 'support' in terms of the type of and philosophy of provision, which will be considered in Chapter One. Suffice it to say here that both categories are included in our very broad definition of 'support' used in this book.

The book was stimulated by the relative neglect of this area in housing research, which contrasts with its importance in the lives of many vulnerable people. Therefore the book is intended as a review of the research that has been undertaken and a stimulus to further research. The objectives of the book have been severely constrained by the lack of research evidence. Even in the more popular research areas, such as supported housing for older people, Croucher et al (2006) note the lack of research that takes an evaluative stance rather than just being a description of a particular form of provision. A major objective of the book is to provide a framework to guide future research, which needs to be focused on the impact of supported housing on the well-being of vulnerable people, and the following chapters will show how little is known about this to date. But research also needs to focus on the philosophies and discourses underpinning supported housing. Important questions include: Why is it being provided? What are its objectives? Who is meant to benefit and in what ways? The answers to these questions may seem to be self-evident but, on close inspection, this does not always prove to be the case. Exploration of the policy context of supported housing shows that the existence of provision and the forms it takes are influenced by particular discourses or understandings of the nature of the problems of vulnerable people and of appropriate ways of tackling them. These discourses may be contested and may not be shared by the residents of supported housing themselves. Therefore any study of supported housing should be aware of the context within which provision is located and the underlying discourses that shape it.

Another stimulus for the book was the realisation that some supported housing continues to be provided, sometimes at great cost, even when research evidence and the views of residents seemed to indicate that the provision does not meet the preferences or the needs of residents, or provide good value for money. An example may be the provision of sheltered and extra-care housing for older people in Britain. At the same time, there is a policy presumption against institutions, when it is clear that many older people need and want to live in them. So important questions for the book are, on what basis are some forms of supported housing promoted by government policies and why?

Also, there is a tendency in policy towards supported housing to promote particular forms as panaceas for the needs of a particular group, whether it is older people or young homeless people. I have long been a critic of the tendency to categorise and stereotype the needs of particular groups in this way (see Clapham and Smith, 1990; Clapham, 2005). So a crucial theme of this book is the need to acknowledge the differences between people in their perceptions, attitudes, attributes and lifestyles, as well as in their material resources, given that inequality is becoming the predominant feature of many western countries including Britain and Sweden.

Another reason for writing the book was the desire to encourage more debate and innovation in the way the impact of supported housing on the lives of the residents is measured. There are a number of possible ways of doing this, but some of them do not seem to relate to the lives that people wish to live or to be sensitive to the differences between people. A fundamental assumption in the book is that supported housing is primarily justified on the basis of achieving increases in the subjective well-being of those who live in it. As we shall see in the book, some discourses and models of supported housing are predicated on the assumption that society knows better than the individual what is best for them. This approach is criticised here on moral grounds and the focus is primarily on what is best for the individual as they define it. This does not deny the existence of 'conditionality' in access to supported housing, and progress in or from it. By this is meant the desire to change the behaviour or attitudes of the resident as a condition of entry or progress from a particular setting. We shall see in Chapter Seven how the 'staircase model' for homeless people in Sweden has been based on this approach. The achievement of behavioural change can be linked to subjective well-being if it is shown that the change is in the best interests of the person concerned and so can be justified by reference to the increased well-being that would result. This case is stronger if any behavioural changes deemed to be necessary are agreed by the support staff with the resident and are seen by the resident themselves as in their best interests. Therefore, the book advocates the use of the concept of subjective well-being as an appropriate tool for evaluating the impact of supported housing on those who live in it, while being aware of the existence of social control objectives. Nevertheless, the concept of well-being needs further development before it can be used in a useful and meaningful way in this context and the book is intended to be a contribution to this process.

The focus on well-being is also considered to be vital in reviving political support for public provision of services such as supported housing. Judt (2010) is critical of some features of traditional state services that did not give primacy to the individual consumer. It is argued in this book that the use of a concept of well-being as a goal of public policy in general, as well as in particular public services such as supported housing, is crucial to the survival and growth of social welfare services and to the life chances of those who depend on them, because it places at the forefront of attention the impact of policies and services on individuals, in terms of their identities and lifestyles.

The final aim of the book was to bring some evidence to help policy makers and providers to make judgements about the appropriate forms of supported housing that should be provided. Two themes of the book are the need for flexibility to meet individual needs and preferences, and the importance of the attachments to homes and neighbourhoods in the lives of individuals. Some forms of supported housing are better in coping with these elements than others and it is argued that these are the forms that should be prioritised in the future.

The context for the exploration of supported housing in the book is the experience in Britain and Sweden. Britain was chosen because it is the location where I have studied and taught about supported housing for over 30 years and so the area I know best. Sweden was chosen to illustrate differences and similarities between different contexts and was the country where I also have some knowledge of supported housing. Although Britain and Sweden are similar in many ways in their policies and practices towards supported housing, and have a long history of provision, there are differences that help to shed light on some interesting and important elements. Seeing supported housing in different contexts allows us to show the importance that this context plays in influencing the form of provision. It allows us to question what may be taken for granted in one country and not in the other. If experiences are shared (say, of one form of provision), then it may show that there are inherent flaws or advantages in that form of provision that may be important for the future. However, there are many problems, which we will engage with, in reaching simple conclusions from the study of just two countries as well as in transferring lessons from one country to the other. Nevertheless, the exercise can be illuminating and lead us to useful conclusions. It is always difficult to undertake research in a country that is not one's place of residence. I was particularly hindered in Sweden by my lack of any Swedish language proficiency. Therefore, the book has been restricted to the use of English-language literature, supplemented with interviews with policy makers, practitioners and academics in Sweden, and visits to a number of supported housing schemes.

Supported housing is provided for people with a wide range of needs and it is impossible to cover all of these in the space allocated to this book. Therefore, the focus in the book is on older people, homeless people and people with disabilities. Although a theme of the book is the problematic nature of the categorisation of needs, it was recognised that most supported housing provision and policy are organised in this way and so it was decided to follow convention. These three categories were chosen to reflect as wide as possible coverage of different forms of supported housing, and of different needs and lifestyles. However, it does not cover the whole of the field and this must be borne in mind. Nevertheless, the coverage does draw out interesting and important differences between supported housing provision for the different categories that shed considerable light on the objectives and outcomes.

Outline of the book

Chapter One sets the context for the rest of the book by describing the main similarities and differences in forms of supported housing. First it examines the definition of support and looks at the many different kinds of support that can be provided and their objectives. A key element of this is the fact that support may be aimed at achieving social objectives by changing behaviour to accord with societal norms. In other words, well-being may be defined in a way that emphasises societal discourses that may conflict with the subjective well-being defined by the resident. For example, young people may be expected to get a job and abstain from drugs before they are judged to be worthy of permanent and secure housing. It is a core argument of the book that the subjective well-being of the resident is the primary objective of supported housing and that practices of social control can best be accepted if they impact on subjective well-being and have the agreement of the resident. Nevertheless, it is important to identify and examine social control elements of supported housing and be aware of their impact.

The chapter then focuses on the different models of supported housing by identifying the diverse ways in which different forms of accommodation can be mixed with various forms of support. A number of models are identified, and they are described and some general issues that influence their impact are identified. This discussion is intended to set the scene for the more detailed discussion of supported housing models for particular 'categories' of people in the following chapters.

The analysis of supported housing begins in Chapter Two with a review of the philosophies, concepts and discourses that underpin provision and form the basis for the evaluation of its impact. Discourses are situated in particular social and political settings and so the chapter starts with a discussion of the nature of postmodern societies with an emphasis on diversity, identity and lifestyle. It is argued that the individualism and diversity of postmodern societies places emphasis on the need for personal responses to individual problems and for people to be in a position to take control over their lives. The focus then shifts to the discourses that have shaped supported housing, although a more detailed description is offered in chapters that consider particular officially designated categories of need. Most emphasis here is placed on the discourse of well-being, which forms the basis of the evaluation framework used in the book to examine particular supported housing forms or models. The history of the well-being discourse in studies of health inequality and happiness is described, and the underlying rationales for the discourse assessed. It is argued that the discourse is of most use if the psychological concepts that underpin it are uncovered and operationalised. The main concepts of personal control, identity and self-esteem, and social relations are described and applied to the situation of supported housing. The final part of the chapter examines the way that the discourses and concepts have been used to assess the outcomes of supported housing, either through inspection by regulatory agencies or through performance measurement regimes. Tools such as the Activities of Daily Living (ADL) scales are introduced and examined. It is concluded that the discourse of well-being and its underlying concepts are useful tools in the assessment of different supported housing options, whether this is at the level of an individual judging which option is best for them, or at the level of a government agency trying to assess the best value for money. However, well-being has been used most often in a social care setting, whereas supported housing involves both support and accommodation. Homes and neighbourhoods are important locales for the achievement of well-being and so need to be considered in any evaluation. Therefore, it is argued that more emphasis needs to be placed on the attachment between people and their homes and neighbourhoods in the evaluation framework.

The next two chapters focus on the locales of respectively home and neighbourhood. In Chapter Three the research on the relationship between people and their houses and homes is reviewed. It is clear that our homes mean much to us: they are an important symbol of our identity and enable us to live our preferred lifestyle. However, there is a distinction in thinking about homes between the social and the physical dimensions. Homes do carry important meanings for us, but they are also the physical locale of many of our daily activities. The chapter puts forward a perspective based on the concept of 'affordances' to provide a holistic analysis that includes both the physical and meaning elements of a house.

In the following chapter (Chapter Four) the same 'affordances' approach is used to analyse the relationship between people and their neighbourhoods. Again the theme is the need to integrate analysis of the physical attributes of a neighbourhood (for example its amenities and accessibility) with its meaning elements, such as the potential for a feeling of belonging and attachment. A key element of the discussion in this chapter is the important issue of segregation. Vulnerable people are likely to live in neighbourhoods with many other vulnerable people. This may be because of a choice to live near to people like themselves, or it could be because of a lack of choice for financial or other reasons. The key question to be posed is whether vulnerable people's well-being is improved by living in a balanced community or in a segregated one. The chapter argues that there is no universal answer to this question as it depends on individual preferences, situations and lifestyles.

The chapter concludes by bringing together the discussions of well-being, and the locales of home and neighbourhood to form a framework that will be used in the rest of the book to evaluate the outcomes of supported housing.

Chapter Five begins the examination of particular supported housing models by explaining the focus of the book on two particular countries. It explains the reasons for choosing an international comparative approach and justifies the choice of Britain and Sweden as the two countries studied here. Reference is made to the welfare regimes approach that seeks to identify and explain the differences in welfare expenditures and policies between countries. In this analysis, Britain and Sweden are usually placed under different categories, with Sweden being classified under the social democratic model and Britain under the neoliberal one. However, it is argued that there are many similarities and differences between the two countries and that both show elements of each regime. This conclusion is justified through a description of the main support and housing policies in the two countries. There are many similarities in support policies, although Britain has gone further in the directions of marketisation and personalisation. In housing, both systems are 'monstrous hybrids', with elements of market and state provision and regulation that often combine to create problems, such as low housing supply and inadequate accommodation, as well as unequal distribution and segregation, that can make life difficult for some vulnerable households.

In the following chapters, the evaluation framework, based on the concept of well-being and the locales of home and neighbourhood, is used as a way of structuring the analysis of supported housing in Britain and Sweden. Three 'groups' are examined in turn. Chapter Six focuses on older people. It reviews the changing discourses, identities and lifestyles that characterise this group, before examining the housing and support policies towards them in Britain and Sweden. This is followed by an evaluation of the supported housing options available in the two countries using the headings of 'home', 'neighbourhood' and 'well-being' to structure the available evidence. The same approach is used to examine the situation of homeless people in Chapter Seven and people with a disability in Chapter Eight.

Chapter Nine concludes the book by drawing some general conclusions about the value of supported housing in general and its different models from the analysis of the previous three chapters. The chapter begins with a comparison of Britain and Sweden. The analysis started in Chapter Five with a discussion of welfare regimes and the position of the two countries in this categorisation. This section reflects on the welfare regimes approach and comments on the position and trajectories of the two countries in the light of the evidence presented in the book.

The chapter continues with a discussion of the discourses that are associated with policy and provision, and reflects on similarities and differences between the two countries. Also, the chapter focuses on examples showing the impact of discourse in shaping policy and provision, and the agents that attempt to influence this. The section attempts to answer some questions on the existence of particular forms of provision. For example, why have extra-care housing and foyers been adopted in Britain despite being expensive forms of provision that do not maximise the well-being of residents? In Sweden, the continuance of the staircase model as the cornerstone of provision for homeless people is discussed. Although it is under threat from the Housing First approach, it is still the predominant way of thinking about supported housing provision.

The focus of the chapter then moves onto the well-being framework that is used in the book to evaluate forms of supported housing. This section reflects on the usefulness of this framework and its future application. It is concluded that subjective well-being is a very useful framework for decisions at the level of national or local policy, or for individuals to use in choosing what is best for them, although the framework needs further development.

The penultimate section considers the findings in the individual chapters on the evaluation of the different models of supported housing. In each of the individual chapters conclusions have been reached on appropriate forms of supported housing for the people considered there. In this section the focus is on the general models and the attempt is made to determine whether some models are better than others across the field. This leads to a final surmise on the future of supported housing. Based on the findings here, what should it look like in the future and are there general philosophies that should underpin policy and provision?

It is argued that the overriding emphasis in future policy and practice should be on the need for flexibility to meet individual needs. This is best met through models that do not tie particular elements of support to particular accommodation, because this allows support to be flexible and responsive to changes in individual preferences and needs. Models that support people flexibly in their own homes are usually preferable to those that require people to move from their preferred home and neighbourhood, although there is a place for both, especially where the existing accommodation or neighbourhood is inappropriate. Most flexibility can be achieved by models based on a 'core and cluster' approach that can link particular accommodation easily to different levels of support or to domiciliary forms of provision.

The analysis in the book was hindered by the lack of research in this area and the book ends with a plea for further work on this relatively unfashionable subject in academic and policy circles.

ONE

Models of supported housing

The subject matter of this book is supported housing, where accommodation and support are linked together in some way. There are many different ways in which these elements can be linked together and the aim of this chapter is to briefly review the main ways and to begin an assessment of the issues that have emerged in relation to their use. An assessment of the impact of the different models of supported housing on the well-being of residents cannot be undertaken at this general level because of the different factors that may impact on different individuals and groups. Therefore, the options for different people will be discussed in more detail in later chapters that refer to particular groups identified by professionals as in need of supported housing. This chapter sets the general context for the chapters that follow.

The discussion begins with a brief review of the main factors involved in both the accommodation and support elements of supported housing. Accommodation may vary in its form and facilities, and the support provided may vary considerably in its nature and objectives. Also, the way that the two are linked may be different and may have a bearing on the service provided and the experience of residents.

The main focus of the chapter is a description of the different forms of supported housing and a general discussion of the factors that may influence the well-being of the people who live in them. The discussion is framed by the categorisation of different supported housing forms into four groups: shared living; own housing with linked communal facilities; core and cluster models; and domiciliary models. The examples used in the discussion of these categories are the ones that most often feature in housing and support provision in Britain and Sweden, which are the two countries considered later in the book. They were also chosen because they have particular resonance for the groups considered in more detail in later chapters, such as older people, homeless people and those with health problems. The choice of examples was also based on providing a reasonable coverage of the possible ways of linking housing and support. The discussion here is in very general terms and will focus on the context within which the particular model is used, the accommodation provided and the support services. Some important general issues that have arisen in consideration of the particular form of provision are raised. The discussion starts with shared housing, which is the closest to institutional living, because this is the form that many governments have been trying to move away from. Despite this policy preference, there are still many people living and receiving support in this type of setting.

Accommodation

The accommodation element of supported housing may take many forms. At one extreme will be shared accommodation, such as in some institutions, hostels or group homes. This may consist of communal dormitories where each resident has just their own bed and no private space, to situations where each resident has their own room and en suite bathroom facilities, or, in-between, the situation where residents may share a room with one or two others. Activities such as cooking, eating, and watching television may be undertaken in private or communal space. In some supported housing, residents have self-contained accommodation in the form of a house or apartment and so the variation is wide.

The facilities of the accommodation may also vary. Some rooms or apartments may be the same as mainstream housing, but others may be specially adapted, with features such as wide door spaces and corridors in order to manoeuvre a wheelchair, or lower kitchen worktops, or adapted bathroom facilities with grab rails, and possibly hoists, to enable residents to get on and off the toilet or in and out of a bath or shower. Some supported housing schemes will have communal facilities, such as guest bedrooms, hobby rooms or gyms, or rooms for socialising. Some may have spaces for the support activities, whereas in others residents may go elsewhere for activities such as training or lunch clubs and so on.

Schemes may also vary in the extent to which residents have rights over their accommodation. Any rights may be permanent or, alternatively, may be temporary, limited by time or conditions that may focus on adherence to certain rules of behaviour. For example, residents of a hostel may be evicted if they consume drugs or alcohol on the premises. The rights that residents possess will vary according to the tenure of their accommodation. In many supported housing schemes the predominant tenure is rental, in which residents have a lease. However, owner occupation may be the predominant form in some models, such as forms of retirement housing like retirement villages in Britain. In Sweden cooperative tenure is common in some forms of supported housing. However, some residents may not have full tenancy or ownership rights over their accommodation. In Britain residents are often given a residency licence that gives limited rights of occupation and often contains clauses that include residency conditions. Licences are more common in shared housing, and the conditions may reflect management's view of the need to ensure the good functioning of the scheme, and that it operates in a manner conducive to the comfort and well-being of residents. Nevertheless, temporary and conditional occupancy rights are liable to hinder the affordances of home that residents may experience, and to have a negative impact on their feelings of security and well-being. In Sweden, it is common for some households in the secondary housing 'staircase' (see Chapter Five) to live in ordinary rented housing, but to only sublet from the municipal social services authority, which holds the primary lease. Full tenancy is seen as a state that has to be earned through adherence to behavioural conditions and to approval from the municipal authorities.

Schemes will vary in their potential to offer the affordances of home for their residents. As we shall discuss in Chapter Four, the potential for home may be influenced by the physical attributes such as space and privacy, and the residential status offered. Some supported schemes are designed to look like mainstream housing, to minimise feelings of difference that may be experienced by residents or neighbours. However, others may be designed to look different and may have a clear symbolic meaning that could be positive or negative. Well-being through the locale of the home may also be influenced by the social relations that take place in the formation of the social practices of everyday living. For example, privacy may be influenced by the physical form and layout of a building or home, and by the social practices inherent in situations such as the behaviour of support staff in entering the resident's home – for example, whether they knock on the door or ask for permission to enter.

Also, supported housing may vary in terms of the affordances of neighbourhood that are available to the residents. In some cases the scheme may cater for a particular group of people, such as older people or people with disabilities, and so constitute a homogeneous community within it. In others there may be a mix of different residents and so they may mirror the general society to a larger extent. Some schemes may be insular, in that people from the neighbourhood rarely enter, or they may be very permeable, with facilities that are shared with people who live nearby. Also, the regime of the scheme may foster interaction with the neighbourhood or may encourage isolation. The physical size and layout of the scheme may encourage or discourage these factors. For example, a single dwelling, as in the domiciliary category discussed below, may offer more opportunities for engagement with the neighbourhood than a large cluster of dwellings which is physically distinct from the surrounding dwellings and residents.

Support

We have used the term 'support' to describe the services provided to people in 'supported housing', largely because of its use in the latter term. But there is a definitional confusion around the services provided, with other terms such as 'care' and 'help' also being used. Each of these terms carries a different emphasis. For example, 'care' tends to denote more personal and professional services than 'support'. Therefore nurses and doctors provide health care but housing managers or sheltered housing wardens may provide support. 'Help' and 'support' tend to signal a more controlling role for the person receiving it than 'care' does. A helper or one providing support is supporting a person to cope rather than in the more intimate role of a caring doctor or parent. Despite these differences, it is difficult to draw any clear dividing line between 'care', 'support' and 'help'. Factors involved in distinguishing between them could be the type and intensity of the support provided, who provides it and the relationship between the giver and recipient. For the purposes of this book the term support is used to cover the spectrum of functions discussed, although the different aspects of provision will be considered.

In the British White Paper *Caring for our future: Reforming care and support* in 2012 (Department of Health, 2012) the two terms in the title were used together throughout without defining the difference. Care and support:

> enables people to do the everyday things that most of us take for granted: things like getting out of bed, dressed and into work; cooking meals; seeing friends; caring for our families; and being part of our communities. It might include emotional support at a time of difficulty or stress, or helping people who are caring for a family member or friend. It can mean support from community groups and networks: for example, giving others a lift to a social event. It might also include state-funded support, such as information and advice, support for carers, housing support, disability benefits, and adult social care. (Department of Health, 2012: 13)

Support is provided for many reasons. Franklin (1998: 170) highlights seven objectives for providing support in a supported housing context. These are:

- *control* – maintaining discipline and authority, albeit in a velvet glove, suggesting that the recipient is naughty, stubborn or childlike;
- *containment* – keeping difficult people and problems under restraint and away from others who may be offended;
- *protection* – of the individual from society or of society from the individual, suggestive of violence, danger or contamination;
- *order* – re-establishing order in a life which appears disordered and in danger of disintegrating;
- *rehabilitation* – attempting to enable the sick or disabled to return to the position they were in before an episode of sickness or disability, even though this may not be achievable;
- *modification* – the transformation of 'unacceptable' to 'acceptable' behaviour, whether by therapeutic or behavioural means;
- *compensation* – to compensate for the independence which cannot be achieved, making up for something which, sadly, is not possible.

An important point raised by this list is that some of the categories involve acting in what is judged to be in the interests of society rather than the individual. For example, a person may be in supported accommodation to protect society from the consequences of their behaviour, and attempts may be made to contain and modify this behaviour and to reinforce societal behavioural norms. As we shall see in the following chapters, the extent to which a societal interest agenda is pursued varies between different groups. For example, we shall see that it is more prevalent in supported housing for young people than it is for older people. We shall see later that the emphasis in welfare services in Britain and Sweden on personalisation and individualisation is being pursued at the same time as an apparently contradictory emphasis on increasing conditionality in service provision, based on behavioural norms.

The approach in this book is to argue that subjective well-being, as defined by the resident, is the appropriate criterion for the assessment of supported housing. This is argued on moral grounds, because it should not be the role of government to act against the subjective interests of vulnerable people unless there are very strong reasons, and that these should be identified and justified. The criminal justice system exists to define and police behaviour that is considered to be against the interests of society as a whole, and so gives sanction to government action to challenge, punish and change the behaviour of individuals subject to accountability to an independent judiciary. The supported housing considered in this book does sometimes fall within the criminal justice system. For example, there is a link between homelessness and criminality and so some homeless people living in hostels may have links with the police and courts. However, it is assumed here that the primary aim of the criminal justice system should be to rehabilitate offenders and to prevent re-offending through integration into mainstream society. As a consequence, improvement in the well-being of the offender is a key element in rehabilitation and is likely to help in the prevention of re-offending, so the well-being framework used here has relevance even in these circumstances.

It can be argued that support is often designed to bring about changes in behaviour that are in the interests both of society and the individual resident. For example, it could be argued that it is in the interests of society that a young person abstains from alcohol and drugs and gets a job, as well as being in the interests of that young person themselves. In most cases it can be argued that what is in the best interests of the individual is also in the best interests of the society. In most instances in supported housing, the resident concerned will have agreed to the objectives set and this is an important element of the 'outcomes star' approach discussed in Chapter Two. Nevertheless, in principle there could be differences between what an individual would choose to improve their well-being and what people in authority over them, such as those administering supported housing, would judge to be appropriate. These possible conflicts between different definitions of well-being need to be borne in mind in all that follows. The implication of the argument outlined here is that support that does not have the aim of improving the individual, subjective well-being of the resident should be explicitly stated and justified in each specific circumstance and should be minimised wherever possible. Adoption of well-being as an evaluative tool leads to the identification of these instances and can lead to questioning their justification and value to the individual and to society.

The list of objectives of support also shows the broad spectrum of tasks that support can encompass and suggests the wide range of skills needed to deliver them, which in practice may be provided by many different professionals. In Sweden, where the profession of housing management is less developed and professionalised than in some countries such as Britain, most supported housing will be run by social work or health staff. Supported housing in Britain is usually managed by housing officers, who may also have responsibility for other forms of accommodation. There is usually held to be a divide between what housing officers do and the role of support workers, although this division has proved to be difficult to define and to maintain in practice.

In a study of housing management in Britain, Clapham and Franklin (1994) identified nine different roles of housing management in supported housing. The categories were as follows:

- *Core housing management* – these were functions any landlord would have to undertake, whether in the public or private sectors, and included issues such as ordering repairs, collecting rent and letting properties.
- *Intensive housing management* – where tenants are vulnerable in any way it may take more time and effort to undertake the basic functions. For example, for tenants on low incomes rent payment may be difficult and housing officers may get involved with a wide range of issues. Older people may have problems in coping with a repair process and may need extra help.
- *Housing advice and information/assessments* – this may include giving advice to tenants on whether to move or stay put, or advice on the tenancy options available. It may also include involvement in the housing elements of wider assessment processes, such as community care assessments.
- *Community support* – the provision of services, advice and support to ensure the community functions in an effective way. Included are the promotion of tenants' groups and the implementation of tenant participation.
- *Brokerage* – acting as a contact for the tenant with other agencies and acting as a tenant advocate. This may involve contact with social services agencies to arrange domiciliary services or trying to contact an energy company regarding electricity supply.
- *Practical, non-personal, dwelling-related support* – these are simple tasks related to the property, such as internal decoration, gardening, changing a light bulb and caretaking tasks.
- *Practical, personal, non-dwelling-related tasks* – examples are doing shopping, preparing food or training tenants in these tasks.
- *Practical personal support or care tasks* – these are usually undertaken by social services or health agencies rather than housing staff, although they may get involved in emergencies.
- *Physical health services and emotional support* – ranging from nursing, physiotherapy or care from doctors to counselling or psychiatric care. Housing officers usually only get involved in these functions

in a non-professional way, by befriending tenants, listening and giving sympathy.

In their survey of housing officers in Britain, Clapham and Franklin (1994) found staff performing each of these roles either routinely or in an emergency. Often housing staff felt themselves dragged into providing services that they thought should be under the category of support, but felt that if they did not do them no one else would and they took pity on the resident. However, housing staff recognised that they were not trained to undertake many support tasks and were often forbidden to do them by their employers. The chance of being drawn into more personal and intensive support tasks were higher when housing staff were specialised rather than generic, as they were more aware of what needed to be done and became more confident in undertaking these tasks. Some staff in this category had worked previously as nurses or elsewhere in health services.

Franklin (1998) identified the following categories of support tasks:

- *rehousing processes* – such as advising on accommodation options;
- *functional skills* – enabling a person to function effectively in the neighbourhood and gain access to private facilities, such as shops and public services such as health care, employment services and so on;
- *financial skills* – income maximisation, budgeting, dealing with debt, gaining employment;*household skills* – such as cleaning, laundry, shopping, preparing food, decorating, changing a light bulb;
- *personal skills* – such as personal hygiene, health care, appropriate dress, socialising, taking medication, abstaining from abuse of alcohol or drugs;
- *self-actualisation* – development of self-worth and identity, forming relationships, sense of purpose feeling safe and at home.

The Care Standards Act 2000 in the UK, which created a new regulatory framework for social care, identified the following four elements of care:

1. non-physical care
2. emotional and psychological support
3. assistance with bodily functions such as feeding, bathing and toileting
4. care that just falls short of assistance with bodily functions but still involving physical and intimate touching, including activities such as helping a person get out of a bath and helping them to get dressed.

The last two categories fall within the requirement for registration as care providers with the Commission for Social Care Inspection (CSCI), which has implications for many supported housing providers, as many include these categories in their schemes of extra-care housing.

Support can be provided by professionals working for statutory, private or voluntary organisations, but also by family and friends or by other residents. The type of support provided varies widely and depends on the needs of individuals and groups (for example, the support offered to older people is usually different from that offered to young people) as well as other factors, such as the finance available and the objectives and organisation of the supported housing, and the skills available.

Different categories of supported housing

The accommodation and support elements of supported housing may be combined in a number of ways. The aim of this section is to describe some of these common ways through a discussion of four common categories. Evaluation of the different models that comprise these categories will be considered in Chapters Six, Seven and Eight that focus on particular groups of people. Therefore, the focus here is to describe the key features of the categories, which may show up in different ways as they are modified to suit the requirements of different groups.

Table 1 shows some of the key factors in support and housing that are present in different models of supported housing. The aim of the table is to aid identification of the differences and similarities of different types of schemes in order to be able to make a simple categorisation to aid description and analysis. It is difficult to include some of the more subtle, varied and subjective elements. For example, it would be good to include factors such as the symbolic meaning of the scheme and the philosophy of support in this table, but it is difficult to pin these down to a simple binary divide like the other factors, as they may be subtle and may vary considerably between different contexts. Therefore, the table covers some of the most important factors that differentiate schemes and that can be relatively easily identified and classified. It must be borne in mind that some forms of accommodation are restricted to particular groups or categories of vulnerable people, whereas others may be more open to a number of groups. The forms of supported housing included in the table are the ones that are important for the vulnerable people considered in Chapters Six, Seven and Eight, namely older people, homeless people and people with a disability. They have been grouped

Table 1: Models of supported housing

	Accommodation					Support		
Category	Shared	Grouped or scattered	Linked communal facilities	Integrated or segregated	Rights	Extent of support	Linked or domiciliary support	Flexible or fixed support
Shared living	Yes	Grouped	Yes	Segregated	Limited	Usually extensive	Linked	Fixed
Linked housing with communal facilities	No	Grouped	Yes	Segregated	Full	Can vary from extensive to limited	Linked (sometimes with domiciliary extra)	Fixed (sometimes with add ons)
Core and cluster	No (although may be in the core)	Both	Yes	Integrated	Usually full in cluster and limited in core but may be limited throughout	Can be extensive or limited, but usually same in core and cluster	Linked but may be domiciliary add on in cluster	Flexible
Domiciliary *support as in ch text*	No	Integrated	No	Integrated	Full	Varies	Domiciliary	Flexible

into a number of categories where the features identified are shared among a number of forms of supported housing. For example, the category of 'Shared living' includes residential care for older people and hostels for homeless people because they share many common characteristics in the form of housing and support provided, even if the residents are in different categories. The aim of this categorisation is to aid the analysis of different forms and the identification of factors that improve or constrain well-being.

Five housing elements have been included. The first is whether the accommodation is shared with other residents or is in individually occupied dwellings; the second is whether the accommodation is grouped together, whether in one building or in connected apartments or flats, or, alternatively is scattered around a neighbourhood with no physical link between them; the third is the existence or not of physically linked communal facilities such as social spaces, dining facilities and so on; the fourth is whether the supported housing is integrated with the community at large or is segregated into a homogeneous environment with one group of residents (such as a retirement village); the fifth factor is the rights held by residents (that is, whether they have full occupancy rights through ownership or a lease, or whether they have more limited rights, such as a sub-lease or a form of limited occupancy rights). This factor can also include whether the accommodation is temporary or a permanent home.

Three support elements are identified; the first is the extent of support with a simple (and necessarily arbitrary) division made between extensive and limited support; the second is whether the support is linked to the accommodation or whether it relies on domiciliary support provided to others (for example, whether it is provided by staff who are on-site and only provided to residents of the scheme or not); the third factor is whether the support is flexible in order to meet the demands of individual residents or is fixed by the limits of the support and facilities provided.

Shared living

Many supported housing schemes have shared living as a key element of the provision. Key features of shared living include the provision of non-self-contained accommodation, often of one room, grouped together usually in one building. There are usually linked and often extensive communal facilities and support services, and a segregated environment, usually containing one group of people who are physically (and often socially) isolated from the wider neighbourhood, although in some schemes efforts will be made to attempt to reduce this isolation through the service regime (for example, through organised visits or sharing of some facilities with people in the wider neighbourhood). Shared living is usually associated with more limited occupation rights as residents do not have their own self-contained accommodation and so do not have full ownership or leasing rights. In some cases residency will be temporary, but in others it is permanent. Support is usually linked to the accommodation and so primarily fixed and standardised or common to all residents. For example, if meals are provided, every resident can access them.

Shared living is the nearest categorisation to institutional living and, as we shall see in the following chapters, the current support policies in Britain and Sweden have developed from a desire to move away from institutional living. Institutions were considered to be expensive to build and run, and to lead to problems of institutional neurosis; they were also considered to have regimes that focused control on the staff and robbed residents of privacy and control over their lives. This was argued to lead to a loss of autonomy and the ability to cope in everyday situations outside the institution. Rather than being agents of rehabilitation, institutions were characterised as agents of decline and loss of functional capacity. For example, it is argued that, if residents are never given the opportunity to exercise judgement and choice, they will lose the capacity to do so.

Despite the clear focus in policy away from institutional living in most countries, many people are still resident in settings that could be described as institutions. These include older people in nursing or residential care homes as well as people with health problems in hospitals. Older people with dementia are one particular group that is receiving substantial interest and provision in both Britain and Sweden. The community care policy pursued in Britain was always ambiguous as it referred to providing care and support in people's own homes or in 'homely settings'. It has never been clear as to what constitutes a homely setting and substantial efforts have been expended in trying to make some institutions into homely settings and to overcome some of the perceived disadvantages of institutions in the past. In Sweden, policy has been much more successful in the sense that shared living has been largely superseded by the provision of self-contained accommodation, even though the communal facilities and support services may be very similar in form and content to shared living. This is an important issue that will be considered further in following chapters.

Examples of shared housing cover a wide range of user 'categories' including the three covered in following chapters, namely older people, homeless people and those with a disability. The three forms covered in more detail here are residential provision for older people, hostels for homeless people, and group homes for those with a disability.

Residential homes for older people

This category includes forms of provision with many different names. In Britain there is a difference between residential homes and nursing homes, the difference being in the extent to which medical support services are provided. In Sweden institutional provision of this form has been largely phased out and residential homes are now usually based around self-contained accommodation and so do not clearly fit into this category.

Accommodation and support

The accommodation in an institution is usually in the form of individual rooms with bathroom facilities, although there are a large number of examples, particularly in Sweden, of institutions where residents have their own small apartment within the complex with separate sleeping and sitting rooms. It can be argued that the presence of an individual apartment changes the nature of the provision, which should no longer be classified as an institution and may be closer to the British model of extra-care housing than the traditional institutions. It is for this reason that Nord (2011) uses the term 'assisted living' to differentiate new institutions with separate apartments from the traditional model with just individual rooms. Here we have included schemes where residents have their own, self-contained accommodation in the 'Linked housing with communal facilities' category.

Rooms usually have some special adaptations such as handrails, hoists and easy-to-use fittings. The rooms are usually designed with space to manoeuvre, often with wheelchair use in mind. The institution normally has resident staff, who are primarily, if not entirely, focused on the residents within the institution. However, additional help and skills (such as from medical practitioners) can be brought in as appropriate. Perhaps the unique elements of an institution are the relatively fixed nature of the support packages, and their close link to the residential accommodation. These two features mean that people usually move into institutions in order to receive the support on offer rather than for the accommodation. This support tends to be extensive and residents of institutions are usually frail and vulnerable people who need substantial care, possibly on a 24-hour basis, and who find it difficult to cope at home.

Some issues

One of the major criticisms of shared living has been the financial cost. However, one justification for the linking together of the accommodation and the support elements is that there are economies of scale in provision. The argument is that staff have more time to spend with residents when they do not have to travel to different homes. In the early days of community care in Britain it became apparent that the provision of extensive care in a person's home could be more expensive financially than care in an institution (see Means et al, 2008). However, the counter-argument is that the relatively fixed nature of the support services in shared living schemes can lead to a lack of targeting, being only loosely related to need. So if meals are provided, then all residents receive them, even if they could cook for themselves. Attempts have been made to overcome this by undertaking assessments of individual need and devising individual care packages, both elements of which are incorporated, to varying extents, in the British and Swedish systems. But there are limits to the flexibility that can be achieved given the relative fixity of support staffing. Therefore, the attempts at targeting have more potential where staff are also caring for others outside the institution as well as residents, and so there is more scope for flexibility as the extent of care given to residents can more easily be varied. The model of forms of supported housing being used as a base for care and support services provided more widely is one that will be explored later as an example of the 'Core and cluster' model.

The linking of the accommodation to the support in shared living gives rise to another common criticism, which is that people may have to move accommodation to receive support if there are not equivalent services available for people in their own homes. The argument runs that the support should be available to anyone wherever they live and some places have taken this as their objective.

The above discussion highlights that the affordances of home and neighbourhood provided by shared living for many people may be limited. Nevertheless, the specific circumstances of individuals, such as their physical and mental abilities and their lifestyles, may mean that other alternative forms of provision may not offer more affordances.

Hostels

Hostels are a form of shared housing usually used for vulnerable young or homeless people, but also for people fleeing domestic violence and for others. Hostels are usually seen as emergency accommodation for those who have no immediate shelter and have been common in Britain. Hostels are also common in Sweden, although there has been a different philosophy of provision for homeless people as we shall see later. A particular form of hostel in Britain has been 'foyers', loosely based on a model taken from France. The idea is to provide small bedsits or apartments in a modern building with communal facilities and attached support, usually geared towards living skills and training and employment issues. Foyers became very popular with the government in Britain during the first decade of the century, but problems became apparent and they have fallen out of favour recently.

Accommodation and support

The emergency nature of hostels means that the accommodation is often sparse, with small single rooms or dormitories, as the accommodation is seen as temporary to overcome a particular crisis situation. Meals are usually provided and hostels are often linked to particular support services that may be especially concerned with the assessment of the needs and the devising of appropriate support and accommodation packages to overcome the crisis situation. Other longer-term support services may be provided to deal with the problems experienced by the residents. Hostels may be the focus for drug rehabilitation programmes, other health services, independent living schemes and so on. Foyers may provide a better standard of accommodation, with bedsits or sometimes self-contained accommodation that would take them out of this category, but others are very similar to hostels in the form of accommodation and support offered.

Most hostels and foyers have support workers who both manage the accommodation and also work with the residents. Tasks may include assessing the accommodation and support needs of the individual and help in achieving an appropriate solution for that person. People entering hostels may have a wide variety of support needs and may have accommodation and employment problems, as well as issues with drug abuse or physical or mental health. Hostels are usually associated with independent living programmes, enabling residents to get support in managing independent accommodation. In foyers for young people, there is an emphasis on daily living skills and on employment-related issues. There may be in-house training and support programmes, or residents may be able to access provision outside the supported scheme. It may be the case that accommodation in the scheme is made dependent on certain kinds of behaviour or attendance at training sessions. For example, in hostels, accommodation may be contingent on abstinence from drugs on the premises or in general, and possibly attendance at an appropriate treatment session. In foyers, accommodation may be dependent on employment-related behaviour, such as attending training or searching for or accepting employment opportunities. Therefore, conditionality has played a large part in this form of provision.

Some issues

Although the rationale for hostels is the provision of temporary help, in practice they have often become 'silted up' with longer-term residents who are not able or willing to move on. As a consequence, the emergency element of provision becomes more difficult as accommodation is in short supply and additional support services have to be provided for the longer-term residents. The emergency model is predicated on success in moving people on to alternative forms of accommodation once their initial crisis is over and their needs assessed. However, this depends on the appropriate accommodation and support services being available and hostel residents being willing and able to take advantage of them. In practice, these conditions have not been met and in Britain there has been a programme to change the nature of hostel provision. This has emerged in response to criticism that hostels had become 'holding stations' for people who relied on them and so did not move towards independent living. The government re-branded hostels as 'agents of change' and placed emphasis on training of support staff and on achieving change towards independent living in residents (see Chapter Seven).

In Glasgow, the decision was made to close the majority of their hostels and to pursue a programme to prevent new hostel entry and to re-house existing residents. The prevention programme consisted of an enhanced and holistic assessment system coupled with increased community support services, in particular for those with drug-related and other health problems. The aim was to ensure independent living for those who otherwise would have entered hostels and for those already there.

Common criticisms of foyers in Britain have included the high capital costs (they have often been in new purpose-built schemes); the problem of silting up, as young people are not able or willing to move on; and the financial disincentives for young people in the benefits system, which means that if they do get a job they cannot afford to pay the full cost of the provision and so have to leave.

Group homes

Group homes are defined here as consisting of a number of people living together with their own rooms, but not in self-contained dwellings, in a supported housing setting. Examples may be houses for people with learning difficulties, where there is a need for substantial support that may need to be provided 24 hours a day. Such accommodation was developed from the 1970s onwards in Britain especially as part of the programme of closure of the old mental hospitals or institutions. Those residents thought to be capable of supported living were often moved to shared housing of this form, either as a temporary solution until they were thought capable of independent living, or as a more domestic alternative to institutional living. Shared housing is seen as a way of preventing future institutional admissions by providing a supported, yet 'homely' environment. In Sweden there were 'Boarding flats' for people with learning disabilities, consisting of living accommodation in the form of individual rooms, but they have largely been superseded since 1986 by forms of provision in which residents have their own individual apartments. Other provision for people with mental health problems in Sweden is similar to group homes except that residents have their own apartments rather than individual rooms and so do not fit into this category.

Accommodation and support

Each resident usually has their own room and shares kitchens, bathrooms and living areas. There may be support workers there during the day and perhaps a bedroom for a worker to stay overnight. Shared housing provides an environment in which substantial support can be given to the residents. This may be in daily living skills, such as cooking or washing, or may be more training-based to develop capacities and confidence. There may also be the use of outside facilities, such as day centres, where more support can be offered. Support workers may be resident in the shared housing or just be there during the day. It is usual for there to be one bed space for a worker to stay overnight on a rota with the other care workers where there is a need for 24-hour support. Otherwise residents may be left on their own together for certain times of the day or night.

Some issues

Shared housing does not offer self-contained accommodation for the residents, although it is usual for them to have their own bedroom. There can be issues of privacy and security for them as well, as the need to coexist with others who may have different needs, abilities and lifestyles. Communal living of this form is not the usual way of living for most people so there may be problems of stigma and difference for the residents. Shared housing is expensive because of the extensive support offered, although it may be less so than institutional living to which it is most often considered to be the alternative.

Linked housing with communal facilities

The category here is a large one and contains supported housing schemes where residents have their own self-contained accommodation that is linked together with others and with communal facilities. In Sweden much supported housing is of this type as, even for frail people in what may be thought of as institutional living, residents have their own self-contained accommodation. Only some hostels depart from this norm. The model for older people until the 1990s in Sweden was service houses where each resident had their own apartment and paid rent, and received optional communal facilities and support. This form of provision was meant for residents who were supposed to move in when they did not need much support and stay when their support needs increased. However, there was excess demand for the apartments and so incoming residents became more and more frail. In addition, charges were introduced for services and the model was superseded by that of senior housing, which will be discussed in Chapter Six. But even provision for people with dementia in Sweden is usually provided in self-contained accommodation.

In Britain, the major examples of this category of supported accommodation are sheltered and extra-care housing for older people. Sheltered housing has been an option for older people in a number of countries. It became popular in Britain from the 1950s onwards as an alternative to institutional care. Peter Townsend, in his famous book *The last refuge* (1962), painted a bleak picture of life in residential care homes and promoted sheltered housing as the desired alternative that, he argued, would obviate the need for residential care. This form of accommodation is very common in different countries and is to be found in Britain and Sweden, usually in schemes of 20 or more apartments. In Sweden, this form of accommodation may have many different forms and titles, reflecting the different models of the housing companies and the lack of a generally accepted national form, as in Britain. In Sweden, the different models include ones with extensive support services, as well as senior housing where support is much less if it is available at all. In general, there seems to have been a growth in schemes with more extensive provision, because of the perceived lack of a viable alternative to institutions. In Britain, the support within schemes has been increased and the model of extra-care housing is now more popular with policy makers than the traditional model of sheltered housing, that is perceived in many local areas to have lower priority for Supporting People funding (for review of the different models in Britain see Croucher et al, 2006).

It could be argued that the different forms of supported housing identified in this model are different and should not be put together in the same category. It is true that the services offered to residents in the different forms may differ substantially as the following discussion will show. However, they do have a common form in the provision of self-contained accommodation grouped into schemes, with communal facilities and in situ support, and so merit being considered together with an awareness of the differences involved. As Croucher et al (2006) note, the different forms included here have largely evolved from the activities of sheltered housing providers reacting to the changing needs of their tenants and so have a common ancestry.

Accommodation and support

The key elements of sheltered housing in Britain are the accommodation, consisting of a 'small warm home', which, at the beginning, included bedsitter or one room and bathroom accommodation, but later was usually a one- or two-bedroom flat linked to common facilities that often included a communal room, laundry facilities and an alarm system linked to a resident warden or carer. The role of the warden varies, but is often to respond to any emergency situation, arrange social events, look after the common areas and so on. Some sheltered housing schemes in Britain no longer have wardens, as it is considered that remote emergency call systems can address emergency problems and domiciliary services can provide support, as they do for many residents even when a warden is present. For other schemes (such as extra-care schemes), there are support staff and extensive facilities, such as provision of meals, physiotherapy and perhaps even medical care. Therefore, the traditional model has been extensively restructured, with no consistent and general model taking its place. Rather, there has been, in both Britain and Sweden, a growing spectrum of different forms of provision with different levels of support. What they all have in common, though, is self-contained accommodation grouped together and some degree of support.

Some issues

Common criticisms are that the provision is expensive and is inappropriately targeted. Because the warden and other support staff cannot cope if all residents are frail people, and the scheme would be judged to be too much like an institution if this were the case, it is common to have a 'balance' of fit and frail residents within a scheme. In that case, the support staff spend most of their time on a few residents and there have been examples of the 'fit' residents complaining of poor value for money, as they do not receive much attention. There was also evidence of uneven usage of the communal facilities. Perhaps the most difficult criticism to overcome was that the facilities of offered in sheltered housing were not sufficient to prevent people having to access institutional living. Therefore, sheltered housing did not achieve its original objective and was perceived as a stepping-stone to institutional living rather than an alternative to it. The reaction in Britain was to increase the facilities of sheltered housing to what, at first, was a model of very sheltered housing and then became extra-care housing. In these variants, the basic philosophy of linked accommodation and care was retained, but the support element was increased as described above. However, there is evidence that the drawbacks of sheltered housing were retained in the extra-care model. For example, Tinker et al (1999) argued that there was still a balance of fit and frail tenants, with many residents being relatively fit and so not needing the facilities provided. Nevertheless, the support facilities were not extensive enough to prevent entry into institutional care. In addition, it was argued that extra-care housing was more expensive than domiciliary support.

Another criticism of the sheltered housing model has referred to the relatively fixed nature of the support available to residents and the impermeability of the schemes. As a consequence, some providers have made efforts to situate more support workers and carers on the scheme, and to provide services to older people living in the local neighbourhood, allowing them to use the facilities of the scheme in an example of the core and cluster model discussed later. This has proved difficult in some cases where there have been disputes about funding for and about the use of scheme facilities between scheme residents and others.

Reviews of sheltered housing have commented on its popularity among residents (Clapham and Munro, 1990). The security of an alarm and the presence of a support worker, as well as the privacy of self-contained accommodation, the sociability of the segregated environment and the communal facilities are well liked by many. However, it has fallen out of favour with policy makers in Britain because of its expense and the need to focus on more vulnerable older people. Therefore, the recent focus has been on extra-care housing, which can cope with frailer residents, but which is even more expensive to provide and run.

Core and cluster

This model involves the provision of a core facility with a cluster of accommodation linked to it in terms of the provision of support, even though the accommodation may be scattered over the local area. There are examples of this form of provision in a number of fields. In Britain, some retirement villages may fall into this category, as they may be based around a residential home, with support services and other facilities open to those who live in other forms of housing in the village around. In Sweden, some housing schemes for older people have extensive facilities, such as the provision of meals, social events in communal space, hobby rooms and facilities, and health provision that can be accessed by older people living in the local neighbourhood. In Britain, the example of a 'community hub' is similar, where the facilities of sheltered or extra-care housing are shared with older people living in the local community. In addition, the hub contains internal and outreach support services that may include shared health and social services. The essence of the model is that the core facility is a neighbourhood resource that can be accessed wherever one lives, and is a base for care support staff as well as the provision of physical facilities. Therefore, the decision to move accommodation into the core is one taken for accommodation rather than support reasons. It may be that the resident's apartment lacks particular facilities that cannot easily be installed. Also, there may be problems of mobility, making it difficult to access the communal facilities. The basic philosophy is to separate, in principle, the accommodation from the support elements of provision, with the working assumption that the same level of support can be provided in any number of accommodation settings. This allows a more flexible link between accommodation and support than in other models, with fewer constraints on the type and amount of support residents can receive in different settings. In Britain, retirement villages can be an example of the core and cluster model where they are based around an institution, but include ordinary or adapted housing and extensive neighbourhood and support facilities that are shared by all who need them. However, retirement villages tend to be in new-built properties, isolated from neighbouring settlements, whereas community hubs are more likely to be in existing settlements and embedded in local neighbourhoods.

Another example of a core and cluster model is found in provision for young homeless people. In some areas, there is an open-access hostel that provides emergency accommodation and assessment and a base for support staff. The aim of the emergency accommodation is to be a temporary respite until self-contained accommodation can be obtained in scatter-flats in the surrounding neighbourhood. Support is maintained in the independent accommodation to enable the young person to maintain the tenancy. The core houses the provision of training and support facilities that can be accessed throughout by the young people living in the emergency accommodation and those in the scatter-flats.

Accommodation and support

This model is the most variable in the extent and type of support that can be provided because of the more flexible link with the accommodation. Therefore, in principle, any quantity and form of accommodation and support can be provided. Accommodation usually takes the form of self-contained, mainstream accommodation in apartments or houses, although the accommodation may be adapted for the specific needs of the category of residents, as in many retirement villages. In some cases, residents may live in ordinary accommodation but not have full occupancy rights. For example, it is common in Sweden for residents in the upper level of the secondary 'housing staircase' (see Chapter Five) to only hold a sub-lease, with the primary lease being held by the social services authority and full rights being seen as needing to be earned through 'good behaviour'.

The support is linked to what is provided in the core and any domiciliary support. However, the extent and type of support can be varied according to the needs of the individual, and be changed over time as the resident changes, without this impacting on the need to change accommodation.

Some issues

In principle, the core and cluster model offers more flexibility than other forms of supported housing. However, it can require considerable integration and joint working between housing, support and health agencies to provide and run. It may be expensive to provide and may involve a move of accommodation on the part of residents into the scheme, which may be a segregated environment, as in retirement villages. Nevertheless, the core and cluster model offers a greater potential for achieving the benefits of neighbourhood and home for people with support needs.

There have been some problems with the sharing of facilities where the financial arrangements are not clear between residents and others, or where the physical layout is such that residents may feel that others are using 'their' facilities or feel a sense of insecurity. Nevertheless, these problems can be overcome through appropriate design, with clear distinctions between private and shared areas along the lines of 'progressive privacy' and clear funding responsibilities for residents and other users of the facilities.

Domiciliary support

What is meant here is the provision of support in a person's own home. This may be in the form of standard services, such as home care or meals, or nursing care or cleaning and so on. The services may be open to all those assessed as needing them across an area or may be part of a special scheme, such as a floating support scheme to offer services that are not normally available. Floating support aims to provide support services in an individual's own home. Some schemes have a particular menu of services, whereas others will offer an individually tailored package to meet individual needs and wishes.

An example of this model in Britain is the KeyRing scheme, where there is a network of dwellings lived in by those receiving support (usually about 10 properties) and one lived in by an unpaid community-living volunteer, living rent-free, who can provide local support. In addition, there is a call line if professional help is needed, as well as domiciliary support provided by the KeyRing organisation or by other statutory or voluntary agencies on the basis of a personal care plan (or personal budget). This form of provision started for people with learning difficulties but has been expanded to others, such as young people or those with mental health problems.

Accommodation and support

The nature of this model depends crucially on the quality and adequacy of the individual's home and neighbourhood, as this is the site of the support. Of course some people do not have adequate housing and so this is a prerequisite here, as acknowledged by Housing First schemes for homeless people that offer accommodation before consideration of support needs. Support is dependent on the availability of mobile services that may vary in their adequacy and scope. Mobile services may be more expensive because of the need for travelling time and there may be limits to the extent of support that can be provided on this basis. As we shall see in Chapter Three, in both Britain and Sweden the number of older people receiving domiciliary services has been reduced in recent years, with support being concentrated on those in most need.

Some issues

Support in one's own home seems to offer the advantages of allowing residents to enjoy the full benefits of home. Undoubtedly this is generally true for most people, who will not want to move home because of support needs. Their homes may have strong links to their previous lives and form the basis of their family ties and social contacts. However, there are two main caveats that need to be applied. The first is that the house itself needs to be appropriate for the changing needs and lifestyle of the resident. A home will come to mean something different over time if upstairs rooms cannot be accessed or the roof leaks and there are no funds to repair it. The process of the provision of support may lead to changes in the physical form of the house through aids and adaptations, such as grab rails in bathrooms or ramps for outside doors. Alternatively, funds may not be available for needed adaptations and residents may be left in an inappropriate environment. Second, the support may be provided in such a way as to change perceptions of home. For example, support workers will enter the home and will undertake some tasks within it. They may have a key for access and may let themselves in. Residents may feel a loss of privacy and control with another set of people (support workers will not always be the same person) being able to access and move about their home. The attitude of the support workers may be important to the resident. If support is offered in a condescending or controlling way that does not respect the privacy, control, self-confidence or self-esteem of the resident, then this can impact on their sense of home. Home may be associated with shame, dependence and lack of control, which may outweigh the positive elements.

Support in one's home should mean the preservation of existing neighbourhood affordances including social contacts. However, if the existing neighbourhood is low on affordances, and is either threatening or unpleasant or of low status, then staying in that neighbourhood may not lead to high self-esteem or well-being. Some people will favour a move away from an existing neighbourhood into, for example, an age-segregated retirement community or sheltered housing scheme, which could offer the perceived advantages of sociability with like-minded people. Some older people will move house and neighbourhood to locate in an area which offers better facilities for their changing lifestyle on retirement, and perhaps is more age segregated, to avoid any problems arising from a clash of lifestyles with other residents.

Conclusion

The aim of this chapter has been to describe the main elements and forms of the different supported housing models and to briefly review their advantages and disadvantages to residents in relation to their well-being. Clearly this has been a very general account, as many of the factors will vary with the individual scheme, and the individual lifestyle and wishes of the resident. Chapters Six, Seven and Eight will allow a more detailed look at the outcomes of the different models for different groups and this conclusion will outline the framework for this discussion in those three chapters.

Some very general points can be made here. First, the value of the home-related models for some (but not all people) is apparent in that, in general, support in one's own home is more likely to lead to greater well-being. The core and cluster model seems to offer the advantages of independent living with access to support facilities. It also offers the advantages of flexibility and individual targeting of support. Other less flexible models that are associated with standard levels of support are often in living environments that do not offer the full advantages of home and neighbourhood.

However, there is no standard solution for everyone and people will need to weigh up the different forms for themselves in light of their own lifestyles and the particular options available to them. The array of different models open to individuals will vary according to their needs and lifestyles, as well as their abilities.

In order for individuals to judge what is best for them, and for policy makers to make judgements on which forms of supported housing to develop, there needs to be a framework to evaluate the different options. The next three chapters formulate such a framework, based on the concept of well-being.

TWO

Difference and well-being

The aim of this chapter is to introduce the concept of well-being and to work towards a way of using the concept to assess the impact of supported housing on the lives of individuals. The starting point for this discussion is a review of some perspectives on the nature of present society, which some have labelled as postmodern or late modern. Writers in this tradition emphasise the individualisation of life and the importance of the pursuit of individual identity and lifestyle in an increasingly risky and unequal world. The argument is that the construction of our self-identity has become an important life project that reflects our status in society and impacts on our happiness and health. Our identity is reflected in our lifestyle, which consists of the activities and practices that we undertake in our daily lives, including how we spend our time and our money. The two concepts of identity and lifestyle are central to the analysis of supported housing in this book and so are considered in some detail, as they lead to a focus on difference in perceptions and ways of living that are crucial to the understanding of the impact of supported housing on individuals, who may have very different preferences and subjective perceptions.

Identities and lifestyles are influenced by the discourses that shape them and are shaped by them. When related to categories of people such as older people, or others considered here, the categorical discourses shape understanding of the way that people are expected to live their lives and encapsulate societal norms that comprise the socially constructed reality of life. These discourses influence the forms that policies and provision for the different groups take and so are crucial to the understanding of the reasons for the development of specific forms of supported accommodation and their impact on residents. Each of the chapters (Chapters Six, Seven and Eight) that consider provision for particular groups of people will therefore start with a discussion of these categorical discourses and their impact.

The concepts of identity and lifestyle are also important because they lead into a discussion of the concepts of happiness and well-being which are the main focus of the book. These concepts have become popular recently in a number of situations, including judging the happiness of a society. Here we will examine the underlying elements of well-being and focus on the key concepts of personal control, identity and self-esteem, and social relations that are fundamental to well-being. The argument of the book is that the concept of well-being is a very useful framework for evaluating supported housing, because it can help to answer important questions concerning the impact supported housing has on the lives of residents and how it should be measured, but it needs some development before it serves the purpose adequately. The chapter therefore begins to tackle the issue of how we should consider different forms of supported housing and starts the construction of a framework for judging the impact on the lives of individuals through the concept of well-being. It is argued that existing evaluative frameworks, such as the 'outcomes star' and the Supporting People framework, do not give enough emphasis to the relations between people and their home and neighbourhood environments that are crucial to their well-being.

Difference, risk and inequality

Postmodern analysts such as Giddens (1991) emphasise the individualisation of global societies and the ensuing 'opening out' of our societies that enable people to 'make their own lives' by pursuing the project of identity. It is self-evident that there has been less uniformity in lifestyle including consumption patterns, clothing and so on, than in previous decades and centuries. Someone born in a mining village in the South Wales valleys in the 19th century would have had little freedom to choose their religion, occupation, style of clothing, family structure and so on. Much of this change has reflected the growing diversity of employment in the post-Fordist economy where the number of occupations has increased and traditional forms of jobs for life have reduced. There has been an increase in part-time work and self-employment, and large migrations of populations around the globe following the globalisation of the economic system in which flows of goods, people and finance circle the world. At the same time, there has been an explosion in the availability of consumer goods, which are increasingly individualised and carry identity and status messages. To a significant degree, we derive the image that we have of ourselves and that others have of us through our consumption of goods and services. To the long-standing differences of age, ethnicity, gender, functional capacity (the practical ability to undertake common tasks) and social class, have been added ones of beliefs and attitudes, identity and lifestyle, which may cross-cut these traditional categories. This does not mean that the traditional categories are not important, because members may share some experiences, attitudes and perceptions, but that they do not define everything about an individual. Harrison uses the idea of difference within difference to illustrate the commonalities and differences that are associated with ethnicity. With regard to housing, he argues:

> Certainly it is difficult to 'read off' households' choices and housing careers from ethnicity, material positions or racisms in a simple way. Black and minority ethnic households face common problems in terms of discrimination, and also tend to be materially disadvantaged, but this commonality is overlaid or cross-cut by gender, ethnicity, disability and age, and by highly specific differences between households and their goals. (Harrison, 2001: 150)

It is a recurring theme of this book that categories based on a limited field of attributes have very limited use in helping to understand the housing situation, preferences and needs of individual households and, therefore, the policy and practice emphasis should be on individual assessment and planning. Nevertheless, the use of categories is ubiquitous in housing and support policy, and pervades the field of supported housing.

The trends of individualisation described above have been accompanied by an increase in inequality in many western countries, particularly in Britain and increasingly in Sweden (Wilkinson and Pickett, 2009). Growing difference in material resources has therefore left individuals in very different situations in coping with the difficulties in life, such as the need for support, and had profound impacts on their well-being. This point will be considered further later in the chapter.

The increase in inequality has had more impact because of the increase in the scope of market provision, where ability to pay has taken the place of other means of allocation, such as need, as defined in traditional public services. Sandel (2012) has shown how market relations have taken a greater role in many aspects of life. He argues that in many situations this has brought a new set of moral relationships, based on economic incentives, into areas such as support (as we shall see later), which have superseded more traditional values of trust and compassion and have allowed economic inequalities to be more clearly reflected in differences in life chances. Judt (2010) also laments the corrosive increase of inequality and the rise of material self-interest as the dominant ethos of recent times. He argues that the neoliberal discourse of unfettered markets has been responsible for the reduction of public services in the name of economic efficiency, which has resulted in the loss of the 'social protection state' that was based on values of community and trust, and served to alleviate economic and social insecurity.

Following the neoliberal paradigm of increasing market relations, public policy has increasingly been driven by individualisation, which means that individuals have been left more and more to take responsibility for their own situation with decreasing help from the welfare state. In Britain particularly, but also in Sweden, cuts in the real value of benefits and a growing need for financial payments for support have left individuals in a position of greater financial responsibility. Beck (1992) has drawn attention to what he calls the 'Risk Society'. Some of the increased risks he identifies are at the societal level, such as that of environmental catastrophe, but others are at the individual level. Individualisation and inequality have left people at greater financial risk if things go wrong and for those with fewer resources this could cause substantial difficulties. They have also created an environment of anxiety. Judt (2010: 8–9) argues that 'we have entered an age of insecurity – economic insecurity, physical insecurity, political insecurity [...] Insecurity breeds fear. And fear – fear of change, fear of decline and fear of strangers and an unfamiliar world – is corroding the trust and interdependence on which civil societies rest.' He argues that the generalised anxiety circulating in today's media outlets and political discourse can be traced to the elevation of individual responsibility and the denigration of government-funded welfare provision.

Writers in the Foucauldian tradition (Foucault, 2002) have seen this move towards individualism as a change in the mode of governmentality (for example, Rose and Miller, 2008). They point to the perceived move towards individual responsibility as a means of social control by the government of our own conduct, which is reinforced by the increased conditionality of public services and support, which is predicated on the individual acceptance of behavioural norms deemed appropriate by others.

Wacquant (2008) and Standing (2011) have identified an increase in risk that has been focused on what has been termed the 'precariat'. No longer able to find security in an increasingly liberalised labour market with wages that are often not enough to prevent poverty, 'marginal' people have been abandoned by the welfare state, which is increasingly focused on control and containment of behaviour rather than support. The vulnerable people who are the focus of this book will be at the forefront of these changes and are likely to be members of this 'precariat'.

The increase in inequality and the growth of market relations and increased personal risk are the context in which people (such as those who reside in supported housing) live their lives. Individuals can choose the degree to which they engage with the consumer society, but they are likely to be judged by its badges of status. Judt (2010) is critical of some features of traditional state services that did not give primacy to the individual consumer, a flaw that makes any revival of state services more difficult to achieve politically. It is argued in this book that the use of a concept of well-being as a goal of public policy in general, as well as public services in particular, such as supported housing, is crucial to the survival and growth of social welfare services and to the life chances of those who depend on them, because it places at the forefront of attention the impact of policies and services on individuals, in terms of their identities and lifestyles.

Identity and lifestyle

Identity here is taken to be our sense of who we are as well as the way that people view us. These two elements are related because identity is forged through our interaction with others and so identity is not fixed but is a 'process of becoming' undertaken throughout our lives. From early socialisation processes to our everyday interactions with others, we form a sense of who we are and our place in the world. Whatever we think of ourselves it is difficult to hold on to this view if it is contradicted by others. Some of these external views may be based around dominant discourses related to the categories to which we are ascribed membership and may be very influential in our lives. For example, a dominant discourse of 'old age' delineates what is acceptable behaviour and how members of the category are treated by others, as well as the forms of support offered by the state and others. Dominant discourses based on categorical identity, therefore, may shape public policy and specific forms of provision such as supported housing. Categorical identities may highlight perceived similarities between members and may indeed act to reinforce these through the expected behavioural norms. But in the world of increasing difference described earlier, they crucially serve to hide the differences between individuals. Not all older people enjoy bingo or wish to live in a social environment consisting solely of other older people.

Identity is usually embodied in that our view of ourselves and the view that others have of us is shaped by our appearance and our physical attributes. Of course in the internet age it is easier to construct a disembodied identity that exists only in the virtual, digital world. But, in everyday life, the actions which help to shape and reflect our identity are undertaken through our physical bodies, which provide

41

the possibilities and limits of action in particular physical environments. Also, in interaction with others we use the senses of sight and possibly smell and touch. The way that others view us may be influenced by our physical appearance and there are societal norms about attractive bodies. It is often argued that present western societies give high status to the young, slim body and lower status to the body that shows signs of an ageing, or is impaired or unattractive. Many of the residents of supported housing may not have bodies deemed to be 'perfect' in popular discourses, and may have a social and/or physical disability that may limit their ability to fulfil their desired identity and lifestyle.

The concepts of identity and lifestyle are closely linked. Lifestyle can be defined as the playing out of an individual identity in social practices, such as use of time and money, consumption choices and so on. Lifestyle is how we live our lives, and here we are particularly interested in the everyday life of social practices including eating, sleeping, working, buying, interacting with others, relaxing and so on. These activities are often used in defining the 'need' of individuals and have been codified into scales that may be used by support workers or professionals such as occupational therapists to identify support and accommodation needs. As we shall see later, these Activities of Daily Living (ADL) scales have the drawback of being used generally without reference to different lifestyles.

As with identity, lifestyles are influenced by dominant discourses and the words and actions of others. Some lifestyles are given more status in society than others because they more fully reflect societal norms. So a lifestyle based around employment for a young person is given more status in the general society than one based around the drawing of welfare benefits. Of course, society is not a homogeneous whole and it is possible that there may be subcultures or groups within society in which this lifestyle is valued. Groups will vary in their ability to shape the dominant discourse and so the existence of power becomes important in the forming and acceptance of lifestyles.

Dominant discourses shape the way that people think and act, but they are not fixed or immutable. Giddens' (1984) concept of structuration shows how discourses and their related social practices are reproduced by the actions of individuals who re-enact them. Change occurs when many actions alter or amend existing practices. If enough people do this and there are no societal sanctions, it is possible that a different social practice will be formed. An example may be the dominant discourse of ageing that has changed considerably over time as new cohorts of fit and healthy older people have challenged previous stereotypes of inevitable ill-health and dependency. Pressure groups spend much time trying to alter dominant discourses and social practices through changing public perceptions and the attitudes of politicians and government officials through media campaigns and other means. However, it is worth stressing again that the distribution of power resources in society is crucial to the structuration process.

The status of lifestyles may often reflect the resources that can be devoted to them. In societies that value monetary wealth, lifestyles that indicate this through the use of time and the ownership of expensive products will be highly valued, and of course these lifestyles will be only open to those who have the financial resources to access them. It is argued that the importance of individual wealth and income in the adoption of lifestyles makes the concept unnecessary and misleading, and that the traditional concept of social class provides all the analytical power that is needed (Allen, 2008). However, it has proved to be difficult to provide a clear definition of social class that does not include aspects of consumption and status. The inclusion of these factors makes the concept almost indistinguishable from that of lifestyle. The only difference seems to be in the assumption of a hierarchical structure of social classes, whereas the concept of lifestyle leaves open the possibility of a different status for lifestyles of different income requirements. In other words, monetary considerations are only one element in the status of different lifestyles. Spending lots of money indulging your hobby of trainspotting may not bring as much status as spending the same money on a luxury yacht on the Mediterranean. As long as the concept of lifestyle considers economic issues there is no need for a concept of social class.

The related concepts of identity and lifestyle have been recognised in many government discourses and policies. For example, the concept of social exclusion, which informs policies of poverty and area deprivation, usually involves some element of exclusion from 'normal' or mainstream lifestyles (see Chapter Four). The concept of normalisation influenced thinking around government community care reforms in many countries and uses the concept of lifestyle (see Chapter Eight). However, it is in the concept of well-being that identity and lifestyle have their most relevant expression.

Happiness and well-being

Identity and lifestyle are means to an end: namely to increase our happiness. We construct our identity and pursue our lifestyle in order to make ourselves happy and contented. Therefore, any evaluation of supported housing needs to assess its impact in promoting individual happiness and well-being.

Layard (2005) has identified seven factors affecting happiness. Five of these are family relationships, financial situation, work, community and friends, and health. All of these factors are related to where we live, as a house is the setting for family relationships and for community and friends, as well as enabling access to work. It is a major item of family expenditure and contributes to good health. Layard's (2005) final factors in affecting happiness are personal freedom and personal values. He argues that these are instrumental in that they are the means of achieving greater personal happiness, because they allow people to find their own ways to happiness. The concept of happiness has been criticised by Johns and Ormerod (2007) as being vague and unquantifiable. Nevertheless, there is an important and growing literature on the definition and measurement of well-being or happiness. The New Economics Foundation has devised indicators of well-being to be used alongside GNP (gross national product) as measures of societal progress (New Economics Foundation, 2009), as well as indicators of success for public programmes and policies (Thompson and Marks, 2008). The British government has shown an interest in well-being issues in devising and measuring the outcomes of policies (see for example the final report of the Foresight Mental Capital and Wellbeing Project, 2008).

In measuring well-being, there is argued to be a need to move beyond happiness as a temporary mood state (Searle, 2008). Nettle (2005) distinguishes between three levels or concepts of happiness. The first is momentary feelings of joy or pleasure (sometimes labelled 'happiness'); the second, overall contentment with life ('life satisfaction'); and fulfilment of one's potential ('the good life'). Most people report themselves to be happy most of the time even if they are living in a dreadful situation. Measures of happiness, such as the Oxford Happiness Questionnaire (Hills and Argyle, 2002), not only tap into people's emotional state but also address issues related to psychological well-being such as: the ability to make decisions; feeling satisfied; being healthy; showing an interest in other people; having a sense of life achievement; and being in control (Searle, 2008: 13). Ryff and Keyes (1995) see happiness as 'psychological well-being' that has seven elements: self-actualisation; autonomy; personal growth; self-acceptance; life purpose; mastery; and positive relatedness. In their measurement of well-being across different countries, the New Economics Foundation (2009) argues that they are trying to measure more than life satisfaction and are seeking to include people's subjective reports of how they feel in relation to others. In addition, they seek to move beyond good feelings and to seek to measure how well people are doing in terms of their functioning and the realisation of their potential. It is worth emphasising that well-being, as used here, is a deeply subjective concept. It can be measured, but only by asking the people concerned and recording and comparing their responses.

Elstad (1998) identifies what he labels the self-efficacy approach in the study of health inequalities. In this approach an individual's sense of self-efficacy is seen as the important factor in influencing their reaction to social conditions. As with Layard, happiness or well-being is seen as a social construct. It is a reflection of social existence – an individual's response to a collective experience. It is rooted in the structural features of society – its systems of material inequalities – and in the supportiveness of the social environment (Elstad, 1998). Self-efficacy can be defined as 'the extent to which people see themselves as being in control of the forces that importantly affect their lives' (Pearlin et al, 1981: 329, quoted in Elstad, 1998). Self-efficacy is used here in a similar way to other concepts such as mastery and personal control. Elstad (1998) identifies the opposite concepts as fatalism, powerlessness and learned helplessness. Elstad (1998) argues that self-efficacy is closely related to other concepts, such as self-esteem and social support, that have to be seen as a bundle of interrelated and self-reinforcing concepts. The problem is that the precise relationship between the concepts is not identified and so it becomes problematical to separate them out for analytical purposes.

The advocates of the self-efficacy approach, as well as other authors such as Wilkinson (2005) and Layard (2005), emphasise the importance of feeling in control of one's situation in generating well-being or happiness and avoiding shame. Some psychologists have argued that the feeling of being in control is a universal motivation, which is a key element of self-esteem. For example, Renshon (1974) argues that every person has within them the desire to have control over the factors that shape their lives. Shapiro and Astin (1998: ix) argue that 'one of our greatest fears is losing control, and one of our strongest motivations is to have control over our lives'. Layder (2004) argues that a feeling of being in control helps to reduce uncertainty that can feed insecurity; is an important building block for self-esteem; and offers leverage in avoiding a feeling of helplessness. He argues that good mental health requires that we have some control over ourselves and our lives. A feeling of being 'out of control' can lead to poor physical and mental health. Seligman (1992) argues that the lack of personal control can lead to what he calls 'learned helplessness'. This occurs when individuals lose the sense that anything they do helps their personal situation and is a primary cause of poor mental health and depression.

The psychological literature reviewed above seeks to find universal human attributes. However, as Seligman (1992) observes, not everyone suffers from learned helplessness at the same time or to the same extent. People differ in their capacity to cope with challenges to their positive self-image and self-esteem. Identity maintenance is a key activity and, in pursuing their own coping strategies, individuals use what Searle (following Antonovsky, 1974) has called 'resistance resources', which include personal networks and societal resources. Therefore, an absence of these resources through contextual factors such as poverty can have a major impact. Seligman (1992) recognises that poverty restricts the capacity of individuals to exercise personal control. Even if one is sceptical of the psychological emphasis on the universality of human motivation, preferring to stress the social nature of wants and desires, it is easy to see how the need for control is a key element of 'postmodern' society. As considered earlier, Giddens (1991) argues that late modernity is associated with an 'opening out' of social life, in which individuals are more able to make their own lives by actively making choices. This is encapsulated by the concern with 'lifestyle', by which is meant the desire to choose an individual identity that leads to self-fulfilment (Giddens, 1991). The high incidence of perceived risk and uncertainty caused by the insecurity in the labour market and the opening out of social life can lead to great importance being attached to the need for what Laing (1969) termed ontological security. At the same time, the social status attached to the pursuit of a socially valued lifestyle can reinforce the desire for control.

Bartley et al (1998) maintain that the key argument later presented by Wilkinson and Pickett (2009) and Layard (2005), and many writers in the field of health inequality, is that the effect of income and other material goods is not directly material, but psychological. In other words, the impact of social conditions on the health and well-being of an individual is mediated by their personal identity. As applied to supported housing, the proposition is that the physical structure of a house is not necessarily a good guide to the happiness it brings. Individuals may differ regarding the precise attributes of a house that affect their happiness, depending on their identity and lifestyle. Bartley et al (1998) pose the key question which follows from this perspective: what resources does each social form (or social practice) make available to individuals from which they may shape an identity they can live with? Therefore, in relation to supported housing, the question is how different forms and regimes enable different households to frame a valued identity and lifestyle.

Both Wilkinson and Layard also stress the importance of the reference group in feeling valued and achieving status. This builds both on the tradition of work on relative poverty (Townsend, 1979) and on authors such as Hirsch (1977), who stressed the importance of 'positional goods'. Wilkinson and Pickett (2009) argue that inequality is a major cause of poor health as it leads to feelings of inadequacy and shame. Whatever the level of resources an individual has, they are unlikely to feel happy if everyone else has far more than they do.

Wilkinson and Pickett (2009) have summarised much of the evidence of the impact of the degree of inequality in a society on well-being. They draw attention to the Easterlin paradox that, for rich societies, an increase in material wealth is not matched by an increase in well-being. Rather, they argue that differences in a wide range of issues that make up well-being are related to the degree of inequality in that society. The issues they consider are ones that have a social gradient within any country, in other words they are more likely to impact adversely on those at the lower end of the income spectrum. Examples are life expectancy, drug use, physical and mental health, obesity, educational performance, teenage births and violence. They argue that inequality gets 'under the skin', because people compare themselves with others and react to this comparison. Wilkinson and Pickett (2009) point to the increase in anxiety in developed societies stemming from a concern with how we are viewed by others, although it is not always clear exactly who people compare themselves to. Therefore, increased anxiety has been associated with an increase in an insecure narcissism, as people react to threats to their self-esteem or status by becoming more focused on themselves and more insensitive to the needs of others. Wilkinson and Pickett (2009) follow Elstad (1998) and Scheff (1988) in emphasising the importance of avoiding shame as a human motivation, and accepting the link between shame and mental ill-health and depression. The views of others form the evaluative framework by which we view ourselves and feel either pride or shame, and are related to our social status. It is much easier to feel valued the further up the social scale you are and, conversely, much harder the lower your social status. Wilkinson and Pickett (2009) argue that the increase in inequality has increased status differences and consequently has increased these identity anxieties.

If the aim of government is to improve the overall level of happiness in society, Layard (2005) argues that this would best be achieved by improving the lot of those at the lower end of the income spectrum.

This would make them happier, but is unlikely to substantially reduce the happiness of those higher up the income scale. We are continually concerned about how we stand in the eyes of others in our reference group. However, it is not always clear who the reference group is. For example, we do not know whether an older person in supported accommodation compares themselves with others in terms of their housing and support situation; if so, who they choose to compare themselves with; and whether this influences their overall housing satisfaction.

Elstad (1998) sees self-efficacy or personal control as rooted in social status and the supportiveness of the local environment. This places emphasis on the fact that the way individuals cope with social conditions may be influenced by the social support that they receive. Support may be within the household or family, but it may also relate to people in the locality or neighbourhood.

The adoption of ideas of well-being and happiness could have profound implications for supported housing policy as housing could play an important role in achieving (or not) well-being or happiness. But, as Layard and authors in the self-efficacy approach have noted, the physical attributes of housing may not be important in their own right, but largely insofar as they allow one to achieve high self-esteem through living a valued lifestyle. This point is supported by the research on the impact of poor housing on health. The evidence for a direct link between substandard housing and health is limited to specific issues, such as the impact of dampness and mould growth on respiratory problems, particularly in children (see Clapham, 2005). Poor housing conditions seem to interact with a wide range of other factors, such as low income, stress, social isolation, and lack of control or self-esteem.

It is possible to measure the overall happiness that people gain from their housing situation. As Layard (2005: 13) argues, the best way to find out whether someone is happy is to ask them. Of course the result will be deeply subjective and may change as people change their expectations or their reference group. Nevertheless, it is the subjective perception that the measure is trying to capture. In Britain and Sweden, measures of satisfaction with housing are now commonplace, as most landlords will undertake a survey of their tenants to gauge satisfaction and there are a number of surveys at the national level. However, if they are to be meaningful they need to move beyond the consideration of happiness as a mood state, as the New Economics Foundation (and others) has argued. Also, although these subjective measures may give a good picture of success in achieving the overall goal of happiness, they may not be a good guide in showing how to achieve greater success, given the impact of difference in shaping the individual nature of the housing experience. To gain guidance here it may be necessary to examine the process of achieving the goal, rather than focusing on the goal itself. In order to do this it is necessary to examine some of the factors that have been shown to impact on happiness. Three that are drawn from the previous discussion of well-being are identified here as being most relevant to our analysis of supported housing: personal autonomy and control; identity and self-esteem; and social networks. But first it is important to stress the impact of inequality on well-being. Specific supported accommodation schemes may have little impact on levels of inequality, and so it is inappropriate to evaluate them by this criterion. Nevertheless, inequality is such an important issue in the generation of well-being that it is important to ensure that it is not forgotten, as it is likely to underpin the factors identified here and its significance will be returned to in the conclusions of the book.

Personal control

It has been argued that personal control is closely related to social status and self-esteem. Therefore, the aim of this section of the chapter is to formulate a way of thinking about control and the related concepts that is useful for our task of evaluating supported housing.

The starting point for this exploration of control is the notion of a housing pathway (see Clapham, 2005). This is defined as: patterns of interaction (practices) concerning house and home, over time and space. The housing pathway of a household is the continually changing set of relationships and interactions that it experiences over time in its consumption of housing.

In the context of a housing pathway, personal control can be seen as feeling in control of one's housing circumstances and the process of achieving one's goals. An individual may know when they feel in control and when they are not, and it is this personal feeling that is key to self-esteem rather than any objective notion. The literature reviewed earlier emphasised the importance of individual differences in mediating the impact of external conditions. Nevertheless, we may want to generate an analytical framework that enables an investigation of the factors that may influence the personal feelings of control without losing sight of the subjective concepts.

It is important at the outset to make the very difficult distinction between choice and control. Feeling in control may involve having the ability to make appropriate choices and for most people it is probable that feeling in control involves having a degree of choice over, for example, the amount and type of support provided. However, control is more than just choice. It is possible to conceive of someone feeling in control without actively making choices if they are very satisfied with their current housing and support circumstances. Control also focuses on what some authors have termed effective choice. It includes the extent to which choices are possible, wanted and valued. Whereas it is relatively easy to analyse objectively particular choices, control is a more nebulous and personal feeling. Therefore, an analysis of control needs to include an analysis of choice but it is not always reducible to it.

In the discussion of housing pathways a key element is the ability of a household to formulate and pursue a housing strategy. By strategy is meant a forward plan, or set of objectives which a household seeks to achieve. It cannot be assumed that all households have housing strategies or plans. An example of the lack of a strategy is the housing pathways of some young homeless people (see Fitzpatrick, 2000). In this situation some young people may change their housing often as they move between living at home, on a friend's sofa, on the streets or in a hostel. Rather than the result of a long-term strategy, their housing circumstances are the result of short-term reactions to their pressing needs.

There is an interesting and important issue here about whether the young homeless person used as the example above is 'in control' of their situation. In many ways it can be said that they are not, as the options open to them are very limited and would generally be perceived as of low quality. Also, the young person's 'decision space' is small. In other words, the pressing need for immediate shelter is likely to push longer-term considerations out of the decision field. Nevertheless, it is possible to see that some younger people may feel a degree of control in this situation, in that they can make choices and can vary their housing circumstances according to their own wishes. Therefore, although a long-term strategy would seem to show evidence of an individual being in control it is clearly not always necessary.

It is easy to see how the control exercised by the homeless young person in the example above could be improved, either by increasing the resources at their disposal or widening and improving the options available to them. Alternatively, it is easy to see how the small degree of control the person has could be completely undermined by, for example, forcing them off the streets and into a hostel against their wishes. Any intervention in the lives of the young homeless person could be judged on the basis of whether it allows them to think longer-term and enables them to devise and implement a strategy to achieve their housing goals.

A number of factors can be identified which can influence the degree and nature of control that a household may be able to exercise over their housing circumstances. Analyses of the concept of choice have highlighted the importance of different kinds of resources, such as financial resources, and information and knowledge, in enabling choice to be exercised (see for example Brown and King, 2005). As King (1996: 80) argues, effective choice involves 'opportunities for self-creation and the ability to affect the context (that is, one's current situation) itself, and, second, the access to resources that translates choice into empowerment.' It is easy to see how the control that a homeless young person could exercise would be improved by access to employment and a regular income. Similarly, more information about the housing options available would clearly be advantageous. Therefore, a focus on control leads to a policy focus on the key elements that constrain it.

One of the major issues with choice is the differential ability of individuals to exercise it. For example, a household in acute and urgent housing and support need will be forced to accept the first property they can access, whereas a household that is adequately housed and has few support needs may be able to wait for the perfect property to come along. Other resources that may influence the ability to exert control through choice include knowledge of the choices available and their consequences, and the ability to deploy personal skills to negotiate: for example, the ability to find one's way through an allocation system and persuade housing officers to use their discretion to allow choice, or the ability to negotiate with a caregiver to ensure that personal needs are met.

A cornerstone of housing policy in Britain (and increasingly in Sweden) has been to improve choice through enabling households to enter the private housing market and to purchase support from a choice of private and public providers. The underlying assumption is that participation in the market is enough by itself to enable choice. However, in the market situation financial resources will determine, to a large extent, the choices available to the household. Higher income households will have more potential options open to them in the market and will be more able to achieve desirable outcomes in both housing and support. Therefore, one can argue that lower income households are constrained in their ability to exercise control if they have only limited options open to them, which may be low status and which will not meet their desires and aspirations. A low-income household may only have the option of access to low-status public sector supported housing options. If access to owner occupation is made available to them, they are likely to be able to afford only low-price, poor-quality properties that are less likely to experience price appreciation. Another important point is that such households may be placed in an uncertain and risky situation. They may struggle to find enough resources to keep the property in good repair and, if they are in a low-demand neighbourhood, may experience price depreciation, thus reducing future choices. They may also have difficulty in maintaining mortgage payments or service charges, particularly if their income reduces, for example through unemployment. Therefore, the assumption that market participation, by itself, will bring about choice and control over housing and support circumstances is flawed. Nevertheless, this discussion of market choice highlights the importance of resources in general, and financial resources in particular, in enabling differential access to control. It follows that if government wanted to increase choice, it would pursue redistribution towards the poorer households to enable them to join others in exercising it.

In the supported housing context, personal control may also be influenced by the way that support is provided and the social practices undertaken by support staff in the scheme. One of the reasons for the move away from institutions has been the desire to increase the personal control that residents can exercise in the everyday running of their lives, as well as in their choice of accommodation and support. The personalisation agenda in Britain is designed to give people more control over their support arrangements and in Sweden disabled people may be able to choose their personal assistant to provide support.

Personal control is a difficult concept to define and measure, and so is a slippery concept around which to build an evaluation of supported housing. However, in practice the example of the young homeless person shows how useful it is as a guide to action. Any housing intervention that improves physical conditions but decreases control is liable to be counterproductive if the aim is to increase well-being.

The discussion above highlights the importance of the home in realising personal control. It is in the home that we perform many of the important social practices that define our feeling of control and efficacy. People receiving support tend to spend more time in the home and the way that support is provided may have profound impacts on the degree of control over the everyday social practices that a person can exert.

Identity and self-esteem

A positive identity and high self-esteem are essential for happiness and well-being. There is a large literature on the importance of housing in the creation and sustenance of personal identity. However, identity is sometimes 'spoiled' through housing circumstances. Individuals may pursue strategies to protect their self-esteem and a positive identity when it is under threat. For example, Farrington and Robinson (1999) describe the different ways that homeless people cope with the negative identity associated with their situation. Some denied the homeless identity and sought to distance themselves from it. Others sought a positive group identity within the homeless population as a whole and referred to it as a family. Others identified with a subgroup of homeless people and sought a favourable comparison with other subgroups or the general population of homeless people. Farrington and Robinson (1999) identify the paradox that the homeless people who maintained the most positive identities were those who identified most strongly with the homeless role and with a supportive group of friends. However, this identification made escape from homelessness more difficult. It is argued that, for these individuals, opportunities would need to be created for the development of a positive personal and social identity that was independent of homelessness. In their conclusions the authors stress the importance of the acknowledgement of these identity processes by policy makers and practitioners dealing with homeless people. A positive identity and high self-esteem are associated with a sense of efficacy or ability to cope. A focus on happiness and well-being brings efficacy to the fore and highlights the importance for practitioners and policy makers of creating and sustaining this if people are to thrive.

Also, there is an important issue of the dignity and self-esteem that households receive from their housing and support experiences. It was argued earlier that a lack of control can lead to low self-esteem. At the same time, if the only choices available to a household are all of low status, then personal control may not lead to high self-esteem. But self-esteem may also be influenced by the way that people are treated by significant others they interact with. When living in supported housing, people are in interaction with other residents and professionals of many kinds, whether the carer, housing officer or home help. How they are treated by these others may influence their self-esteem. If they are treated with condescension, aggression, disgust or any other negative attitude, then this may hinder their achievement of high self-esteem. The point here is that the way that households are treated by key actors may be as important a part of the outcomes of supported housing as the substantive aspects of the provision.

People may differ in the extent to which their housing circumstances allow them to feel a positive identity. As outlined earlier, Clapham (2005) has argued that many housing options are shaped by general categorical discourses from which stereotypes are constructed. An example would be discourses of old age, which emphasise dependency and frailty and which are linked with housing options such as sheltered housing, which are based on a stereotypical view of the needs of older people. Another would be the discourse of youth that emphasises the primacy of work and the need to use sanctions to ensure that it is not undermined by the 'workshy' unemployed (see Clapham, 2005). Where the discourse is negative, signifying low status, stressing dependence rather than control and over-emphasising the uniformity of need and aspirations, it is likely that the supported housing options associated with it will have similar characteristics.

A key set of discourses relates to tenure. It was argued earlier that impact of the different legal attributes of tenure is mediated by the attitudes of individuals. However, there are clear status differences between tenures related to their societal discourses. Gurney (1999) has referred to the 'normalising discourse of owner-occupation', where owning one's own home is portrayed as the right and proper thing to do and shows that one has achieved a status position.

Categorical discourses that stigmatise the members of the category can impact on well-being through housing design. The external appearance of a building can impact on identity and self-esteem by emitting signals of status, other aspects of difference, or elements of categorical discourses such as frailty or cultural difference.

The key point here is that people do not construct their identity in isolation from wider societal factors, some of which are susceptible to policy intervention. A focus on well-being emphasises the importance of creating and sustaining supported housing options that sustain a positive identity. Improving the material standards of disadvantaged people may have less of an impact if it is associated with stigma and so spoils identity. An awareness of the identity implications of provision is needed and a focus on identity management by the people being helped.

The home is an important element in sustaining our identity and self-esteem as the preceding discussion highlights. In both its practical design and its symbolism, the home can influence strongly our view of ourselves and the way that others see us.

Social relations

One of the factors highlighted earlier was the importance of social relationships in enabling individuals to cope with social conditions and to maintain high self-esteem. Most social support is provided by family and close friends, but there may be some limited ways that housing policy can impact on this. For example, allocation policies in public rented housing have not traditionally given weight to the need for people to be close to family and friends, but could be used as an instrument to improve the local availability of social support. In Britain, the recent concern with the creation of mixed communities may reduce the stigma for disadvantaged people, but may have an adverse impact on social support, as there is little evidence of close ties between inhabitants with different backgrounds (see Chapter Four). The issue of segregation is a key one for the vulnerable people who are the focus of this book, as we shall see in Chapter Four. Will self-esteem and status be influenced by segregation in an environment such as a retirement village? In the abstract, one can hypothesise that segregation could improve social relations with like-minded people, but may reduce contacts with others and could signal difference from the mainstream population and a low-status position. The example of the impact of the isolated Victorian asylums in Britain on the well-being of their residents may have influenced many people's views on segregation, but retirement villages seem to be popular.

In supported housing, there has been a focus on the social relations of those living within a scheme. Clearly, the better the social relations within a scheme the more likely residents are to gain support from their peers, which seems to be crucial in generating high self-esteem. Less attention has been given to social relations between people inside and outside any scheme. Questions exist about the extent to which entering a supported housing scheme may result in loss of contact with previous friends and family. This is, therefore, a crucial issue in the evaluation of supported housing, and we will explore it in more detail in our discussion of homes in Chapter Three and neighbourhoods in Chapter Four.

Evaluating supported housing options

If we are to achieve the aims of this book it is necessary to identify ways of assessing the success or failure of supported housing options in particular circumstances. This need may be at the level of an individual, or their family or support worker, attempting to assess what is best for the individual. Or it may be managers deciding on the appropriate form of supported housing that will meet an identified need in a given locality. Alternatively, it may be government deciding how to make the best use of scarce resources in planning new provision. At these different levels, there is a need to assess the relative worth of different forms of provision. Given the importance of individual identity and lifestyle emphasised in this chapter, it is assumed that there will not be one form of accommodation that is most appropriate for everyone. It is assumed, therefore, that there is a need for a flexible range of supported housing options for people to choose from, although it may be possible that, in practice, some forms are more popular and more effective for more people than others.

Later in the chapter, an attempt will be made to build an assessment and evaluation framework on the basis of the concept of well-being. However, before embarking on this it is necessary to consider two other ways that could be and have been used to make evaluations.

Consumer choice

One possible scenario would be for personal choice to be the touchstone of effectiveness. In other words, effective forms of supported housing would be considered to be those chosen by individuals in a 'quasi-market' situation. It could be argued that if people were dissatisfied with their accommodation and support, they would move elsewhere or choose another form. Providers would be guided by the choices of consumers in terms of the forms of supported housing they would provide. This scenario is one that is envisaged in the original community care arrangements in Britain and reinforced through the personalisation agenda. Consumers are viewed as being assessed on the basis of their expressed needs and a sum of money or personal budget allocated to them, which they are free to spend as they wish (see Chapter Five).

There are a number of problems with this scenario, as touched on in the previous section on control. The first is that doubt has been expressed about the ability of consumers to make the best choices for themselves. This criticism has a number of elements. One is the doubt that some people have the ability to make rational and effective choices for themselves. This criticism has most often been expressed in relation to people suffering from dementia or learning difficulties, where people may not be aware enough to understand the nature of their circumstances or their needs. A related point is that people may lack the confidence or ability to be able to manage their own support package. In response to these issues, a number of advice and advocacy agencies have arisen to help consumers to make effective choices by providing information and offering a management service if required. Therefore this criticism does not really hold, as it should be possible to provide support to enable people to make informed choices and to maximise the extent to which choice is possible.

A second doubt is the knowledge that consumers will have about the options open to them and the impact on their lives. This is one reason why governments have looked to the provision of information that could enable consumers to make more informed choices. For example, in the field of health care, information is provided on success rates for particular operations so that consumers can choose an appropriate hospital and doctor for them. A similar example may be school exam results. Therefore, in the field of supported housing, there is a case for more information on 'success' to guide consumer choice. This is a key argument for the evaluation approach taken in this book, which should provide information on which choices can be based.

A third doubt is a lack of confidence that consumers will make appropriate choices. Where government is funding the supported housing, at least in part, it may be felt that there is an issue of public accountability for public money and it may be considered that government has a right to a say in (or even control over) what the money is spent on. As an example, there was press coverage in Britain a few years ago of a man receiving a direct payment who used part of this to pay a support worker to take him down to the pub to have a drink one night a week. The man justified this on the basis of enjoying a relaxing time with friends in a sociable environment that reduced his isolation, kept him in touch with friends and improved his well-being. The press view was that this was an inappropriate use of public money that should have been spent on more 'pressing' and 'deserving' needs. Of course it is possible to argue that the improvement in well-being that the pub visit was said to bring could have led to improved self-esteem and social integration that would have led to improved physical and mental health and so, in the long run, would have reduced future calls on public finances. However, without a measure of success or outcome it is difficult to make this case satisfactorily.

This example raises an important issue that comes up throughout this book, which is that governments and residents may have different views of what supported housing is meant to achieve. In other words, the government may judge that there is a societal objective to be achieved, which may not be the objective chosen by the resident. For example, a vulnerable young person may be required to abstain from drug or alcohol use or criminal behaviour before being given supported housing, although the young person may not agree that this is in his best interests. There is clearly a social control element in the provision of supported housing that varies between different groups and different forms, and which may limit any approach solely concerned with the subjectively defined well-being of the resident. In practice, many ways of assessing the impact of supported housing, such as the 'outcome star' discussed below, start from the basis that the objectives to be achieved are agreed between the support worker and the resident. In others, such as the Supporting People framework, a list of well-being outcomes is devised by the government in agreement with the providers and contains both subjective well-being factors and behavioural factors that relate to objectives of social control through behavioural change. We will consider some of the societal objectives in more detail in our discussion of particular groups in later chapters. However, it was stated in the introduction that the standpoint of this book is that any deviation from the aim of increasing subjective well-being through supported housing is inappropriate on moral grounds unless it can be agreed with the person concerned, and this position was discussed more fully in the previous chapter.

In addition, the consumer choice scenario is based on the premise that the consumer pays for supported housing, even if some of the cost is met by government subsidy. However, many supported housing schemes are funded directly by government through what may be termed a supply subsidy. In this case, an outcomes measure is necessary for government to decide whether it has received value for money. The consumer choice model is only really applicable when all forms of provision are priced at a level that meets costs, or if all receive the same amount of subsidy. In this scenario, government should be neutral between different forms of provision, which is not currently the case in either country considered here. A more fundamental point is that inequalities in income mean that some people will be more able to exercise choice than others. For example, not everyone can own their home in a retirement village.

In summary, the consumer choice or market model of the analysis can be a valuable approach in enabling people to achieve their own well-being, but it is at best a partial tool for assessing the outcome of supported housing, because of the constraints on choice outlined above. Governments need more information in order to assess the value gained from public money. Consumers themselves need information on which to base their choices and are subject to constraints on the options open to them. Therefore, consumer choice is one element of an acceptable evaluation framework, but a focus on the outcomes of provision on subjective well-being is an important element of that approach.

Quality standards

The second scenario is an approach adopted by most governments, which is to subject supported housing schemes to various statutory regulatory regimes that lay down standards to be met. For example, in Britain some supported housing services, such as some extra-care housing, have to meet the Care Quality Council standards that cover administration of the service. Items covered in the standards include the provision of information and the involvement of consumers; the existence of personalised care and support; safety and safeguarding; suitable staffing; quality of service; and suitability of management. However, most of these measures are of output rather than outcome. That is, they measure the service provided rather than the impact this service provision has on consumers.

The concept of normalisation has provided a set of factors that have been included in many sets of criteria used to assess supported housing. Normalisation was an influential, but strongly contested concept that held sway for a limited period of time and will be considered further in Chapter Eight. Important elements of normalisation are the social value that is deemed necessary for people to have a positive self-identity and to express this in a lifestyle that is valued and 'mainstream'. The concept was criticised by advocates of the social model of disability, who argued that it overplayed the necessity for impaired people to fit into 'mainstream' life, without placing emphasis on the changes necessary in society to reduce the barriers that led to their disability and reinforced their exclusion. The concept was also criticised for being too vague and difficult to use in practice. What exactly is 'mainstream' or 'normal' life? However, despite the controversy, the essential features of normalisation were incorporated into policy and practice. This was helped by the existence of tools that provided a rating scale for judging the extent to which a particular service promoted social identity and personal competence. Normalisation was the forerunner of many different lists of service requirements that have formed the basis of service planning and evaluations of service delivery that we shall consider later in the chapter.

There has been little dispute around the issues included in these lists of important principles of policy and practice. However, divorced from their normalisation roots, the concepts chosen seem to lack a unifying rationale. Why these factors and not others? How do individual factors relate together and what is their relative importance? However, perhaps the most damning criticism of these lists relates back to the roots of normalisation roots in the relative lack of voice of the service user. The criteria of success are not defined by individuals themselves, but by those working with them to a predefined script. The concept of well-being offers a way of dealing with this deficit.

For all the above reasons, there is a perceived need to evaluate the outcome of supported housing on the part of governments and other stakeholders: consumers, producers and managers. So the key question is, what is the outcome of supported housing? One approach to this question is to assess the outcomes of individuals receiving a service.

Well-being and supported housing

There has been substantial interest in Britain recently in finding measures of service outcomes that reflect the individual emphasis of well-being. An example is the use of what became known as the 'outcomes star' (Triangle Consulting, 2014). In this technique a number of goals and achievements are identified for each individual. The goals may relate to the development of personal relationships, gaining employment, reducing alcohol intake, and so on. These goals are to be agreed between the individual and their professionals, and the results rated over time in terms of progress towards the highest rate of the scales. This tool can form the basis of service planning for the individual and a monitor of outcome. There has been some use of the tool for the evaluation of service provision. An important argument made in support of this approach is that the aim of many providers is (or should be) to improve the lives of individuals, rather than just to provide a menu of services. Therefore, services should not be judged on the basis of some externally derived service guidelines (such as those derived from the normalisation approach) but on the sum of the differences made to individual lives. The star has since been developed further for the use of agencies helping homeless people (Triangle Consulting, 2014). It is based on the concept of an individual moving up a ladder from being stuck to accepting help, to believing (that the individual can make a difference to their life), to learning (how to achieve our objectives), to self-reliance. This ladder is related to 10 areas of life: motivation and taking responsibility; self care and living skills; managing money and personal administration; social networks and relationships; drug and alcohol misuse; physical health; emotional and mental health; meaningful use of time; managing tenancy and accommodation; and offending. This is, in many ways, a very mixed list of areas. Some relate directly to the well-being of individuals, such as health, motivation, and social networks, but others relate to specific norms of behaviour, such as offending and drug and alcohol misuse. These elements seem to point to a social control element to the list and, of course, social control is one element of the objectives of supported housing. However, it is not difficult to see that there could be a strong link between, for example, a lack of drug misuse and well-being.

Another approach was taken through the Supporting People framework in England, where national data were collected from 2003 to 2011 and, since then, on a voluntary basis by a number of agencies. This framework involves the collection of service output information (what is provided to consumers) as well as demographic and other characteristics of the consumers. On leaving the service an assessment is made as to whether the consumer has made a successful exit, defined as one that is made in a planned way. Service management information is collected on issues such as utilisation of services, throughput of consumers and success in terms of the achievement of independent living. The key element of the framework is a set of measures to assess the needs of a consumer and the extent to which they have been met. There are five main headings: economic well-being (that covers maximising income, access to paid work); enjoy and achieve (work like activity, training, education or learning, and contact with friends, family or service agencies); be healthy (physical and mental health, and substance misuse); stay safe (secure and independent accommodation, offending behaviour and harm to oneself or others); and make a positive contribution (choice and control). For each of these items, consumers are judged as to whether they require help and whether they achieved a positive outcome (for example, avoided self-harm or maintained paid employment).

The two approaches have different emphases. The outcomes star is primarily a tool for individual assessment and support planning, although it can be used at the level of the individual scheme to assess the effectiveness of provision. For example, it may be possible to try different styles of intervention, and to assess their impact on people at a similar stage on the ladder. Issues such as the impact of staff expertise and training could also be assessed. A key strength of the outcomes star approach is that it focuses attention on the individual consumers and their needs and their trajectory. The trajectory point is important because it stresses the developmental aspect of the ladder. It tends to be used for homeless people or those with health problems, such as alcohol abuse, that can be tackled through intervention. Is it as useful for those with chronic problems, such as older people, who may deteriorate rather than develop? It could be argued that a development focus is still important in focusing on the ability of older people to function, even if they have a declining physical and mental capacity. Alternatively, it could be argued that where people are only maintaining their situation or managing deterioration, the ladder could become a dis-incentivising tool rather than the reverse. Although it is useful at the level of the individual person and scheme, there are questions about the usefulness of the ladder for benchmarking between different forms of support. It is difficult to aggregate from the individual level because of the complexity of the individual data. However, in theory it should be possible to devise a 'value added' measure that assesses the 'distance travelled' by individuals from a starting point of receiving supported housing, and to use this to compare different forms of provision, although this has not been done in practice.

In contrast, the Supporting People framework has been devised specifically to allow benchmarking between different forms of provision. To achieve this, it is much simpler than the ladder, taking into account a much-reduced range of variables and requiring only a simple assessment of the outcome. The framework does not offer a 'distance travelled' tool, so is difficult to use to assess the impact that a particular form of provision has had.

The Supporting People framework is largely focused on the behaviour of the individual, whether this is in terms of employment or work-related activity, or dealing with substance abuse or other problems. Whereas the ladder is based on an agreement between an individual and the provider on what issues need to be tackled, the Supporting People framework is more of a 'top-down' list of normative behaviour rather than an individual's expression of their own well-being. So someone could be conforming to behavioural norms but be lacking in self-esteem and well-being. The outcomes star focuses on behaviour, but also on some of the factors that have been shown to impact on well-being, such as control, social relations and physical and mental health.

Both of the approaches use elements of the ADL scales. On a daily basis, staff of statutory and voluntary agencies have to assess the abilities and needs of people who have a physical disability and their ability to function adequately in specific physical environments such as their own homes. They do this using the ADL. There are many differences in the functions chosen, but those included are usually ones that could be considered to represent the basic needs of individuals to keep themselves safe and healthy. Key elements, therefore, are the ability to wash, eat and use toilet facilities. Domestic tasks such as food preparation and cooking, shopping and housework are included. Mobility both inside and outside the dwelling is also assessed. However, the assessment moves beyond the basic needs to cover motivation as well, and emotional needs such as loneliness, and the existence of interests and activities. It covers relationships with others, such as family and friends, and learning, work and leisure activities and interests. The assessor is also asked to consider the physical, sensory and mental health and functioning of the individual. It is necessary to undertake an assessment of the individual's accommodation in terms of its suitability for their needs, both in terms of its type, facilities, tenure, and its situation in the local environment. The assessment focuses on the relative ease of a particular person being able to undertake an activity. However, the list of activities in the outcomes star and the Supporting People framework covers only basic activities; there is an implicit acceptance that the activities are the same for each individual and little attention is paid to the context of the built environment. Therefore, the concept of lifestyle is not incorporated in the approaches. This can be overcome by accepting that the activities of individuals will legitimately vary and so a particular set of activities needs to be defined for each individual. In this way the individual lifestyle can be incorporated into decisions about appropriate accommodation and support.

Although there has been some criticism of the possibility of measuring the concept of well-being, some studies are now beginning to emerge that have attempted to measure well-being in a housing context. For example, Christian et al (2011, 2012) have used measures of well-being to investigate the use of outreach services by homeless people. They used indicators of social identity, efficacy (or degree of control) and self-esteem. Kearns et al (2012) examine the impacts on well-being of different forms of accommodation and neighbourhood. This study is important because it emphasises a common drawback of the outcomes star and Supporting People approaches, in that both are focused on the support elements and neither focuses enough on the accommodation aspects of the supported housing package. There is a complete absence of any element of the built environment in the approaches outlined. Supported housing, by its very definition, involves both accommodation and support and both must influence the impact on individuals.

Conclusion

The chapter has focused on the ideas that are important in justifying, shaping and judging different forms of supported housing, and has drawn attention to the impact of discourses in shaping the forms that provision takes. Emphasis has been placed on the importance of difference as it is represented in different identities and lifestyles. The achievement of a positive personal identity and a socially valued lifestyle are crucial to the well-being of individuals and so should be the core of supported housing provision.

In particular, the three important factors highlighted here that underpin well-being – personal control, positive identity and self-esteem, and positive social relations – are at the heart of successful provision. The achievement of the well-being of the resident should be the primary focus of supported housing and gives us a way of assessing the impact of different forms of provision. However, existing ways of doing this are flawed in a number of respects. The most important is that they neglect the impact of the physical, social and symbolic setting on well-being, focusing, as they do, on the support elements of provision. The home is the setting for many of the processes that impact on well-being, as it is the place in which we pursue our closest relationships and the base from which we live out all the aspects of our lives. The neighbourhood in which we live is the setting for many functional practices that sustain our lives, such as shopping and the use of other facilities. It is also the place where many of our social relationships take place. Supported housing is a mix of shelter and support and so both elements should be judged in terms of their impact. In the following two chapters, therefore, we focus on the home and on the neighbourhood in which it is situated, as they are the two important elements of the setting of supported accommodation. The aim is to incorporate these elements into our framework for judging provision.

But, finally, the chapter has stressed the impact of inequality on well-being; it is a factor that needs to be borne in mind throughout the book and is one that will be returned to later.

THREE

Homes

Supported housing consists of both a house and support. Therefore, in order to evaluate supported housing we need to consider the relationship between people and their houses and homes, and find a way of assessing whether this meets the criterion of improving well-being. It was argued in the last chapter that previous evaluations of supported housing have neglected the home, even though it is where we spend most of our time, is integral to our achievement of well-being, and is an integral part of the supported housing 'package'. Therefore, this chapter seeks to add to the discussion of well-being in the previous chapter by focusing on the home and its impact on the well-being of those who live in it.

The term 'house' has been used to denote a physical dwelling and there is an important research and policy focus on the impact of physical houses on people with support needs, as we shall see in the following chapters. What kinds of physical houses do people need and how are they different from the houses needed or desired by others? At the same time, there is a realisation that houses are not just physical objects, but have symbolic, emotional and psychological dimensions. The home is a major source of our well-being as it is the locus of our most intimate and private moments and of our closest relationships, as well as a source of identity and self-esteem. The problem with existing research is that the physical and the other elements of home have been examined separately and there is a lack of a holistic framework in which the two kinds of factors can be considered together. The need for such a framework is urgent if we are to understand the impact that houses and homes have on the people who live in them. This general point is particularly apposite for our present purpose in this book. In supported housing, both sets of factors are likely to be important to residents, and there may be trade-offs between the physical and other dimensions. For example, the introduction of adaptations to enable better physical functioning in a house may have an unwanted symbolic meaning for the resident by signalling difference, and may destroy the identity and self-esteem that the resident may have felt.

The construction of an appropriate holistic framework is not easy and needs substantial theorising to reach an acceptable conclusion. The effort is worthwhile, however, because of the importance of the issue for our purpose in the book and its potential for improving the well-being of supported housing residents. The chapter will focus first on the meaning elements of a home and will then search for ways in which these can be combined with the physical dimensions to provide a holistic framework. This is done by using the concept of affordances, which stresses the interrelationship between the perception of physical things and of their meaning.

The meaning of home

There is a substantial literature on the meaning of home (see for example, Saunders and Williams, 1988; Somerville 1992, 1997; Gurney, 1999; Moore, 2000; Easthope, 2004; Heywood, 2005). However, the main point made in this chapter is the relative paucity of studies that combine all of the main elements involved in the relationship between people and their physical home. Some studies have focused on the everyday discourse of home where the aim has been to attempt to describe and analyse the meaning that the concept has for individuals, groups and societies. In some cases this has taken the form of lists of meanings. For example, Somerville (1992) uses six categories of home: shelter, hearth (by which is meant feelings of physical warmth and cosiness), heart (loving and affectionate relationships), privacy (power to exclude others), abode (place to call home) and roots (individual's source of identity and meaningfulness). This list and others like it (see, for example, Sixsmith, 1986) seem to be blind to cultural aspects of shared meanings, but other lists include cultural as well as experiential elements (see, for example, Despres, 1991) and therefore recognise that different aspects of home may be important in different societal contexts.

Homes have important emotional and psycho-social impacts. Kearns et al (2012) found a strong correlation between high levels of mental well-being and four subjectively assessed elements of a person's house that relate strongly to the factors highlighted in the previous chapter as being important to general well-being: their view of its external appearance and what other people thought of it (social status contributing to self-esteem); a feeling of being in control of the home (personal control); the home expressing one's personality and values (identity); and personal progress in that my home makes me feel I am doing well in life (self-esteem). Therefore, in the discussion of supported accommodation it is important for the well-being of the residents that the housing elements of the package are able to deliver these benefits.

Home can also have strong symbolic aspects in particular societal contexts. For example, public housing in Britain in the 1920s, with its garden suburb design stimulated by the Arts and Crafts movement, symbolised 'homes fit for heroes to live in' after the First World War and harked back to a rural idyll. In contrast, public housing in the 1960s, with its modernist design, was linked to political discourse about modernisation and the 'white heat of technology' (see Dunleavy, 1981). Ravetz (2001) sees council housing as a cultural colonisation, in which a vision was forged by one sector of society for application to another. Cole and Furbey (1994: 112) argue:

> The spatial segregation and architectural distinctiveness of many estates, most notably the post-war flatted developments, involved the powerful imposition of producer's meanings and symbolism on working class households. Such architecture announces to society the 'differentness' of the scheme's residents, underlining the marginal status of many inner-city households and prompting the question, in the context of concern about 'problem housing estates' as to why people should be expected to care for the symbols of their own social inferiority.

If a supported housing scheme is substituted for the council housing considered above the same factors may be important. The design of the scheme may carry a strong symbolism of society's view of the people living there, and their status and 'difference' from the rest of the population. In this way, supported housing may carry the categorical identity of the group of people living there. Older people may be cut off from mainstream life in their 'sheltered' housing scheme, which symbolises their low status and difference following the disengagement discourse that sees old age as a gradual withdrawal from life in a preparation for death (see Chapter Six). People with learning disabilities may live in premises that look different from ordinary houses and are isolated from community life, reflecting the view that they should be hidden away from the rest of the population as in the Victorian asylums (see Chapter Eight). The general point is that the form of provision may carry important messages about the way that the residents are considered in society and their status. Given the importance of the perception of others to self-esteem and identity, this symbolism could have a profound impact on the well-being of the residents.

Home is also linked to other social institutions and discourses, such as the discourses of family (see Allan and Crow, 1989). The design of accommodation and the management practices that surround it may send out signals about the appropriateness of family life and family roles. Gender discourses may be reflected in the layout of houses and the positions of rooms, such as kitchens or 'male' studies. In supported accommodation there may be gender or age differentiated provision. In some shared houses it may only be possible to cater for individuals, and there may not be provision for residents to form couple households, possibly reflecting dominant discourses about the sexual relationships of, for example, older people or people with learning disabilities.

There is also a very important strand of literature that links home with patterns of social change. One examples is the proposition that home is becoming increasingly important in a time of time-space distantiation or the stretching out of social relations in space and time (Giddens, 1984, 1990). In this tradition, home is not necessarily associated with a particular place or dwelling. It may be associated with a country or homeland, or may be transportable between locations (see Blunt and Dowling, 2006). This may be particularly important for migrants or ethnic minorities, who may have more than one location they think of as home that may have very different cultural meanings and signals.

There has been a research focus on the relationship between a dwelling and the people who live in it. This is essentially an analysis of the relationship between individuals and one aspect of their built environment and is a common approach in people–environment studies. For example, Porteous (1976) equates home with the dwelling and links it to concepts of territoriality. He argues that home provides individuals with all three of the identified territorial satisfactions of identity, security and stimulation. Moore (2000) notes that early psychological explorations of home examined the affective bonds between people and home places, and produced concepts such as place attachment and place identity. In this literature, Moore (2000) argues that home was nearly always taken to mean a person's dwelling or house, but the focus was solely concerned with the psychological impact on individuals and was therefore decontextualised from the wider cultural contexts or the socially shared meanings or representations, which, in part, may have shaped the subjects' conceptualisations of home. Also, there was a lack of focus on the particular physical elements of places. Moore (2000: 211) states that 'place identity tends to be concerned with the way in which places form part of the self-identity, and less to do with the qualities and evaluation of places'. Moore (2000: 213) points out the irony that, in this approach, 'while home is examined largely because it has physical form, this feature of home has been left relatively unexplored in relation to the personal and psychological aspects'.

In contrast, another strand of work, exemplified by Rapoport (1982, 2000), has examined particular physical forms in the relationship between people and their houses, and has drawn out the symbolic meanings of house design and furnishing. 'It appears that the meaning of activities is their most important characteristic corresponding to the finding that symbolic aspects are the most important in the sequence of concrete object, use object, symbolic object.' (Rapoport, 1982: 33). This strand of work is important in linking together societal and psychological factors in the relationship between individuals and particular physical dwellings. Other work has seen the built form as the carrier of symbolic meaning, whether at the individual or societal level. Good examples of the latter are work by Ravetz (2001) and Swenarton (1981) into the symbolic meaning of particular house forms that were discussed earlier. The – often implicit – foundation of this approach is that the built form of the house or dwelling is a passive carrier of meaning. This fundamental tenet is well defined by Harré (2002), who uses the term 'social objects' to cover material things that are defined in relation to their place in the social world. An object is 'transformed from a piece of stuff definable independently of any story-line into a social object by its embedment into a narrative' (Harré, 2002: 25). 'To become relevant to human life material beings must be interpreted for them to play a part in a human narrative' (Harré, 2002: 32). The focus, then, is on the narrative in which the material object is embedded, such as narratives of home. However, the focus on symbolic meaning seems to ignore the functional use elements of the physical environment.

In conclusion, there is a very diverse and rich literature on home that has illuminated many aspects of the relationship between people and their dwelling. However, what seems to be lacking is an integrating framework that can focus on the people–physical house relationship, and consider together the use and symbolic elements.

Embodiment and home

Despite some recent exceptions (Gurney, 2000; King 2004, 2005), in much of the literature on home reviewed above, the emphasis has been on meanings, but less on feelings, senses or physical actions. Until recently, therefore, the literature on the meaning of home has mirrored that in much mainstream sociology in that the body is an 'absent presence' (Shilling, 1993). It is there, but rarely explicitly considered or adequately theorised. Social constructionism (through the work of Foucault; see for example, 1980) is criticised for treating the body as entirely a social construction that is a passive carrier of meaning. Although this has taught us much about the way that society has shaped the body and made it meaningful, it tells us little about the nature of bodies and how they can shape meaning (Shilling, 1993). In relation to our purpose here, the major issue is the importance of the body as an integral component of human agency. As Shilling (1993: 9) argues:

> It is our bodies that allow us to act, to intervene in and to alter the flow of daily life. Indeed it is impossible to have an adequate theory of human agency without taking into account the body. In a very important sense, acting people are acting bodies.

There has been a relevant debate in geography about the embodied nature of human action. This focus has led to what has been termed 'the emotional turn' in human geography, in which there has been an emphasis on the role of bodily senses and emotions in relation to places (see Rodaway, 1994; Anderson and Smith, 2001; Davidson et al, 2005). Thrift (2004) has argued for a non-representational geography that does not just focus on texts or other symbolic forms of meaning, but examines affect, which encapsulates 'our self-evidently more-than-human, more-than-textual, multi-sensual worlds' (Lorimer, 2005: 83). This has led to a focus on the performance of everyday activities and social practices that enact identities (Butler, 1993), or 'practices, mundane everyday practices that shape the conduct of human beings towards others and themselves in particular sites' (Thrift, 1997: 126–7, quoted in Nash, 2000: 655). The emphasis on embodied experiences and practices within the home is clearly important in the context of supported housing. But the exciting emphasis on performance should not hide the meaning dimensions of home because both are important, as the literature on home makes clear. Home is both a discourse and a physical object within which embodied activities are performed. Nash (2000: 658) argues that even dance, which would seem to be a good example of a performed body practice, has an element of language and thought in the way that it is 'taught, scripted, performed and watched ... even untrained dance is culturally learnt and culturally located'. Lorimer (2005) uses the phrase 'more than representational' to make the point that the focus on performance should be additional to, rather than at the expense of, representational analysis. Embodied social practices need to be socially located in levels of discourse and meaning.

Towards house as a material artefact

The approaches reviewed above all offer some insight into the relationship between humans and houses and homes. Clearly, houses have a symbolic and discursive meaning at both a societal and individual level. Home is embedded in a wide range of societal discourses that shape the meaning that individuals hold. However, the meanings are embodied in the sense that they involve feelings, emotions and actions. Our link to our dwelling is as much of the body and the senses as of the mind. Meaning is shaped by use as well as discourse and our use of dwellings is embodied. We move around and perform social practices in a house using our bodies.

The house is a discourse, but is also clearly a material object that influences our patterns of behaviour and our meanings. Lees (2001) criticises the understanding of a building as a text in which meanings are inscribed, where it is seen as a sign and symbol of something else, such as gender relations and so on. This approach neglects how ordinary people engage with and inhabit the space. She argues that 'consumption [of space] is an active, embodied and productive *practice*' and recognises 'the creativity of consumers in actively shaping the meanings of the goods they consume' (Lees, 2001: 55).

Gieryn (2002) argues that we should try to approach material culture without reducing objects to instantiations of discourse or realisations of cognitive representations, and to avoid the disappearance of the material world behind language. However, he argues that buildings cannot be considered as having agency in that material artefacts cannot pursue intentional action as humans can. He states that:

> buildings do not have agency, but relative fixity. Brick and mortar resist intervention and permutation, as they accomplish a measure of stasis. And yet, buildings stabilise *imperfectly*. Some fall into ruin, others are destroyed naturally or by human hand, and most are unendingly renovated into something they were not originally. (Gieryn, 2002: 35, original emphasis)

Buildings stabilise social life. We shape our buildings and afterwards our buildings shape us. A building can be seen as the object of human agency *and* as an agent of its own through its relative fixity. A building is a site for people and organisations to define themselves and pursue their goals, but also one where those meanings and purposes get structured and constrained. Gieryn identifies three important moments in the life of a building. The first is the design, where the building takes on the meaning of the designers; the second is the shift of agency to the building that structures human relationships; the third is reconfiguration through narration and reinterpretation by users. This reconfiguration may be discursive or material. Lees (2001) uses the example of children playing on the escalator of a library building who, through their behaviour, alter the meaning of the building by using it for a purpose not foreseen or sanctioned by the designers. An example relevant to our subject matter here may be using a domestic house as a group home.

Giddens (1984) argues that buildings become what people actively do with them. The structuring force of built environments comes from the spatial and architectural routinisation of everyday interactions: the design of familiar places evokes and steers patterned behavioural responses. This is not agency, because behaviour is dependent on the interpretations and uses by knowledgeable humans, although buildings can structure practices at an unconscious level without conscious human involvement. Buildings are simultaneously the consequence and structural cause of social practices. Therefore, the house is the setting that influences the embodied action within it as well as a carrier (and creator) of meaning. The difficulty is in identifying and theorising the nature of this embodied action. What kinds of actions are involved? What is the relationship between embodied action and meaning?

The above discussion has profound consequences for the discussion of supported housing. It highlights the way that humans can change the meaning of homes through their actions within them that may alter the use and meaning that was envisaged by the designer or architect or commissioner. The work of Miller (2001) on the material culture of the home gives examples of the ways in which a home and its inhabitants transform one another. Miller details the way in which homes and their inhabitants negotiate a compromise between the house's given order and the inhabitants' preferences in layout and decoration. The following chapters will show examples of the way that the practices of support workers are shaped by, and in turn shape the use and meaning of a resident's home. One example may be the way that staff enter a person's individual room by knocking on the door to show respect for privacy and resident control over a private space. Another example may be the redistribution of furniture in a common room in a supported housing scheme in the way residents want, in order to facilitate social interaction, which may turn a public space controlled by staff into a semi-private space controlled by residents. These social practices may be made easier or more difficult depending on the physical layout of the scheme. Therefore, the interaction between the social practices within a supported housing scheme and the built environment are an important element in the experiences and well-being of the people that live there.

The material house

The general approach towards the relationship between people and their homes that is adopted in this book is to build on the concept of *affordances*, which was first developed by the psychologist Gibson (1986) and later taken up in relation to houses by Coolen (2006). Gibson defined the affordances of a material object or environment as 'what it offers the animal, what it provides or furnishes, either for good or ill' (1986: 127). It implies the complementarity of the animal and the environment. Therefore, the emphasis is on the physical properties of an object (such as a house), but only relative to a particular person, as the affordances are unique to the individual. In the case of a house, the layout may afford different behaviours for different people and different mechanical encounters. He uses the example of the height of a chair, which may mean that it has the affordance of the provision of rest to an adult, but not to a child. Gibson emphasises that an affordance is neither solely objective nor subjective, but is both. In his terms 'it is equally a fact of the environment and a fact of behaviour. It is both physical and psychical, yet neither' (Gibson, 1986: 129). The concept of affordances places a twin focus on the built house and the individual using it. Gibson argues that the approach is incompatible with the unhelpful dualisms of both mind–matter and mind–body.

Gibson's approach has some similarities to the concern in emotional geography with the limits of linguistic meaning. The roots of Gibson's approach lie in his rejection of the representational theories of perception that are based on the concept of a filter between humans and their perception of the environment. In other words, in the representational view, humans see the material world through their own lens of constructed meanings, whether shared or individual. This emphasis creates a dualism between the subjective and the material world, and places the focus on the social construction of meanings and away from the environment as much research on the meaning of home has done. In contrast, Gibson argues that perception of the environment is direct.

> Departing from the long-held position in the philosophy and psychology of perception that the meaning of objects

73

and events for a perceiver is imposed on sensory input by cognitive processes, Gibson argued that this meaning is directly perceived; that it is objectively specifiable in the environmental information available to a perceiver. (Heft, 1988: 29)

Heft (1988, 1989, 1998) argues that the concept of affordance can help to transcend the dualism of people and environment, and enables the development of a framework that can integrate the two through a focus on social practices. This is an important insight and one that will receive much attention in a later section. The concept of affordance focuses attention on the possibilities that the built structure of a house opens up for human use; the task of identifying the many and varied uses, however, remains to be achieved.

The criticism of the direct approach by representationalists is that it fails to take into account the social construction of meanings. For example, Dunn (2006) criticises Coolen (2006) and the ecological approach for the statement that: 'The meaning of objects resides in the functional relations between features of the environment and the needs and intentions of human beings' (Coolen, 2006: 3). Dunn criticises the sole focus on use as the definer of meaning. As the 'meaning of home' literature shows, the house may have symbolic meaning which is not reducible to the use made of it by individuals. Dunn argues that the approach seems to ignore social discourses and meanings that are wider in scope than individual use. The approach therefore needs to be extended to incorporate the meaning beyond use.

The concept of affordances allows the built structure to be considered as influencing human behaviour through its physical form as well as its meaning. It offers a way of combining the factors considered above in the relationship between people and their houses while overcoming the unhelpful dichotomies between mind/body and mind/matter.

Towards an integration of meaning and use?

It was argued above that the representational approach to perception is based on a dualism between people and the material environment, and that the concept of affordances may offer a way of pursuing a more integrative perspective that focuses on practices. As Heft (1997: 81) states, rather than a dualism where the physical and mental realms are ontologically distinct, with mind standing outside the environment, Gibson's approach conceptualises the perceiver–environment relationship as a 'fittedness' rather than a separateness and a reciprocity rather than a dualism. The relationship between human and environment is reciprocal and continuous, with learning leading to refined perceptual-action skills and the revelation of new affordance possibilities. The environment can also be changed through human action to create new affordances. In the relationship between an individual and the environment, the environment has meaning to that individual in terms of the affordances that are perceived. Therefore, the environment does not have meaning imposed on it, as in the representational approach, but it is perceived as a meaning-laden object. However, a key question is the extent to which the framework can satisfactorily include symbolic meanings, which have been prominent in the literature on the meaning of home, as well as use meanings. The usual examples of affordances given in the literature relate to what may be called practical uses. For example, a chair affords sitting or an escalator affords play for children. But we have seen that the home environment can have meaning in terms of cultural symbols and psychological goals such as higher self-esteem and status in the eyes of key others. So can this element be incorporated within an affordance approach? Perhaps we can pose the problem of analysing the situation of an older person sitting in a comfortable chair in their sitting room that they have furnished and decorated in a style they have chosen and which contains material objects that have good memories for them.

Heft (1989) argues that it is necessary to overcome the, often assumed, dualism between the natural and cultural world. He argues that they are one and the same, and the perceiver directly sees both use and cultural meaning in their environment. For example, a person in Britain sees a red metal container by the side of the road and knows that it affords posting a letter. This knowledge is the product of an understanding of cultural practices, which are perceived by individuals so socialised as an affordance of the object. However, as mentioned earlier, affordances are usually stipulated in terms of actions. Can sitting still in a chair in a particular environment be analysed in the same way? One way forward is signalled by Heft (1989), who sees affordances in relation to the intentionality of action. He emphasises the point made by Gibson that the meaning of an object resides not in the object or the person, but in the relationship between them. When an individual perceives an object they see it in relation to their objectives. For example, a knife may have a different meaning if one is about to prepare food than if one is being physically attacked. Heft applies this approach to socio-culturally defined meanings. He sees intentional acts as situated within a particular cultural context and with respect to particular objects. 'Enculturation can be viewed as acquiring a repertoire of acts, each act being situated with respect to a particular set of environmental features, the functional significance of which are socially conveyed' (Heft, 1989: 18).

> The fact that another person teaches the perceiver the behavioural significance of an environmental feature, or that a feature has a socially shared and conventional meaning, does not make its significance any less real from a functional standpoint. If affordance is defined relative to the body in an intentional sense, then an extension of the concept to this type of functional meaning is warranted. (Heft, 1989: 17–18)

The concept of intentional action goes some way to providing a framework for analysing our person in the chair, but further progress can be made by unpacking the concept of intention. People act to meet their needs. 'Needs control the perception of affordances (selective attention) and also initiate acts' (Gibson, 1975: 411, quoted in Heft, 1989: 26). Needs can be viewed through the lens of the earlier discussion of the concept of well-being. The key point here is that actions are oriented towards achievement of the elements identified as key to well-being, such as self-esteem and identity. So sitting in a chair in a personalised setting can be seen to afford self-actualisation, autonomy, self-acceptance, life purpose and so on. Of course, each of these elements is socially situated, as are many of the meaning elements of home. So self-acceptance may depend on the positive evaluation of significant others and a feeling of contentment in one's home may be influenced by visitors' perceptions of it. But the linking of intentionality with the concept of well-being allows the affordance concept to be used beyond the functional meaning of action, in relation to the meaning elements that have traditionally been associated with home. However, a key element of the concept of well-being is its subjectivity. Therefore, meaning cannot be read off by any culturally aware analysis, as suggested by Rapoport (1982), but has to be investigated in each individual case and is socially situated.

The concept of social practices can be used to bring together the elements discussed here. As mentioned earlier, Thrift (1997) urges us to focus on the mundane everyday practices that shape the conduct of human beings towards others and themselves in particular sites (one can think of the activities of daily living incorporated in the ADL scales discussed earlier). Giddens (1984) uses the concept of social practices to emphasise the interrelationship between the agency and structure elements of action. He also sees social practices as being situated in time and place. The affordances of a particular place (a house) for a particular individual at a particular time can be seen as social practices, containing structural and agency elements and being specific to that particular physical environment and individual. The key task then is to discover and unpack these social practices.

Heft and Kytta (2006) suggest that the starting point of any empirical research using the affordance approach should focus on the uses (social practices) as identified through observation or communication with the individuals concerned. This in contrast to the approach suggested by Rapoport (1982), who suggests that anyone familiar with a particular culture is able to read off the symbols in a residential environment. The approach suggested here would involve the observation of practices within the home and communication with those undertaking these practices.

One difficulty with this focus on social practices is that in some instances more than one person may be involved, whereas the concept of affordance is based on individual perception. Where a household is made up of one person who copes without support, there is no problem. But where a person lives with another, or receives support in activities within the home from others, there may be differences between the perceptions of affordances. In this case, the social practices may be the outcome of a process of interaction between individuals such as a resident and the support workers. The concept of affordance therefore focuses attention on the process by which individual affordances are translated into social practices.

Embodiment and the material home

The above discussion has shown in sharp relief the factors that need to be taken into consideration in a holistic analysis of the relationship between people and their homes. It has shown the lack of a theoretical framework that can include the physical body and the material house as well as the functional and well-being elements. The physical body is important in the use of housing, but which elements of bodily functioning need to be taken into account? The material form of the house is important in the affordances it does or does not offer to individuals. But which affordances should be considered among the many potential ones?

A beginning in answering these questions can be sought in the practice of assessing and caring for some people with physical disabilities. On a daily basis, staff of statutory and voluntary agencies have to assess the abilities and needs of people who have a physical disability, and their ability to function adequately in specific physical environments such as their own homes. They do this by assessing the ability of people to function adequately in their home environment in the ADLs. There are many differences in the functions chosen, but usually those included are ones that could be considered to represent the basic needs of individuals to keep themselves safe and healthy. Therefore, key elements are the ability to wash, eat and use toilet facilities. Domestic tasks such as food preparation and cooking, shopping and housework are included. Mobility both inside and outside the dwelling is also assessed. However, the assessment moves beyond the basic needs to also cover motivation and emotional needs, such as loneliness, and the existence of interests and activities. It covers relationships with others, such as family and friends, and learning, work and leisure activities and interests. The assessor is also asked to consider the physical, sensory and mental health and functioning of the individual. It is necessary to undertake an assessment of the person's accommodation in terms of its suitability for their needs, both in terms of its type, facilities and tenure, and its situation in the local environment. In a development of the concept of affordances, the assessment focuses on the relative ease of a particular person being able to undertake an activity. In other words, affordance can be used as a relative concept. A particular house may afford a particular use on a scale from 'easily' to 'with great difficulty'.

In theory, assessors such as occupational therapists can examine the interaction between the person and the environment. Any particular problem in an ADL could be dealt with by changing one or other of these. For the person, there may be physical and bodily interventions through medical procedures, training through physiotherapy, or more general training through the teaching of skills or knowledge (such as for cooking and preparing food). Also, the person may be able to use aids or tools in order to be able to undertake the activity (such as a wheelchair or other mobility aid). Of course, the person may also be given help or support in undertaking the task by family or paid helpers, such as home carers.

Alternatively, or in addition, the environment could be changed to enable the activities of daily living to be achieved. Adaptations may include kitchen facilities, or remodelling the layout of the dwelling. In theory, an assessment should examine the affordances of the particular dwelling, related to daily living of the individual. One may dispute the exact factors included and want to add other factors beyond those needed to achieve basic daily living, but the general approach seems to offer a way forward in assessing the affordances of a house for a particular individual.

In generalising from this example a number of points need to be considered. First, the affordances taken into account in an assessment are those considered important by the assessors and their employers. They are generally considered to be the basic needs of individuals. These need to be expanded to cover other, higher-level needs (to use the terminology of Maslow, 1954) included in the concept of well-being. A starting point here could be the literature on the meaning of home that has provided lists of the factors that people think are important in their home, such as security, shelter, warmth and so on. Alternatively, the starting point could be the elements of well-being identified earlier. Indeed, the focus of government policy towards disabled people in Britain has been around the idea of personalisation, in which services are tuned to the subjectively defined needs of individuals and designed to improve their well-being.

Heft and Kytta (2006) suggest that the focus of any empirical research should be the uses of home, as identified through observation or communication with the individuals concerned. The ADL scales can be used either as an alternative to this approach, or as a checklist to ensure that possible uses are covered. The approach chosen may differ according to the precise research objectives or the practical constraints.

The second point concerns incorporating elements of well-being into the consideration of functional use. It must be borne in mind that many of the use aspects considered in the example of disabled people have a meaning element. For example, adaptations to the house to improve use may have negative connotations for the individual. A ramp outside the dwelling to enable access in a wheelchair may be considered to be a symbol of unwanted difference and stigma to the person living there, in their own eyes or in the view of people that they interact with. The literature on the meaning of the home and that on the social model of disability (see Chapter Eight) emphasise that these meanings may be general ones, derived from society, rather than just individual ones, derived from the interaction between an individual and their own dwelling. In practice, there is an understanding of the importance of the meaning elements of adaptations and of dwelling layout. For example, the Micasa Fastigheter showhouses in Stockholm[1] have adaptations to everyday appliances and utensils, such as cookers, sinks and worktops, showers and toilets that are designed to look beautiful as well as function effectively for individuals with disabilities. Many of the features, such as hoists and hand supports, are hidden in a way that disguises their functional purpose. Many features of the apartments would be considered desirable for people of any abilities. The only drawback is that the adaptations are very modern in their style and fit well into modern apartments, but would look out of place in an existing older house. Also, the modern style may not fit with the sensibilities of older people. I saw many examples, in supported housing schemes, of modern facilities side by side with the more traditional furniture and style adopted by the older people in their apartments. Modern styling does not fit with everyone's identity and lifestyle.

A third point is the extent to which these factors of use and meaning can be assessed objectively. Their subjective nature is often recognised in the assessment process in practice, which is why there is often a space on the assessment form used by occupational therapists for the individual concerned to express their own views and preferences. However, the nature of the assessment process means that it will entail at least some element of the rationing of resources between different uses. Therefore, either explicitly or implicitly, the assessor will be asked to judge the relative need of one individual compared to another. So the concept of objective need is likely to be more paramount in this situation. But, even for the purpose of this book, there needs to be some way of aggregating and comparing different subjective uses and meanings. The best way of achieving this is probably to start from empirical data and so this is an empirical rather than a conceptual question.

A fourth point is the process of interaction that translates individual affordances into social practices in the home. Some affordances of a particular dwelling may be conditional on the relationship between the resident and support workers. For example, a house may afford bathing, but only if a support worker is there to employ a hoist. Therefore, in the eyes of the resident the affordance may be considered to be conditional or to have a particular meaning because of the social relationship needed for it to be operationalised.

Conclusion

This chapter has focused on the home because it is the locale in which we spend much of our time and which has a major influence on our achievement of well-being. The literature on the meaning of home shows the impact that homes have on the factors such as self-esteem, identity and personal control that are major elements of well-being. However, the chapter has shown that the existing approaches to home have been partial, only covering some elements of the meanings and uses that homes have for individuals. Therefore, a more holistic approach has been put forward that is based on the concept of affordances. The focus is on the social practices within the locale of the home that are built on the affordances that the home offers to the individual resident.

The example of the use and meaning of homes for people with physical disabilities puts a sharp focus on the embodied use of the material home. The argument has been that the practical assessment of some physically disabled people has necessitated an analysis of their embodied use of material homes by social care and other agencies. What is missing here, though, is the meaning or symbolic dimension. In contrast, some of the literature on the meaning of home (as well as the social theory of disability see Chapter Eight) has provided an analysis of the symbolic meaning of the home and of action.

It has been argued in this chapter that the concept of affordances can be used to provide a framework for the integration of the elements discussed here in a holistic analysis of the embodied practices in the material home. However, the concept has needed development in two major ways. The first is acceptance of the importance of the intentionality of action. Affordances will depend on the objectives, identities and lifestyles of the individuals concerned. The second is the use of the concept of well-being to frame the analysis of intention in a way that incorporates the elements of meaning identified in the literature on the meaning of home. Well-being can be unpacked into its constituent elements of self-actualisation; autonomy; personal growth; self-acceptance; life purpose; mastery; and positive relatedness. All of these elements have been identified in previous literature on the meaning of home. If added to the functional requirements identified in ADL scales, such as preparation of food, bathing and so on, there is the potential to construct an extensive inventory of objectives and practices of everyday life within the home.

The chapter has argued that it is possible to bring these elements together in order to provide a more holistic analysis of the relationships between people and their houses by using the concept of social practices, which has a number of elements. A tool such as the ADL scale, revised according to the precise research question being pursued, operationalises the concept of affordances and allows the impact of the physical body on action within a specific material home to be analysed. It focuses on the social practices around daily living that are the routines of everyday life. In addition, this analysis has to be supplemented with an analysis of the meaning dimensions of behaviour. Each action will both be influenced by and will influence symbolic meaning. Societal discourses of family and home will be lived out through the embodied actions of individuals within specific material homes. However, this is not a one-way relationship because the embodied action within the material home will influence societal meaning structures and discourses through what Giddens (1984) calls structuration. A way of defining and assessing the importance of these meanings can be found through the concept of well-being, as it identifies the factors that we seek to achieve in our pursuit of happiness. Heft's (1989) stress on the intentionality of affordances brings these elements together as an individual seeks to achieve practical functioning and well-being through social practices afforded by a particular physical environment (house).

The concept of social practices in the home also focuses attention on the social relationships involved in turning affordances into social practices where residents are receiving support. The nature of these relationships may alter the meaning of a particular affordance and have an impact on the well-being of the resident.

The aim of the chapter has been to develop a way of conceptualising the use and meaning of home in order to incorporate its analysis into the assessment of supported housing models. As argued earlier, approaches such as the 'outcomes star' have been blind to the fact that support is delivered in homes that have both a physical and a meaning impact. Homes communicate our identity and influence our emotions, as well as providing the physical environment in which we undertake the social practices of our everyday lives. However, homes do not exist in physical isolation, as they are part of the neighbourhood in which they are situated. This element needs to be considered, therefore, before we can progress further.

Note

[1] See: www.micasa.se/sv/in-English/Display-apartment/-Display

FOUR

Neighbourhoods

The previous chapter considered the relationship between people and their homes. But of course people's lives reach outside their houses and are partly played out in the neighbourhood around them. The apocryphal estate agent's mantra that the three most important factors in a house are 'location, location and location' highlights that houses are in part used as staging posts for our life outside. People leave their house to earn money, to use local facilities such as shops and doctors' surgeries, and to visit leisure and recreational facilities such as restaurants and bars. In Chapter Two it was shown that social relations are an important element of well-being and it is in the neighbourhood that people meet and many social interactions take place. Therefore, the neighbourhood is an important locale for social relations, which are vital for individual well-being, and so should be incorporated in the well-being framework used to evaluate supported housing.

The chapter considers the changing nature of neighbourhoods and reviews the proposition that neighbourhood is less important to people than it used to be, with a decline in a sense of community. The approach in the chapter is similar to the previous discussion of homes in that it uses the concept of affordance. It is assumed that people have a meaningful relationship with the neighbourhood as a place, as well as using it in a practical way. In other words, the neighbourhood affords many uses, which have both practical and meaning elements that should be considered together. The chapter examines the changing pattern of neighbourhoods and the growing segregation that is occurring. A key question concerns the impact of segregation on the lives of vulnerable people. Do disadvantaged people want to live close to others like themselves or are they forced into this by factors outside their control? How does segregation change the affordances of neighbourhoods for people in need of support and what impact does this have on their well-being? The focus is on the implications of these factors for the role and form of supported housing. Do particular forms of supported housing help or hinder integration with the neighbourhood and social relations within it? In other words, does supported housing afford a full range of neighbourhood uses?

What is a neighbourhood?

There are many definitions of a neighbourhood (see Galster, 2012, for a review). Most definitions refer to a particular geographical area or a physical or geographical entity, although it is difficult to define the extent. It is commonly accepted that the boundaries cannot be defined in any objective sense and so concepts such as symbolic or subjective boundaries are often used. Galster (2012) argues for the importance of perceived boundaries of residents (and others) in defining neighbourhood, rather than any objective measure. He also follows Suttles (1972) in conceiving of a multi-level spatial view of the perception of neighbourhood boundaries, depending on the particular attribute being considered. Pebley and Vaiana (2002) use three classifications of levels of perceived boundaries of neighbourhood. The first and smallest is the area in which children can be left to play without supervision; the second level was labelled the 'defended neighbourhood', which was the smallest area that was perceived as having a meaning in opposition or in contrast to another area. The third and highest level was usually congruent with local government boundaries and was a segment of the city in which social participation was selective and voluntary.

Galster (2012) sees a neighbourhood as a cluster of attributes that may have different perceived spatial boundaries. He conceives of individuals having a perceived 'externality space', which is defined as the area over which changes in neighbourhood attributes are perceived as altering the well-being the individual derives from the particular location. These externality spaces may be congruent with particular geographical boundaries or not; may be general in the sense that the spaces for different attributes correspond; or may or may not correspond with the externality spaces of others.

The concept of a neighbourhood consisting of a number of attributes that may have different externality spaces for individuals is a very useful one. Using the concept of affordance outlined earlier, these attributes can be seen as affordances of neighbourhoods that may (or may not) impact on the well-being of individuals.

Galster's (2012) attributes are as follows:

- physical characteristics of the buildings; for example, design, density, state of repair;
- infrastructure characteristics – for example, roads, pavements utilities, streetscaping;

- demographic characteristics of the resident population – for example, age, family composition, ethnic mix;
- class status characteristics – for example, income, occupation, education;
- public service characteristics – for example, quality of public schools, policing, parks, health facilities;
- environmental characteristics – for example, extent of noise, air or other pollution, views, topography;
- proximity characteristics – for example, access to major destinations of employment, entertainment, shopping;
- political characteristics – for example, organisation and influence of local residents;social-interactive characteristics – for example, extent and quality of social interactions, perceived commonality or community, extent of local voluntary organisations, strength of socialisation or social control forces; also, sentimental characteristics – such as residents' sense of identification with place, historical significance of buildings and so on.

The list is an interesting one and a good starting point for our discussion here. However, its main drawback is the clear distinction made between the 'objective' categories and the single all-inclusive item for 'subjective' or sentimental characteristics that are only mentioned as a sub-category at the end. In our discussion of affordance we made the point that people perceive the physical and meaning elements of phenomena together. Therefore, it is more useful to see each of the above categories as having both physical and meaning elements that are indivisible. Thus the physical characteristics of buildings in the first item also contribute to the meaning that individuals ascribe to the place and their identification with it, and similarly for each of the other categories.

In summary, the concept of neighbourhood alerts us to a number of attributes or affordances that may have different spatial dimensions, but which contribute to varying degrees and in different ways to the well-being of individuals resident in the neighbourhood. The relative impact of the different affordances will depend on a number of factors, such as the age, family circumstances, income, physical capacity and lifestyle of the individual. Therefore, it is possible in theory for a particular neighbourhood to afford a high level of well-being for one person and a low level of well-being for another, depending on their individual circumstances. For example, proximity to facilities may vary on the basis of access to a car or other means of transport or the ability to drive. The use of some facilities may be made physically difficult or emotionally demeaning because of physical barriers to entry or humiliating procedures of entry for people who have a physical impairment.

The concept of the affordances of neighbourhood attributes outlined here gives a good framework for the discussion of the impact of neighbourhoods on the well-being of those who are in need of support. These people may share many of the same responses to the neighbourhood affordances as others who are not in need of support and may not share any or many with those who also receive support. Nevertheless, there may be some common factors that we can identify which may be important in our assessment of different forms of supported housing. An important one may be the affordance of social interaction in the neighbourhood and it is here that we start the discussion.

Neighbourhood social interaction and community

Much has been written about the perceived 'decline in community' (for a review see Clapham, 2005). The argument is that a traditional working-class community once existed, built around overlapping ties of family, friends and neighbours, that flourished in particular neighbourhoods in Britain at particular times (see Young and Willmott, 1957). In the 1980s, this particular form of neighbourhood interaction seems to have been an anomaly rather than the norm, and numerous studies have not found this pattern in other places and at other times. There is a strong argument that community in this form is unlikely to exist to any great extent in the future, as physical and social mobility has dislocated ties of family and friends from those of neighbourhood. Many people are increasingly mobile through the use of cars and other forms of transport, and can pursue hobbies and leisure activities and maintain friendships over a wide geographical area. In addition, new technologies have meant that shopping and leisure activities and social networks can increasingly be pursued at home through the internet, thus obviating the need for physical mobility.

Local neighbourhood relations are now characterised as 'weak or loose ties' (Granovetter, 1973; Henning and Lieberg, 1996). Nevertheless Henning and Lieberg (1996: 22) argue that the value of these weak ties should not be underestimated: 'The significance of loose ties was underlined by the inhabitants who stated that these contacts meant a "feeling of home", "security", and "practical as well as social support".'

Importantly for our focus here, Henning and Lieberg (1996) stress that these weak neighbourhood ties are particularly important to vulnerable and marginal groups who are likely to be less geographically mobile than others. Willmott (1986) argues that there is an ebb and flow of interaction with neighbours over the life cycle. High levels of interaction tend to occur at stages when more of life is undertaken within the neighbourhood, such as in childhood, early parenthood and old age. The perceived decline in community could be due, in part, to the decline in the number of households in these categories with the increase in single-person and childless-couple households. In addition, the increased employment of women and increased access to a car also reduces the number of those who live out a large proportion of their lives in the neighbourhood. One result of these trends is the growing separation of those who are limited to the neighbourhood from those who live most of their lives elsewhere. We will return to this potentially very important issue later.

The weak ties that characterise many neighbourhoods could lead one to the conclusion that the locality does not matter in many people's lives. There has been much emphasis on the globalising influences that have meant that people increasingly are not tied to localities in their everyday functioning. Shopping and socialising can be undertaken on the internet and modes of physical mobility mean that neighbourhoods are driven through in a car rather than actively used. Nevertheless, there has been increasing interest in the way that people relate to their neighbourhood despite these globalising tendencies. Savage et al (2005) draw attention to the way that middle-class people in Britain associate themselves with their place of residence in a process they call 'elective belonging'. People want to feel that they belong to a place and weave it into their biographies in an active process of identity formation. People relate the places they live in to their lives and construct their personal identity in part around their relationship with the place. They do not have to use the place in any physical way, but it has meaning for them that is a constituent of identity formation. As Forrest and Kearns (2001: 2130) put it: 'in a sense the neighbourhood becomes an extension of the home for social purposes and hence extremely important in identity terms: "location matters" and the neighbourhood becomes part of our statement about who we are.'

In the view of Giddens and other late modern or postmodern writers, neighbourhood becomes an important counterpoint in the lives of many to the insecurities of a globalised world. Scase (1999: 54) argues that: 'In an uncertain world where jobs are insecure and futures are unpredictable, living in a risk society reinforces the importance of community in a symbolic sense. Individuals obtain a sense of "place", of attachment to the communities in which they live.'

Kearns et al (2012) examined the psycho-social environment, which they defined as the nature of social interactions within the neighbourhood context, and how these interactions made people think, feel and behave. They argue that a good psycho-social environment promotes a positive experience or view of oneself in relation to others, for example in terms of control, confidence, self-esteem and status. In their study of deprived areas of Glasgow they found a range of neighbourhood factors associated with high levels of mental well-being. These included the perception of attractive buildings and environment in the area; feeling safe walking at night; community influence on decisions; and a sense of personal progress (in other words a positive view that the neighbourhood represents a good personal progression).

Scase argued in 1999 that neighbourhoods would become increasingly segregated by demographics and lifestyles as well as income and occupation. Older people would continue to move to areas that match their lifestyles and provide facilities for hobbies, socialising and shopping. Young and middle-aged single households would gravitate to the inner city for the cosmopolitan and fashionable lifestyles based around leisure facilities of all kinds. Those with more traditional family patterns and lifestyles would live in the outer suburbs, where provision of quality education and child care would be concentrated. Other neighbourhoods would consist of the culturally and economically excluded who are constrained into locality-based lifestyles, dependent on the quality of local facilities. These trends are clearly apparent in both Britain and, to a lesser extent, in Sweden.

The analysis above places emphasis on the choice element of residential location decisions. However, choices are made on the basis of available options and these may vary according to the position of the household involved, whether this refers to their economic situation, employment, family structure, ethnicity, and their physical and mental health and abilities. The factors around the dichotomy between choice and structural forces have been explored in the example of ethnic minority segregation. There is evidence that ethnic minority households tend to be concentrated in particular neighbourhoods, but is this because they choose to live together for cultural, lifestyle or family reasons, or are they forced to congregate together by discrimination or economic factors?

Musterd (2012) identifies four traditions of thought in the study of residential segregation. The first focuses on individual behaviour and the choices that households make within their economic constraints and the supply of dwellings available (see, for example, Clark, 2009). The second tradition focuses on the impact of major economic transformation processes such as globalisation on different spatial patterns (Sassen, 1991). A third perspective refers to institutional structures such as welfare state regimes and institutions that produce segregation (Musterd and Ostendorf, 1998). The fourth perspective focuses on the specific factors of place, time and context that create variations in places over time. The most useful way forward is to use an integrated perspective that incorporates all these levels of analysis. The concept of a housing pathway (Clapham, 2005) achieves this by focusing on the decisions that households make and the context within which they make them. Using this perspective, segregation becomes a complex interplay of household choice and the wider discourses and other factors that frame the choice.

Musterd (2012) draws attention to the disputed nature of the concept of segregation. He follows Johnson et al (2007) in drawing a distinction between the two elements of separateness and location. Separateness concerns the degree to which members of a particular group live apart from the remainder of the population. Location concerns the degree to which members of the group are congregated into high-density or low-status and low-affordance neighbourhoods. The distinction between the two elements of segregation is important when examining its impact. Most of the attention in the literature on the impact of segregation focuses on ethnic minorities and, in particular the element of separateness. The disadvantages to the ethnic minorities themselves of separateness are said to be stigmatisation and isolation from the opportunities and social networks of the wider society. Also, the concentration of economically disadvantaged people in a neighbourhood can lead to a shortage of facilities because of the overall lack of spending power. From the viewpoint of society, there has been concern that separateness can lead to a lack of integration and the continuance of a minority culture. The advantages of separateness for ethnic minority households may relate to the maintenance of social and family networks as well as the continuance of a particular culture. Separateness can facilitate the development and maintenance of specific cultural facilities, such as religious buildings and specialist shops. It can also provide reassurance and defence in a situation of discrimination. The mixing of people with different norms and values can lead to problems of conflicting lifestyles. As van Kempen and Bolt (2012: 450) note:

not everyone likes garden parties with loud music at night and not everybody thinks that public squares are for children playing football and the bus stops are for hanging out. The use of alcohol in public may annoy Muslims, while Muslims wearing a burka may annoy natives. Confrontations between different groups are more common in areas with a mixed population than in mono-ethnic areas. Living closer together may mean that people are more aware of differences between themselves and others.

Interestingly, van Kempen and Bolt (2012) note evidence that members of minority ethnic groups living in areas that are almost entirely native have a higher chance of developing schizophrenia than minority groups living in areas of a concentration of ethnic minorities. Although the precise causal factors have not been explored, it seems to offer evidence for the supportive impact of living next to people who are like ourselves.

   The political concern with the existence of segregation among ethnic minorities has been coupled with a focus on the segregation of poor households. There has been a long-standing policy concern in many countries with the concentration of disadvantaged or poor people in particular neighbourhoods. The extent of this problem is dictated by the way that statistics are collected and analysed. The common use of small-area statistics leads to a focus on those areas that have a higher proportion of deprived people than others. However, as Holtermann (1975) pointed out for Britain, the majority of poor people do not live in poor neighbourhoods and the majority of people in most poor neighbourhoods are not poor. Despite the clear evidence of the inefficiency of an area-based focus as a mechanism for reaching poor people, it has been adopted by many governments as one of the primary instruments for the alleviation of poverty, usually under the umbrella of the concept of social exclusion (or social inclusion). As Hulse et al (2011: 5) write:

> There is increasing recognition of the role of home and place in contributing to social inclusion. Having a home involves not only having a roof over one's head but also provides a safe and private environment in which intimate relationships can be developed and children nurtured. A home is the base for the routines of daily life, from shopping and socialising to schooling and working. A home is connected to place through a physical dwelling,

and place may be important for self-identity, attachment and a sense of belonging. More practically, place shapes access to transport, facilities, jobs and services. Home and place thus provide a foundation for participation in social, economic, cultural and political life.

There are many definitions of social exclusion, but Hulse et al (2011: 13) offer a useful one as follows:

> social exclusion refers to current circumstances in which some people are marginalised and unable to live a full life for a variety of reasons that may include, but are not restricted to, a lack of material resources. These reasons include lack of family support, social isolation, ill health and disability, not having a home or living in unsafe or inadequate housing, low levels of education, and inability to get a job.

There has been some interesting research on the impact the life chances of those living in a neighbourhood with a high concentration of poor people. The results of this so-called 'neighbourhood effects' strand of research seem to be that living together with other poor people has a small but measurable negative effect on life chances, all other things being equal (van Kempen and Bolt, 2012).

Wacquant (2008) has drawn attention to the advanced marginality caused by the growing inequality in many developed societies. He identifies a marginal group (the precariat) who can no longer find security in a liberalised labour market, where often wages are insufficient to alleviate poverty, who have been abandoned as a result of the cuts in the welfare state and who are increasingly disconnected from trends in the macro-economy. He argues that increasing inequality is being reflected territorially, with marginal people being segregated in poor-quality neighbourhoods, with a lack of community organisations and cultural history to provide support. These neighbourhoods are 'symbolically spoiled zones', where people suffer 'territorial indignity'. The result is spatial alienation, where people lose the humanised and culturally familiar place where they can feel 'at home'. These places are socially fragmented and symbolically splintered as individuals try to distance themselves from the source of their shame by disowning the area and their neighbours. Therefore, in such 'symbolically spoiled zones' it would be difficult to achieve well-being as their inhabitants are subject to stigma and there is a lack of social integration.

The concern about the concentration of poverty and the discourse of social exclusion has led to many countries introducing policies designed to create 'balanced communities'. This term has not been clearly defined, but the policies in Britain have sought to promote mixed developments of owner-occupied and social housing through the mechanism of section 106 planning agreements. The outcome of this mixing was interesting (Jupp, 1999; Atkinson and Kintrea, 2002). Contact between owner occupiers and social renters appeared to be very limited. Owner occupiers tended to spend most of their time outside the estate and had few contacts within it. This contrasted with tenants who, probably because of the greater likelihood of unemployment and the constraints of lack of money and lower car ownership, tended to spend most of their time on the estate and to have more ties with others in the same situation. Contact between the two groups was greater when mixing was on a street rather than a neighbourhood level, and in this case it was also likely there would be fewer problems between the groups. In some neighbourhoods, where the two forms of tenure were physically distinct, there were problems and social tensions created by issues such as vandalism, noise and the behaviour of children. Jupp (1999: 11) concludes that: 'The hope that the current models of mixed tenure estates will foster widespread mutual support between people of different economic groups, considerably broaden understanding between groups and introduce role models into an area appears largely misplaced.' Indeed, as van Kempen and Bolt (2012) point out, social interaction seems highest in neighbourhoods where the social makeup is more homogeneous. This is not surprising as the research on friendship shows that we tend to make friends with people like ourselves, whether this is in age, lifestyle, ethnicity, or on the basis of shared norms and values. Social contacts within a neighbourhood also increase with the length of time a person has lived in the neighbourhood.

Nevertheless, Jupp (1999) did find that mixing, particularly at the street level, did reduce problems of stigmatisation. Skifter Anderson (2002) argues that the image and problems of a neighbourhood often influence the self-identity of residents. The image of a neighbourhood can be divided into three categories: the internal image held by residents; the external image held by outsiders; and the self-reflecting image which is what insiders think outsiders think of their neighbourhood. Dean and Hastings (2000) show that each of these images can be fragmented, but the continuous dialogue between them and the different groups who hold them shape the reputation of the area. Little is known about what shapes these images, and they seem to be to some extent independent of personal experience. The role of local media may be important in forming images of these places. The main point here is that where someone lives may have an impact on their self-identity and well-being through the perceptions and actions of themselves and others.

Neighbourhoods and support

The impact that neighbourhoods have on individuals will vary according to the circumstances of the individual and the affordances of their local neighbourhood. We have presented above arguments about the impact of segregation on the well-being of individuals, which point to both advantages and disadvantages. Most of this discussion is centred on the situation of ethnic minority and low-income people. However, the more general discussion of the impact of segregation on social exclusion can offer some insight into the situation of people who need support. Our discussion is centred on two questions. The first is whether segregation is harmful for people in need of support. The second is how and to what extent different forms of supported housing mediate the affordances of neighbourhoods.

Neighbourhoods are important to many people, and particularly those who are vulnerable and less mobile and so spend more time in the local neighbourhood. Some people receive considerable support from neighbours. However, this is almost always for a short period of time, usually in an emergency. Willmott (1986) found that help between neighbours was extensive, with two thirds of his sample saying that they spoke to one or more neighbours every day and 40% visited the home of a neighbour weekly or more often. Neighbours often performed small useful services, such as looking after keys, plants or pets, lending food or sometimes shopping. In a small number of cases in Willmott's survey, help was much more extensive, with neighbours helping with house maintenance or repairs, helping during illness or looking after children. For most people, and for most of the time, neighbours are people who we are friendly with and may ask to do small practical tasks such as taking in a parcel or perhaps feeding the cat. The neighbourhood is therefore an important, but limited, source of support. Nevertheless, the evidence is that many people value what they receive from neighbours, even if it is just a cheery greeting. For some people the neighbourhood is their major source of social contact. People also value the identity that belonging to a neighbourhood can give them, as well as the practical use that neighbourhood facilities can provide.

The affordance framework presented here has been based on the attributes of neighbourhoods identified by Galster, and this framework will be used in the remainder of the book to answer the two questions posed above. The approach, therefore, is to treat the two questions as empirical ones that have to be determined for each individual and in each supported situation. Nevertheless we can discuss the parameters of the debate here.

The pros and cons of segregation for ethnic minorities were discussed earlier, but it may help as a prelude to our discussion of supported housing in the following chapters to rehearse some of the general arguments as they apply to people receiving support. Most discussion of this topic has revolved around the situation of older people. The key question concerns whether the well-being of older people is best served by them living in an age-segregated environment. Scase and others were quoted earlier as arguing that neighbourhoods were becoming more segregated on age (as well as other) lines. The argument was that some older people are increasingly choosing to live in areas that afford the uses attuned to their particular lifestyle. These may be access to health or care facilities, or leisure activities such as walking along the coast or attending community events. Segregation could offer social contact with others in similar situations and with similar lifestyles. It enables the concentration of private and public resources for older people, such as specialist health and support facilities, or specific retail facilities giving economies of scale and improving targeting. It avoids problems of conflict of lifestyles with younger people over issues such as noise. Such a rationale underpins the development of retirement villages in Britain and other countries, where older people can move secure in the knowledge that the facilities are available if they become frail. However, the disadvantages of being in a segregated environment could be a lack of contact with people of different ages. This could include family, such as children and grandchildren. Also, many older people may not want to give up lifestyles they have maintained through their life to adopt an age-specific lifestyle. Segregation may create problems of stigma. The move to an age-specific environment may lead to the loss of existing social contacts and the move from meaningful neighbourhoods. The discussion earlier highlighted that commitment to a neighbourhood and social contacts within it tend to increase with the length of residence. The balance of these advantages and disadvantages is likely to vary between specific housing and support environments, and between individuals. The affordance framework gives a way of evaluating the impact of those differences.

Whereas the issues of segregation have been relatively well explored for older people, they have received less attention in discussions relating to homeless (young) people or people with a physical disability. Nevertheless the issues involved are similar. For example, age-specific forms of supported accommodation such as foyers and hostels have been created for homeless young people. These may have the advantages of separating young people from inappropriate influences in their previous neighbourhood and of reducing lifestyle clashes with other sections of the population. On the other hand, there may be disadvantages in removing some young people from their families and supportive friends. Supported accommodation schemes may place young people with chaotic lifestyles together and this may create situations of fear or lead to inappropriate collective behaviour. Many young people have found age-specific environments such as hostels threatening places in which they feared for their safety. Age segregation in this situation may also lead to an increase in the stigmatising of young people in an identified scheme among the population at large.

In contrast, the predominant approach for people with a physical disability has been to enable them to maintain existing housing and neighbourhood connections in order to facilitate informal support from family and friends and to maintain social networks. For people with mental health problems there has been a different approach. Some supported housing has adopted the model of a therapeutic environment, in which healing is facilitated by taking people away from their everyday lives and placing them in a protected and supportive environment away from mental stresses. However, again there has been a mixed approach, with many others being supported in their own homes. Segregation for people with learning disabilities and mental health problems has been overshadowed to a large extent by the negative image of the Victorian asylums that dominated provision for many years and encapsulated an image of exclusion and stigmatisation. As we shall see in Chapter Eight, recent government policies in both Britain and Sweden have sought to reject this model in favour of the integration inherent in the concept of normalisation.

Conclusion

The chapter has shown the importance of neighbourhoods in the well-being of people. However, they can be even more important for people in need of support, as their lives can be more restricted to the locality. As a consequence, an important element in the impact of supported housing on its residents is the impact on their relationship with their neighbourhood. This impact may have both physical and meaning elements. The attributes of the neighbourhood identified by Galster show the extent of the possible impacts on residents' lives, but each of those identified has both use and meaning elements. The affordance framework is useful in bringing together these two elements in the examination of the impact on the well-being of the people concerned of different supported housing situations.

The potential impact of the home and neighbourhood on the well-being of residents of supported housing means that the two factors need to be considered as key elements in any evaluation of the outcomes of different models. Therefore they need to be combined with the frameworks discussed in Chapter Two to provide a more holistic framework for judging the impact of supported housing. So, in each of the chapters on supported housing for a specific 'category' (Chapters Six, Seven and Eight) the evidence on the impact on residents is considered under three headings. The first is 'Home' in which the affordances of home and their resultant social practices will be discussed. In the second section, on 'Neighbourhood', the same approach is taken, with a discussion of the affordances of neighbourhoods associated with the different models, focusing particularly on the social relations afforded by different models. The third section, entitled 'Well-being', draws together evidence on the outcomes of the different models, focusing on the psychological factors that constitute the foundation of subjective well-being.

Before focusing on specific groups or people and forms of supported housing, it is necessary to map out the context by examining the general housing and support policies in the two countries of Britain and Sweden that are the focus of our attention in the rest of the book.

FIVE

Housing and support in Britain and Sweden

The aim of the rest of the book is to use the evaluation framework outlined in the first four chapters to examine supported housing for older people, homeless people and people with a disability in Britain and Sweden. This chapter will set the context for this by outlining the housing and support policies in the two countries. Making international comparisons of this kind can shed considerable light on the subject matter. The experience of different countries can open our eyes to new possibilities and can help us to understand how and why things have turned out the way they have. Important questions can be asked such as: Have different forms of supported housing emerged in different countries and why? Are there some forms of supported housing that seem to be successful in different contexts and which show general principles that may be widely applicable or does the context in a country determine the form that supported housing takes and its success? Our analysis needs to heed the problems of attempting to learn policy lessons from one country to another. The problems are illustrated by the literature on the transfer of policy between countries. For example, Dolowitz et al (2000) highlight a number of reasons why the transfer of policy from one country to another may be problematic, as we will discuss later in the chapter. Despite these potential problems, comparing supported housing in different countries may serve to open our eyes to new possibilities or help to identify lessons that can improve policy and provision. The important factors to bear in mind are an awareness of possible problems with potential transfer and the importance of the context within which specific forms of provision, such as supported housing, are embedded in a particular country. Individual countries differ in the political cultures that set the context for policies as well as in their policy-making processes and structures. The institutions that deliver policies in housing and support may also differ substantially between countries. Therefore, it is important to start with a discussion of the nature of these differences and how they are formed before focusing on the situation within our chosen countries.

Supported housing brings together two policy areas, namely housing and what we have labelled here support, which incorporates health and social care as well as informal sources of support. Although they are related in many ways, housing and support policies have often been considered by governments to be separate spheres that only come together in certain specific circumstances. In many countries, therefore, there are different policy dynamics in the two spheres and so each needs to be considered separately before being brought together. Of course, as we shall see, this policy divide creates many problems for the design of policies and practices that attempt to bring them together for individuals.

The chapter begins with a consideration of the research on the nature of the welfare state in different countries, as it sets the context for the discussion within the individual countries considered here. The predominant approach in comparison between countries has been that of 'welfare regimes', where countries are divided into groups depending on the relationship between society, economy and welfare in each one. The different regimes are ideal types that delineate a particular view of the extent and nature of state action in the fields of support and housing. Housing and support policies may be expressions of the regime and thus the nature of the regime, with its underlying political cultures, institutions and practices, sets the context for policies towards supported housing and, as a consequence, the forms it takes and the mechanisms for delivering it. Therefore it is taken as a starting point in comparing the two countries. The chapter continues with a discussion of support and housing policies in Britain and Sweden. In this chapter only a very general outline of housing and support policies will be given, as more detailed discussions will take place in each of the case study chapters (Chapters Six, Seven and Eight), which discuss housing and support for older people, young homeless people and people with disabilities respectively.

Welfare regimes

The discussion of welfare regimes was sparked by the work of Esping–Andersen (1990), who identified three regimes in western capitalist economies. The first was the liberal regime, in which he includes much of the Anglo-Saxon world such as the USA, Australia and, increasingly, Britain. The second was the social democratic regime, in which examples came from Scandinavian countries such as Sweden and Denmark. The third regime was the conservative or corporatist regime, in which the examples were Germany and France. Since this original work a number of other regime types have been identified. There is substantial writing on a southern European 'rudimentary' welfare regime (Leibfried, 1992), where state provision does not cover all classical social service areas, there is great reliance on the family, the influence of the Catholic Church is strong and there is a very large degree of commodification. Also there has been some discussion of an East European model, particularly in the housing field. For example, Clapham (1995) has identified an East European model that charts the movement from a communist to a market-based housing system. Much debate in the welfare regimes approach has focused on the position of East Asian countries that have been argued to need their own additional category (see Matznetter and Mundt, 2012). However, some authors have denied that the 'Asian tigers' have enough similarities to constitute a single regime and that they differ widely and fundamentally in the nature and extent of their welfare policies, practices and institutions (Peng, 2008).

The foundation of the regimes approach is that countries have different political cultures that define the relationships between the state, the market and the family, and which result in social institutions that delineate the approach to housing and support. In liberal regimes the predominant belief is that families should take responsibility for meeting the needs of their members, although it is recognised that the nature of a postmodern society makes this difficult because of labour market practices that result in many traditional carers such as women being in employment. In addition, the growing importance of the nuclear family, and the increasing making and remaking of families through marriages and divorces, can create complex family relationships in which the responsibility for support can be unclear and the capacity to deliver it limited. Despite these problems, the role of the state is seen as being that of the last resort provider of only modest means where other mechanisms have failed. Support is withdrawn once need reduces or incomes rise, and is often conditional on being in a certain category, being in particular defined circumstances or exhibiting particular forms of conduct. Markets are seen as the primary mechanism for deciding on needs and providing for them. The minimal role of the state is to regulate the market where major problems occur and to step in only as a last resort where markets fail to deliver the outcomes perceived as acceptable. This regime has also been labelled as residualist, because policies and programmes are focused on strictly circumscribed groups and situations and are usually set below the level and quality of market provision. Therefore, state provision is generally only for those in most need and on low incomes. Means testing and strict entitlement rules are generally applied and the dominance given to the work ethic means that provision cannot be seen to weaken work incentives.

In a social democratic regime, the predominant political culture is for the state to assess, plan for and meet a wide range of needs, and to provide universal services not subject to market principles. The state is held to have the primary responsibility for the well-being of its citizens and provides services that meet the needs of all citizens and not just those who are unable to provide for themselves. There may be ideologies of equality and citizenship that shape the political priorities for reducing inequalities through the provision of services free at the point of delivery and which seek to achieve positive discrimination in favour of disadvantaged people. The state takes on a comprehensive responsibility for services such as housing and support, although it may not deliver the services itself and may rely on families, voluntary organisations or markets as delivery mechanisms. The social democratic regime generally relies on high tax revenues to fund the universal services provided.

In a conservative or corporatist regime, traditional roles of families and institutions such as the church are given prominence. Therefore, the state does not seek to provide comprehensive services, but applies a principle of subsidiarity and acts itself only as a last resort safety net. Responsibility for vulnerable people is usually taken by the family, supported by organisations such as the churches. This regime provides graded services according to class, status and gender distinctions, and has a strong tendency to reproduce income and wealth differentials.

The welfare regimes approach is useful as a starting point for comparing experiences between countries because it highlights the importance of the context within which particular services and forms of provision operate. However, the approach has been strongly criticised (for a review see Matznetter and Mundt, 2012). One criticism is that the regimes are ideal types and so individual countries do not bear a strong resemblance to the general ideal. Therefore reliance on the general category over-emphasises the similarities between different countries classified under the same regime. Another criticism is that very different welfare policies and institutions can exist in countries that share the same overall philosophy. For example, it is not possible to read off the approach to supported housing just from the welfare regime, although it may give some understanding of the philosophy of provision. Another criticism is the relatively static nature of the regime types. It is assumed that there is path dependency (Malpass, 2011) and that radical change is unusual. However, in practice, political choices have changed the nature of regimes in particular countries and even moved them between regimes. An example of this may be the Swedish move away from the social democratic regime after the reforms of the early 1990s, although there is dispute about how far this move has gone, as we shall see later. It can be argued (Bengtsson and Ruonavara, 2010; Malpass, 2011) that there are 'critical junctures' at certain times in some countries that lead to fundamental change in the welfare path, and that the original regime typologies are overly dependent on what has been termed the 'golden era' of welfare state development in the 1970s. Since then, there has been a welfare crisis driven by lack of public funding, which has been reduced because of the dominance of the globalisation discourse based on the belief that countries have to have low tax rates to attract investment (Clapham, 2006). Many countries, therefore, have moved towards a liberal welfare regime, and the experiences of Britain and Sweden would seem to support this. We will see in the following sections that Britain and Sweden are moving in similar directions in housing and support policies, and share similar neoliberal policy rhetoric. The different starting points of the two countries, however, have left them in very different circumstances now. For example, Sweden is a much more equal country in terms of household incomes than the UK. The usual measure of this is the Gini coefficient, with the smaller number reflecting less inequality. According to Organisation for Economic Co-operation and Development (OECD) statistics, Sweden in 2010 was the 10th most equal country, with a coefficient of 0.269, while the UK was 28th out of 34 countries, with a coefficient of 0.341. The OECD average was 0.313. The difference between the two countries may be significant as it was shown in Chapter Two how important inequality is with regard to the well-being of the population. Despite the public expenditure cuts of the 1990s, public expenditure in Sweden in 2012 was 28.2% of gross domestic product (GDP) compared to 23.9% in the UK. In 2009, government social expenditure in Sweden was $11,134 per head compared to $8,365 in the UK.

The role of housing in welfare regimes is subject to particular debate (see Matznetter and Mundt, 2012). Housing was not part of Esping-Andersen's original research, which formed the basis of his classifications, and its status as the 'wobbly pillar' of the welfare state (Torgerson, 1987) means that it has needed and received special attention. Kemeny (1992) used the welfare regimes approach to argue for what he called a 'divergence' approach to international comparisons in housing, in contrast to the 'convergence' approach that emphasises the similarities in the direction of change of housing systems. Some convergence analyses are based on views about the common development of welfare states (see Donnison, 1967) and others focus on the impact of general forces such as globalisation (see Clapham, 2006). Kemeny argued that political choices meant that housing systems took on different forms in different countries, and he examined the tenure structures (such as the extent of owner occupation) and the extent of commodification. He drew a distinction between unitary rental systems, where there was a large public sector open to many classes of the population that is competitive with the private sector (as in Sweden), and dual rental systems, where public renting was a residualised sector that was prevented by the state from effectively competing with private renting (as in Britain). Countries in this latter category tended to have small public sectors reserved for the poorest people, and high rents and insecure private renting.

Hoekstra (2003) related the characteristics of the welfare regimes to particular aspects of housing systems. For example, he linked the concept of decommodification to the housing subsidy and price regulation system; stratification to housing allocations; and the mix of responsibilities between state, family and market to the systems for the production of new housing. The nature of housing systems is therefore susceptible to the welfare regimes approach, and can be related to the nature of the support system within regimes.

The focus in this book is on two countries in particular, Britain and Sweden. The major focus is on Britain, which can be characterised as having moved from a social democratic towards a liberal regime of welfare, reflecting decisions of governments brought about by changes in political culture. The social democratic legacy has been universal services such as the National Health Service, but these services are increasingly being commodified through privatisation and the use of market delivery mechanisms. Recent political changes, such as the introduction of quasi-markets in health and social care services, and the more recent extensive cuts in public expenditure under 'fiscal austerity', have reduced welfare state expenditures and made them more subservient to dominant market principles.

Sweden is often held up as the exemplar social democratic state, but even here commodification has been evident. In both of these countries, supported housing has taken many diverse forms. When examples of supported housing are used in the text, the individual context in each country needs to be borne in mind. These diverse circumstances also militate against any simple policy learning between countries. Because one model of supported housing works in one country does not necessarily mean that it will work in another, with a different political and social culture and a different institutional framework.

Dolowitz et al (2000) highlight a number of reasons why the transfer of policy from one country to another may be problematic. One is what they term 'unknowledgeable transfer', where there is not enough information about the original situation or the destination to ensure that transfer is made successfully. Another is 'incomplete transfer', when elements crucial to success in the original situation are not included in the transfer. The final one is 'inappropriate transfer', where not enough attention is paid to differences in the context between the countries. Despite these potential problems, comparing supported housing in different countries may serve to open our eyes to new possibilities or help to identify lessons that can improve policy and provision. The important factor is to be aware of possible problems with potential transfer and to be clearly aware of the importance of the context within which particular forms of provision such as supported housing are embedded in a particular country.

Support in Britain

It is becoming increasingly difficult to describe housing and support systems for Britain as a whole, because social care, health and housing are all functions that have been devolved to the administrations in Scotland and Wales since the early 2000s. The result has been differences that have been widening over time, although the limited tax raising powers and the lack of resources and limitations of powers have constrained the extent of the divergence. However, the systems have a common root that will be described here.

To understand the system of support in Britain it is necessary to go back as far as the Poor Law Amendment Act in 1834, which enshrined the role of institutions in the care of vulnerable people (including the older, homeless and disabled people who are the focus here). This was a response to the perceived expense of 'outdoor relief' (cash payments paid by local parishes) and the perceived lack of incentive said to be given to people to take up paid employment. Support was to be confined to the workhouse, where it was based on the principle of 'less eligibility', that is, worse conditions than people would experience outside. It can be argued that the policy on support since this time has been an extended attempt to depart from this model and to move away from institutional living and to provide support that is of a high quality. However, the legacy of poor-quality institutional living has bedevilled support policy and has prevented a balanced approach that embraces good-quality institutions.

The major move away from institutional living occurred in the late 1960s and 1970s, with the policy of community care and the creation of integrated local authority social services departments (subsequently divided into children's and adults' services departments). The policy was driven by a number of factors, although there is some disagreement over their precise impact. The first factor was a political belief that the state was taking a role that should be undertaken by families and voluntary activity. Thus community care was seen by some to include a discourse of care *by* the community as well as care *in* the community. In echoes of the conservative approach outlined above, the family home was seen as the best place for vulnerable people to be cared for by their families and by volunteers.

At the same time there was a powerful discourse questioning the value of institutional living that had a number of constituents. One element was the critique of the quality of life in institutions made by academics such as Peter Townsend (1962) and through the revelations in the media, and consequently through a series of official enquiries, of cruel and inadequate care in the converted workhouses and asylums that provided much of institutional living for older people and those with a mental illness or learning disability (for a review see Means et al, 2008). These institutions were old and were considered inadequate and lacking appropriate facilities for high-quality care. They were also very expensive to manage and maintain, and required substantial repairs and improvements if they were to meet the standards considered to be appropriate. Part of the predominant discourse therefore saw community care as offering a cheaper alternative in terms of the cost to government than remaking the institutions, although it was not long before it was evident that high-quality community care could also have a high price.

The move away from institutions was a general one that took place in support for many vulnerable groups and took particular forms in each case. For older people it represented a move away from residential care in 'old folks' homes', the conditions in which were vividly described by Townsend in his book *The last refuge* (1962), where he paints a picture of residents sitting around with nothing to do and waiting to die. Townsend promoted the alternative of sheltered housing as a form of supported housing that would obviate the need for residential care.

In the 1970s, the media highlighted many scandals concerning conditions in large 'mental institutions' that were found to be home for people with a wide range of needs and abilities. Some residents had profound learning difficulties or mental illnesses, but others were incarcerated because of situations such as an unwanted pregnancy. All were considered to suffer from 'institutional neurosis' – a condition said to be the product of a lack of autonomy, control and activity in institutions, which were seen as the 'total institutions' as defined by Goffman (1968). This institutionally caused neurosis was said to be the cause of the behaviour usually associated with people with mental health problems in institutions, but was independent of the original problem that resulted in admission. The belief was growing that institutional living did not alleviate people's problems but exacerbated them and prevented 'normal' life. In the new community care discourse these environments were considered to be inadequate to promote 'therapeutic communities' for people with mental health problems or training sites for those with learning disabilities. The widespread availability of a new range of drugs to alleviate the symptoms of mental illness and to control behaviour also contributed to the view that high-quality care could feasibly be best delivered outside institutions.

One of the principal outcomes of community care was the closure of many institutions, particularly the old 'mental hospitals'. New admissions were stopped and so new forms of provision were needed for those who were newly recognised as being in need.

Therefore, the closure of institutions was coupled with a move to more diverse forms of provision, often based on particular forms of supported housing. This diversity reflected the lack of an accepted model of non-institutional care. Commentators such as Tyne (1982) and Henwood (1986) pointed to the essential negativity of the community care discourse. There was a clear idea of what was not appropriate (institutional care) but little thought or agreement on what should replace it, what appropriate care should consist of and what principles it should be judged by. For a while the concept of 'normalisation' seemed to offer a way forward, but the concept was heavily criticised for its perceived emphasis on changing vulnerable people to reflect widespread conceptions of what was normal behaviour, as well as the difficulties in defining what is normal (see Chapter Eight for a further discussion). Despite these reservations, many of the principles enshrined in normalisation formed the basis of thinking about appropriate forms of supported housing and so we will return to them later.

The government definition of community care was laid out in the White Paper *Caring for people* in 1989 (Department of Health, 1989: 3).

> Community care means providing the services and support which people who are affected by problems of ageing, mental illness, mental handicap, or physical or sensory

disability need to be able to live as independently as possible in their own homes, or in 'homely' settings in the community.

This official definition owed a little to the normalisation discourse in its use of the concept of independence, but this term was not clearly defined and it soon became apparent that there were different definitions. For example, Heywood et al (2002) argue that the meaning of independence in the legislation was largely seen as independence from state care and living independently was seen as living outside an institution. It was assumed that living at home or in a homely setting was enough to ensure independence and a good quality of care. Heywood et al (2002) argued that older people have a different conception of independence, which is based on the idea of personal control. They point to situations where some older people feel more independent in institutional living because they do not have to rely on family. They also argue that some older people can feel a lack of independence at home if they are isolated and lonely and have to rely on their family for support.

Two other issues are worth mentioning at this stage. The first is the coverage of community care policy. It was assumed that the policy was appropriate for a wide range of people in different circumstances. This caused problems later as the impetus for community care differed between the categorised groups. For example, there was something of a withdrawal from community care for people with mental health problems after some criminal incidents that were widely reported in the media. Despite the wide coverage of the community care categories, some people were left out, such as young people, women suffering domestic violence and homeless people, unless they were included in the overall categories. As a consequence, many people in supported accommodation, both before and after the legislation, were not covered by the community care label, with consequences for the funding stream available.

Second, there is no definition in the government policy of a 'homely setting'. This could be interpreted as meaning supported housing, but this was not made clear and reflected the lack of a positive view of the nature of a non-institutional setting. What differentiates a homely setting from a home or from an institution? Can institutions be homely settings? These questions have never been satisfactorily confronted and answered and so there has been a lack of clarity at the heart of the policy.

The community care discourse was formalised in policy through the NHS and Community Care Act 1990, which had a number of elements. The first was the obligation on local authorities to produce a community care strategy that examined needs in their area and contained a forward plan to meet them. Each local authority was to set a budget to fund community care. Within this overall framework, individuals were to be given a community care assessment designed to uncover their needs. The assessment was supposed to be undertaken without consideration of resources or forms of provision available and to be based on the articulated needs of the person themselves. However, there has been considerable dispute about the nature of assessments in practice, which have been argued to be resources and service rather than user led (for a review see Means et al, 2008). On the basis of the needs assessment, an individual care plan is compiled consisting of the services required. This is then purchased either from the local authority or from another agency. There was some debate about the nature of the purchasing with an emphasis on 'spot' purchasing for an individual rather than 'bulk' purchasing on a longer-term basis. In other words, rather than purchasing one supported housing place when required, the local authority would pre-purchase a number of places for when they were needed. The latter option was argued to give the security needed to ensure supply came forward and enabled the authority to undertake better financial management.

One increasingly important strand of policy that has developed from the community care agenda has been the provision of cash rather than services to vulnerable people. This was first instituted through the Independent Living Fund (ILF), which was primarily aimed at people with a physical disability following political pressure from the Disability Living Alliance and other pressure groups. The fund provided money for individual disabled people to pay for their own support either by employing their own support assistants or by purchasing services from charities or other organisations. Evaluations of the ILF showed that it was popular among recipients and enabled them to exercise considerable control over the form of their support (Glasby and Littlechild, 2009). Despite its success, the ILF is currently being phased out in 2015 as part of the coalition government's welfare reforms. Following the community care legislation, an option of direct payments was introduced for local authorities for community care recipients. Needs were to be assessed in the usual way, but people were given the option of taking a cash sum and using this to purchase services, either from the local authority or, more usually, by employing their own carers. Voluntary organisations provided help to direct payments recipients to undertake the employment of staff and other practical tasks associated with organising one's own support. The evidence from evaluations of direct payments showed that, as with the ILF, they were appreciated by recipients for the increased ability they gave them to personalise the support received to suit their individual needs and lifestyles (for a review see Glasby and Littlechild, 2009). However, the uptake of direct payments was low and there were substantial misgivings from some social care professionals about the ability and willingness of people to take on responsibility for their own support. A different version of payment for care was implemented in 2003 and has gained increasing emphasis through the personalisation agenda of the last Labour government (HM Government, 2007). This mechanism was called 'personal budgets' and involved social services care managers being clear with the recipient about how much money is available for their support and giving them the maximum choice over how this money is spent and the degree of control that they want to take themselves over its spending. This could result in the direct provision or purchase of services by the local authority or other agency, or the provision of cash for individual support, or a mixture of both.

The direction of change towards personalisation has not been universal across the 'categories' of people who use supported housing. For example, homeless young people are not included in the community care categories and are more likely to have conditions placed on their access to and continued use of support that may involve changes in behaviour, such as abstinence from drugs or alcohol. So conditionality has existed alongside the increase in empowerment through personalisation for some people, thus reconstituting the traditional divide between deserving and undeserving poor.

The community care legislation gave supported housing great importance. Housing was commonly described as the cornerstone of community care and most focus was on appropriate forms of supported housing to deliver the community care objectives (see Purkis and Hodson, 1982). However, the development of supported housing was a difficult task because of the many different agencies and funding streams involved. For the closure of existing institutions it was possible to implement phased programmes to re-house the existing residents and to devise specific funding mechanisms to achieve the new provision before the existing institutions were closed. Where the provision was not part of a closure programme, financing became more problematic with many different agencies and sources of funding involved. For example, a new supported housing project would typically require the involvement of the social services authority, the health authority, voluntary management and support agency, and a housing association (for a review see Clapham et al, 1994). Capital finance for the building would typically come from a housing association grant, private sector loans and possibly also from the health and social services authorities. Revenue finance would come from rents and a service charge paid by the residents, who might be eligible for housing benefit, in addition to any support provided by the statutory agencies, such as health authorities concerned to reduce health expenditures or social services as part of their community care plan. During the 1990s it became evident that there was a revenue funding gap in that housing benefit was being used to fund support costs. The result was the introduction of the Supporting People programme in 2003 that was meant to bridge the gap between housing benefit payments (that were reduced in scope) and care payments from the community care process or elsewhere.

The Supporting People funding regime was introduced in 2003 to provide revenue funding for people with support needs. As in the community care mechanism, local authorities were obliged to produce a Supporting People strategy, incorporating health, housing and social care agencies, that was based on assessed needs and laid out plans to meet those needs. Within this strategy, funding could be made available for the provision of supported housing and for low-level support to people in their own homes. The new regime was implemented along with an attempt to reduce the scope of housing benefit payments and to regularise them, where previously different rules had applied in different areas. Supporting People funding was designed to fill the gap between housing expenses, which could be met for low-income people through housing benefit, and support expenditures financed through community care or by local authorities, voluntary organisations or health authorities for those outside the community care framework. It paid for low-level support activities associated with housing provision for vulnerable people, such as providing help with money or debt management, providing access to hobbies, liaising with other services or helping with employment. Supporting People funding therefore became crucial to the development and running of most supported housing projects, but problems with it have bedevilled the growth of supported housing. One issue has been the devolution of Supporting People to the devolved administrations of Britain. The result has been different policies and practices in each devolved region. For example, in England during 2011 and 2012, there were substantial reductions in Supporting People funding, along with an earlier abolition of the ring fence that ensured that local authorities spent the money only on these purposes. The result was a substantial reduction in financial support. However, in Scotland, and Wales, the level of funding was subject to much less reduction, although each administration developed its own policies and procedures for it.

The problems with Supporting People reflected its introduction. Government did not know how much was already being spent through housing benefit and other funding sources for activities due to be covered by the new regime. It asked local authorities to undertake an audit of current provision, but also allowed an interim period in which new forms of provision could be funded through transitional housing benefit and could be eligible for funding alongside existing provision. The result was an explosion of new supported housing provision that meant that, on initiation of the regime, the funding allocated was insufficient to cover all commitments. From that point on, funds for Supporting People have been reduced even further. One avowed aim of the fund was to stimulate a questioning of existing forms of provision in terms of their value for money in meeting need and to stimulate new and innovative forms of provision. Innovation was very difficult in a situation where funding was insufficient and declining, as making funds available for new developments can only be done by closing others. It was made more difficult by the fact that funding allocations reflected current provision rather than any assessed need. The introduction of the Supporting People regime does not seem to have overcome the uncertainty surrounding the development of supported housing.

Housing policy

British housing policy has been dominated since the 1980s by the privatisation of public rented housing and the growth of owner occupation as the dominant tenure. The 'right to buy' for council tenants at a large discount enacted from 1980 and rejuvenated in 2010, coupled with financial restrictions on the ability of local authorities to build new housing, has resulted in a residualisation of the council sector with its size substantially reduced and its role restricted to catering for the most vulnerable households. Although council housing in its early years in the 1920s catered mainly for the skilled working-class and lower middle-class households, who were the only ones who could afford the only lightly subsidised rents, for most of its existence priority has been given to people in the greatest housing need, even when it became a major general tenure in the 1970s, housing almost one third of the population. It must be remembered, though, that access to British council housing has never been subject to a test of income, just of housing need (although those in most housing need are likely to have low incomes).

Many local authorities have transferred their housing stock either to existing non-profit housing associations or new bodies created for this purpose. Although the housing association sector has increased in size, partly through stock transfer and partly through new building with government subsidy, it has not made up for the loss of council stock. Also, although there is great diversity in the sector, housing associations have seen their role change, with more emphasis on market or close to market housing in response to pressure from central government, and changes in the grant regime. Housing associations have been seen by governments as an answer to the lack of investment in private renting and government policy has resulted in some associations providing housing at market rents, thus blurring the difference between the social and private rental sectors. Some housing associations have become more commercial or 'businesslike' in their operations, and there has been criticism in some quarters of the high salaries being paid to chief executives, reflecting their increasing private sector ethos.

Owner occupation has been the predominant tenure since the 1950s and had increased to 69.2% of the stock in 2002, although it then reduced to 64.1% by 2012 (Wilcox and Perry, 2014). The financial crisis of 2007 resulted in a considerable housing market slump, with some reductions in house prices and a substantial reduction in the number of transactions. In response to the financial crisis the mortgage lenders restricted the availability of new loans and increased the deposit requirements. This was at a time of economic hardship, again because of the financial crisis that resulted in reduced living standards for all but the richest, and increasing unemployment, especially among young people. As a result, the proportion of households in owner occupation has decreased in the last few years as problems of affordability have reduced the ability of many first-time buyers and young people to enter the market. Nevertheless, the size of the sector means that many people in need of supported housing will be living in the owner-occupied sector.

Private rented housing (private rented sector – PRS) has undergone a renaissance with the deregulation of rents and the problems of access to other tenures. Although there has not been investment from many of the large-scale investors that characterises the PRS in some other countries, there has been a growth in 'buy-to-let' properties often from people owning only a few dwellings. Over the past decade, the PRS has experienced dramatic growth, increasing from 9.5% to 17.8% of dwellings between 2000 and 2012 (Wilcox and Perry, 2014). This growth has largely been due to the success of 'buy-to-let' mortgages (Ball, 2006). Buy-to-let mortgages are usually taken out by individuals and their growth has done nothing to alleviate the individualistic nature of landlordism in Britain. Properties have usually been those on the owner-occupied market and few properties are newly built specifically for private rental. Investment in the sector has therefore become problematic and, although the government has introduced a number of measures to deal with this, such as providing tax breaks for new investment through mechanisms such as the Business Expansion Scheme, HITS and HEITS, this has had mixed and generally small-scale results (for a review see Crook and Kemp, 2011).

Most tenancies in the PRS are assured shortholds (Kemp, 2009), which means that there is little security for tenants and tenancies are generally short in duration (unlike in Sweden). In 2007/08 40% of private tenants in Britain had lived in their properties for less than one year and 70% for less than three years. Rents in the sector are no longer controlled and so landlords are free to set the rent. This has resulted in relatively high rental costs in the sector. According to CLG (2012), in the private rented sector on average 43% of household income is spent on accommodation, which compares unfavourably to owner occupation and social renting, where spending is 19% and 29% respectively. In addition to relatively high costs and insecurity, some 45% of PRS dwellings in England in 2007 were non-compliant with the official Decent Homes Standard (CLG, 2009a). Despite some recent improvements in perceptions of the PRS (Kemp, 2009), there has been a general reluctance to act to improve conditions in the sector by governments because of the perceived impact on supply.

Traditionally, the PRS has acted as a point of easy access to owner occupation for young or professional people and there has also been a strong student sector. There is also a low-income segment of the PRS made up of those seeking an alternative to social renting and people in receipt of welfare benefits. In private renting, housing benefit is paid through a Local Housing Allowance (LHA), which is calculated on the basis of household size and composition, income and the level of rents in the locality. Allowances are not tied to particular properties and tenants can choose a property with either a higher or lower rent than the allowance.

Given the continuing affordability problems in owner occupation and the relative decline of the social housing sector (Pattison et al, 2010), growth in the PRS looks likely to continue with no significant interventions set to address concerns over security, affordability or standards. Despite this anticipated growth, there is some concern about levels of supply. It is likely that 'buy-to-let' mortgages will be restricted by the recessionary economy and credit restrictions. Also, any decline in the profitability in the sector due to housing benefit restrictions could also detrimentally impact upon supply.

There has been increasing concern about the supply of new housing in Britain and reforms have been made to the planning system that has been blamed by developers and government for holding back housing supply. Economic problems and the decline in the housing market after the financial crisis in 2007 have resulted in historically low levels of new house building at a time when demographic pressures continue to build through immigration and people living longer. Housing shortages are concentrated in the more prosperous regions, such as London and the south-east of England, and have been exacerbated by the impact of growing income inequality and the purchase of many properties in central London by people domiciled abroad.

The focus on supported housing in the community care agenda arose in the 1980s at a time when housing policy in Britain became more commodified, with a reduction in the size and role of public rented housing and a growth in the scope of housing markets and, in particular, the consolidation of owner occupation as the 'normal' tenure. Housing problems have been increasingly characterised as personal rather than political. In other words, if people cannot achieve a decent housing standard then this is the result of personal failing rather than government recalcitrance. Government help is focused on those who cannot help themselves rather than in the form of general entitlements. As a result, housing policy in Britain has become more targeted on people such as those in need of community care (and this is true also in Sweden, as we shall see later in the chapter). Potential recipients of help have to show that they are deserving and this is normally done through proof of membership of a vulnerable community care group, such as being an older person or a person with a physical disability. The result of this has been a focus on the group attributes, rather than those of individuals, and specific forms of provision have been developed for older people or for other groups. Because of the wide range of needs and resources in any particular group, the needs to be met and the provision have usually been based on stereotypical attributes based on dominant discourses of the groups concerned (specific examples will be shown in the following chapters). One example is the provision of housing for older people (such as sheltered housing) based on the perceived need for the company of others of the same age, small warm homes, which are physically accessible, and provision of support services such as a resident warden. So particular forms of supported housing provision have developed, for members of particular groups, based on dominant discourses regarding their needs and preferences. Clapham and Smith

(1990) have termed this approach the 'special needs discourse'. The assumption is that members of the designated groups have needs that are 'special' when compared with others. The problem with this approach is that it tends to hide the needs of individuals that may vary from those of others in their group. For example, the individual needs of some older people may vary considerably from others in the same category who have a different health status, or lifestyle or set of preferences. The needs of many older people may be the same as those of others of different ages. In the 'special needs' approach, the focus is on group membership rather than individual needs and preferences. This can lead to the unequal treatment of people with similar needs, but membership of different categories.

The deserving status of the category is determined in part by its perceived vulnerability. Therefore, pressure groups for older people, for example, are faced with a dilemma. On the one hand they have an interest in stressing the vulnerability of the group and their need for 'special' care. On the other hand, they are aware that this reinforces negative stereotypes of the group and downplays the positive contribution they can make to society. At the same time, the 'special needs' approach tends to implicate individual or group characteristics as the cause of housing problems, and can, therefore, divert attention away from the need for more comprehensive interventions through mainstream housing policy. The approach, with its emphasis on group inadequacies, fits badly with the social model of disability that focuses on the societal barriers to mainstream life (this will be considered in more detail in Chapter Eight).

Finally, it is worth noting at this stage that Britain has a very different homelessness system from Sweden's. In Britain, there is a statutory framework of rights given to people assessed as being homeless, although these are circumscribed in practice and now vary considerably between the devolved administrations. However, the key difference between Britain and Sweden is that, in the former, homelessness is considered to be a housing problem with responsibility given to housing agencies, whereas in the latter it is considered to be primarily a social services issue. More detail is given in Chapter Seven, but it is worth noting here that the homeless systems in both countries have resulted in the provision of many different forms of supported housing.

Support in Sweden

Sweden has often been held up as the epitome of Esping-Andersen's social democratic welfare state or what Korpi (1978) labelled the institutional welfare state. Korpi identified 10 elements of this model:

- social welfare spending makes up a high proportion of GDP
- public services reach a substantial proportion of the population
- services are of a high quality so that higher income people want to use them
- priority given to full employment
- prevention of social problems considered important
- universal services and benefits
- the level of benefits high
- user fees are non-existent or low
- progressive taxation
- social control limited because of the universal nature of benefits.

Up to the financial crisis of the 1990s, Sweden was considered to be very close to this ideal, with public services making up 60% of GDP, but now the ideal seems to be a long way off. The commitment to full employment can be questioned, with historically high rates of unemployment at present being justified as efficient for the economy. The level of state benefits has been reduced in real terms, universal services and benefits have been cut back and fees for consumers of social services are ubiquitous. The incidence of taxation has become less progressive and, as we shall see in the following chapters, social control through the design and implementation of public services has increased. Nevertheless, as outlined earlier in the chapter, public social expenditure in Sweden in 2009 was 150% of that in the UK and overall public expenditure as a proportion of GDP almost 5% higher.

The key to the primary welfare state system is labour market participation, as entitlement is based on employment record. A marginal position in the labour market or total exclusion from the labour market also means, by and large, that you are excluded from the primary welfare system and are assigned to the secondary one that is administered by local social authorities and where social support is means-tested and subject to official assessment of needs.

One example of this secondary system is the public system for the care of older people that dates back to the poorhouses of the 19th century, but was modernised after the 1940s. By the 1980s it was among the most comprehensive in the world and based almost completely on public care providers – largely the almost 300 self-governing municipalities. One of the key characteristics of the Swedish governance system is the relative independence of these municipalities, which can generate their own funds through a local income tax and are not dependent on central government funding. This is unlike Britain, where central government provides most local authority funding and can set upper limits on what can be raised locally through the property tax. In Sweden, central government can influence local authorities through legislation and regulation, and by providing targeted subsidy. However, the extent of local independence has resulted in substantial variation in type and quantity of provision in different localities.

Criticism of the universalist model began in the 1970s as economic problems provided financial restrictions on provision which left long waiting lists for some services. The centre and right political parties adopted policies of privatisation couched in terms of consumer choice. During the late 1980s the Social Democratic party became open to the introduction of 'quasi-markets' in public services to counter perceived problems of inefficiency and lack of consumer choice and so, from the 1990s onwards, governments of different persuasions pursued an agenda of deregulation and privatisation (Blomqvist, 2004).

However, the financial crisis of the 1990s put the social democratic model in Sweden under stress and the election of non-social democratic governments for periods since this time has resulted in change. Blomqvist (2004) quotes Lindbom (2001) as arguing that cutbacks in welfare benefits have been relatively small and that the basic structure of universalism has been retained. However, Blomqvist (2004: 140–1) takes a contradictory view, arguing that far-reaching changes have taken place in the delivery of social services following the adoption of ideas of 'new public management', which were also very influential in Britain:

> The previous system of public provision of uniform services, allocated through bureaucratic planning, has been profoundly transformed, replaced with a system where the choices of service users play a much bigger role, where private providers have re-established themselves (especially in the bigger cities) and where relations between actors within the system are conducted in an increasingly market-like environment.

Although provision by the private sector is low (Blomqvist estimates between 5% and 15%) the effect has been to undermine the universalist ethic and has given more affluent people the opportunity to opt out of the public services.

In contrast, Hajighasemi (2004) argues that the extent of privatisation has been modest and that changes from the 1990s have been to the level of benefits rather than to the nature of the system itself. He argues that there is still strong support for the welfare system both among political parties and among the general population. 'Even in the case of social, health and other services the Swedish model has kept its essential principles. In providing services, huge areas of welfare state activities continue to respect the critical features of comprehensiveness, universalism and generosity' (Hajighasemi, 2004: 265).

The predominant discourse adopted in Sweden for the vulnerable people discussed in this book has been normalisation, as in Britain, but, as we shall see in the following chapters, Sweden has been more successful in implementing the move away from institutions and into community care. Few examples of institutions still exist outside of hospitals and even in supported housing residents generally have their own apartments rather than any form of shared living.

In 1992, the statutory responsibility for support for older people was given to municipal authorities for all types of institutional housing and support facilities. This included long-term care hospitals, nursing homes, old-age homes, service houses, group dwellings and day care facilities. The municipalities were also given the statutory responsibility to provide health care to older residents living in the institutional housing and care facilities mentioned above. By agreement with the county councils that provided most hospital and health care, the municipalities could also take over the responsibility for home nursing care. However, the responsibility to provide health care does not include medical care provided by doctors, which is a county council responsibility. Therefore there is an institutional split between social services and health and housing responsibilities, which is also the case in Britain. The municipalities were also given financial responsibility for all other types of long-term institutional care even if they did not run the schemes themselves. The responsibility also includes patients in short-term psychiatric hospital care and in geriatric hospital clinics.

During the 1990s the majority of municipalities adopted the purchaser–provider split that was also prevalent in Britain, with the local state assessing and purchasing services, but provision being from a mixture of private, voluntary and public providers. The assessment process is the key to unlocking resources for many vulnerable people and there are separate systems for those who have been assessed as needing help and those who are not, as we will see in following chapters. For those assessed as needing care, the Act on Free Choice (2008: 962) gives people the right to choose support and the Public Procurement Act (2007: 1091) enables municipal authorities to procure support from a wide range of providers. However, assessments are very detailed, with little flexibility, and the choice of provider is limited to those on a local authority list, so few people exercise their choice in practice. These reforms are not as extensive as the personalisation policies in Britain so the system does not give the same emphasis to personal choice and decision making.

The extent and type of provision of support is determined by the local authorities with little control from central government apart from in the enabling legislation that stipulates that services should be of good quality, provided by people with appropriate training and experience, and that services should be based on respect for the people's self-determination and privacy. Assistance to the individual is to be designed and implemented together with the person in question. Regulation of provision is through the National Board for Health and Welfare (Socialstyrelsen), which assesses whether providers meet regulations and grants licences to private providers. However, regulation is much less developed than in the British system and there is less emphasis on value-for-money audits.

The municipality is obliged to plan for and provide supported housing in which support for the residents is available 24 hours a day. The places are allocated by the municipality and assigned according to the Social Service Act and must be based on the person's needs for housing and support, and not through a waiting list. If an application for special housing is rejected, it is possible to appeal against the decision in an administrative court.

In 1993, an Act of Support and Services for people with certain functional impairments (LSS) was passed that is effectively a bill of rights for people with various kinds of disabilities, regardless of whether they are genetic or caused by accidents or traumas, or whether they are displayed in physical, mental or social dysfunction, as long as they are durable and not associated with normal ageing. Problems associated with age are therefore separated from those resulting from other causes, while at the same time those with mental and physical disabilities are subsumed under the same legislation as people with mental health problems and people who, for reasons such as alcohol or substance abuse, have disabilities which hinder their functioning in society.

The measures for special support and special service specified in the LSS include advice and other personal support, which requires trained personnel; help through personal assistants; housing through foster care or in housing with special services for children and young people who should not remain with their families; daily activities for adults who have no work and are not involved in education; and housing with special services for adults or other specially adjusted homes for adults. This concept covers all kinds of housing needed by a disabled individual included in the categories outlined in Chapter One, with the exception of domiciliary provision as the Act does not entitle individuals to acquire an 'ordinary home', which therefore distorts the options available to individuals away from domiciliary provision.

An important difference between Britain and Sweden is that disabled people and older people in Britain are all considered under the community care system. However, in Sweden, older people are explicitly excluded from the LSS system for disabled people, where there is substantial choice over the choice of personal assistants and the work they do. Another important difference from Britain is that social services authorities have a legal obligation in the LSS system, laid down in the legislation, to provide the support needed by disabled people. Unlike in Britain, this obligation cannot be avoided because of the shortage of financial resources. Therefore in Sweden, the authority has to generate the resources necessary to meet all assessed needs of disabled people, whereas in Britain the authorities can place a resource cap on the needs that are to be met. However, this obligation in Sweden does not apply to older people, where municipal authorities just have a general duty to provide services to meet needs and they are the people who decide on appropriate needs through the assessment process. Therefore, as in Britain, older people do not have the right to receive services regardless of resources as disabled people in Sweden do.

The Social Services Act (valid from 1982 but recently revised) gives the municipality the 'ultimate responsibility' to see that their residents get the support and help they need. This 'ultimate responsibility' refers to emergency help, including the provision of temporary night shelter for people who would otherwise sleep rough. The Act explicitly states that this does not reduce the responsibilities of other authorities, such as the county councils, which run the hospitals, or the state, which is in charge of prisons, probation and institutions for compulsory treatment.

The Act also gives an individual who cannot satisfy their own needs themselves under certain conditions the right to 'other assistance'. This help should be designed in a manner that increases the individual's ability to lead an independent life. The assistance stipulated includes social welfare services, work or training as prerequisites for welfare, and help provided in the home and supported housing. The Act also covers housing for older people, and obliges the local authority to work towards acquiring dwellings suitable for older people and provide them with support and assistance in their home. It further obliges the municipality to arrange supported housing for older people in need of it.

The Act is based on ideas of normalisation (see Chapter Eight) and it places the obligation on local authorities to provide opportunities for individuals to take part in the community and live like others, as well as to obtain a meaningful occupation and be housed in a way that is adjusted to their individual need. The municipality is given the obligation to arrange the provision of supported housing with special services for those who need such housing.

Beyond this needs-related, municipal, secondary welfare system (the primary one being the universal state provision based on labour market participation), there is a 'tertiary' system designed for people who fall through the safety net and are excluded from both the primary and secondary systems. The tertiary system consists mainly of non-profit organisations working beyond the public sphere and supported by the public, philanthropists and some private companies, but at the same time very much dependent on financing from the local public authorities. Although the Social Services Act gives municipalities the overall responsibility for people in emergency need, dealing with homelessness, especially through the provision of emergency shelters, has historically been, and still is, a niche occupied by non-profit organisations and charities in the larger cities. Their involvement dates back to long before the Swedish modern welfare state began to take shape around the time of the Second World War. At that time the welfare state took over many tasks from the non-profit sector and became the dominant producer of social welfare services.

This tertiary sector is relatively large by international standards and fulfils several different roles. The long tradition of the Swedish non-profit sector is membership-based ownership, democratic organisational structures and voluntary work. Since the 1930s non-profit organisations have been regarded as schools for democracy and citizenship and instruments for political mobilisation, as well as sharing the responsibility for developing and carrying out employment policies (Olsson and Nordfeldt, 2008). They have been given a greater role since the reforms from the 1990s onwards.

Housing policy

The 1990s were also a watershed in Swedish housing policy, which, from the 1970s, was close to the social democratic model, with a policy based on tenure neutrality and generous general subsidies to all tenures.

Bengtsson (2013: 169) argues that the Swedish housing system from the late 1940s up to the beginning of the 21st century has five distinctive characteristics:

- a universally oriented housing policy directed at all tenure forms without individual needs or means testing;
- a public rental sector with housing companies that are owned by the municipalities and professionally managed at arm's length from political influence;
- a so-called 'integrated rental market' whereby both public and private rental housing is available for all types of households, and formal links exist between rent setting in the public and private sector;a 'corporatist' system based on centralised rent negotiations between (public or private) landlords and representatives of a well-established national tenant movement;a large cooperative sector based mainly on the specific tenure of 'tenant ownership'. The prominent role of housing cooperatives can be linked to a legal prohibition (until 2009) against owner occupation in multi-family buildings.

Bengtsson (2013) argues that it is the combination of these five factors that makes the Swedish housing system unique, as many of the individual factors are found in other countries. The only really unique factor is the corporatist system of rent setting, whereby tenant unions represent the individual tenants at the negotiating table.

The large public sector was administered by municipal housing companies that allocated properties on the basis of waiting time without any financial means test or assessment of housing or social need, unlike in Britain. However, this tenure acted as a place of last resort as well as a general tenure for a substantial proportion of the population. There was an important private rented sector, similar in size to the public sector, which was subject to rent control through the corporatist negotiation system. In some areas, particularly in the larger towns and cities, private rented properties were allocated through the municipal housing exchanges run by the local authorities, which used a system of allocation of properties based on waiting time. Sweden had what Kemeny (1992) labelled a unitary rental system, in which the private sector is secondary to the public sector and is subject to the same kind of regulation.

The cooperative sector enabled people to own apartments and houses, although with price restrictions on sale until 1968. Since this date the tenure has become more similar to the British leasehold ownership of flats or the US condominium system, although the communal management arrangements are different from those in the other two countries.

Bengtsson (2013) divides the establishment of the current housing system in Sweden into four phases. The first establishment phase was from 1900 to 1945, which saw the establishment of the National Union of Tenants in 1923, partly in response to the abolition of the first attempts at rent control in that same year. In 1933 the 'historical compromise' between the Social Democrats and the Farmers' League (now the Centerpartiet) created the political framework for left-of-centre political governments from 1936 to 1956. A first sign of this was the creation of the municipal housing companies in 1935, which at first were given the task of providing subsidised housing for families with low incomes and many children. The second phase, from 1945 to 1975, laid the foundations for the universal housing system, with the introduction of state housing loans for all tenures and the consolidation of the position of the municipalities as the major implementation agents of housing policy. Also during this period, the corporatist rent setting system was established, based on the use value of dwellings. However, the major issue of the time was the shortage of housing and so the Social Democratic government introduced the 'Million Homes Programme', when a million dwellings were built over a ten-year period, often in large-scale municipal housing projects. The third phase, from 1975 to 1990, is called by Bengtsson the saturation phase, when problems started to be felt in some of the large housing estates and vacancy rates increased, stimulating a growing interest in the management of these estates. Also, new forms of general subsidies were introduced to balance the interest rate allowances for owner occupiers to create a tenure-neutral financial system. Finally, the period from 1990 onward is named the 'retrenchment phase', where the consensus that had previously characterised Swedish housing policy was broken. Bengtsson identifies this period as a critical juncture in Swedish housing policy, in which substantial change took place. However, the extent of change from the existing system is disputed with Bengtsson (2013) arguing that there is a large element of 'path dependency' and continuity, whereas Christophers (2013) emphasises the extent of change.

During the 1990s there was substantial change to the housing finance system justified on the basis of the perceived threat of burgeoning housing subsidy payments to the national economy. A fundamental element of reform, therefore, was a reduction in general subsidies through state housing subsidies and loans, with reliance being placed on housing allowances in order to focus help on those deemed to need it – largely families with children (Turner and Whitehead, 2002). Rents were increased and were more linked to market rents, although the system of rent negotiation between the tenants' union and the municipal housing companies was retained. However, the housing allowances were not increased enough to compensate for the reduction in production subsidies and so housing costs increased substantially for many people. For example, the rental costs of single people over 65 increased from 18% of income to 32% between 1987 and 1997 and for two-person households from 18% to 25%. The changes resulted in a substantial reduction in the output of new houses and an increase in social segregation.

Christophers (2013) has described the current Swedish housing system as a 'monstrous hybrid'. It is a hybrid because there has been substantial liberalisation, but significant elements of the earlier regulated system exist. It is monstrous, because the resultant system has many flaws, including increasing problems of affordability and a lack of sufficient housing supply. In terms of what he calls the vectors of neoliberalism, Christophers (2013) points to the increased marketisation of the traditional cooperative system through the deregulation of selling prices in the 1960s, thus making the sector owner occupation in all but name. The public rental sector has also been marketised, with the selling off of large quantities of the public stock to sitting tenants at below market prices. The municipal housing companies are usually limited liability companies in form, but they have been required to act in a 'businesslike' or 'commercial' manner, although there is some confusion about what this means in practice. The third vector highlighted by Christophers is the increasing support for owner occupation from government that represents a significant departure from the traditional tenure neutrality. This support is most evident in the scale of tax benefits to home owners, which, when seen in conjunction with the decreasing financial support for renting, both public and private, means that the costs of renting have increased considerably in relative (as well as absolute) terms. One of the owner occupier benefits relevant to our discussion in this book is the ability to offset repairs, adaptations and maintenance costs against tax (this will be covered in more detail in Chapter Six).

Despite these neoliberalising vectors, Christophers identifies three elements of the traditional system that survive. The first is the rent setting system for the rented sector that still involves negotiations between landlords and the tenants' union. Rents are to be set to allow municipal housing companies to make a 'normal' rate of return, although, within the overall total, individual rents are set on a 'use value' principle, which means that rents in popular, inner city Stockholm are well below market levels, although rents elsewhere may not be. Rents in the private sector are based on equivalent use values, but from 2011 the comparisons have been with both public and private sector rents, thus diluting the previous price leadership role of the public sector that was the sole comparator before this change. Also new-built rental housing is now exempt from this system and landlords can charge a market rent. The result is of this rent setting system is what Christophers (2013) labels a 'soft' form of rent control. The second factor identified by Christophers is the allocation system for filling rented vacancies. Traditionally this has been done by the municipal housing exchanges for both the public sector and sometimes for the private sector, but the lack of a requirement to have an exchange since 1991 has seen the subsequent shutting down of most of those in all but a few municipalities. Despite the fact that municipal housing companies have never taken account of housing need in allocating tenancies, their change towards a commercial or market orientation has created the fear that lower income tenants are finding it more difficult to access this tenure. This is in addition to the problems that a queuing system creates for those such as homeless people and new immigrants, whose housing need is urgent. The third factor identified by Christophers is the regulation of letting and sub-letting within both the private and public rented sectors, which means that there is a very heavily regulated framework for the terms and conditions of letting as well as on the rents.

One factor not identified by Christophers (2013) is the planning system in Sweden, implemented in 1947 and not repealed since, that requires all land for development to pass through municipal ownership. This system enables the municipal authorities to exert some control over the location, extent and types of development. In principle this should ensure a supply of cheap development land for housing and so improve the affordability of housing. However, municipal authorities have experienced increasing direction and control by central government on their decision making in this area, and the flow of new housing development has not been enough in recent years to prevent housing shortages in many places, particularly the large cities.

The current Swedish system still has almost all the five features identified by Bengtsson and so change has been evolutionary or 'path dependent'. However, the cooperative sector has now become ownership by another name and the withdrawal of universal subsidies has compromised tenure neutrality. Also, the increasing market orientation of the housing system has created problems. The 'monstrous hybrid' identified by Christophers (2013) has resulted in a system where owner occupation is dominant, but out of reach of many new households. Private renting is heavily regulated, difficult to access in some areas and is short of new investment. Public rented housing is also increasingly difficult to access for many new households, especially those such as young people and immigrants who have not been waiting in a queue for a long time. Coupled with the increasing commerciality of the public rented sector it means that, in practice, the current Swedish system is not functioning as an effective safety net for some vulnerable people and some would argue that the social element of housing policy has been more or less dismantled (Olsson and Nordfeldt, 2008).

The universalist housing policy, with its emphasis on housing for all, has meant that access to housing for the most vulnerable has been dependent on the existence of an appropriate and extensive overall provision. The absence of a specific housing policy focus on low-income and other vulnerable people has left some unable to cope in an increasingly market oriented general housing system. Whereas in Britain households in housing need are given priority for social housing, this has not been the case in Sweden. People who have problems accessing universal provision in Sweden are therefore perceived as having special needs that follow from their individual characteristics in an example of the 'special needs' discourse identified earlier in the chapter. As a consequence of this approach, people with special needs are considered to be primarily the responsibility of municipal social services authorities rather than housing agencies. This shows itself in homelessness provision, but also for people with disabilities who come within the remit of the Social Services Act and the LSS (see previous section). The result has been the existence of supported housing that is the responsibility of social services agencies that makes up the 'secondary housing market' and will be discussed more fully in subsequent chapters. Therefore in Sweden, supported housing for homeless and disabled people has often developed in isolation from the housing system as a whole. This segregation has reinforced the 'special needs' discourse and probably resulted in supported housing that is more distant from the domiciliary model and closer to the institutional model as we shall see later. It has also compromised movement from one system to another, thus making it harder to exit from supported housing and into mainstream housing. Olsson and Nordfeldt (2008) refer to a 'vicious cycle of exclusion' that makes access to the primary housing market for marginal groups difficult. For people who are long-term dependent on social allowances in the secondary welfare system:

> With tougher requirements from landlords for, for example: personal references; a steady income; and a good rent record and credit worthiness, these groups face severe difficulties in gaining access to the primary housing market since they neither possess the economic resources to purchase a house or an apartment, nor do they have an income high enough to be able to get a loan from a bank. This group, which is long-term dependent on social allowances often also becomes dependent on the local social services authorities' secondary housing market. The effect of this is protracted withdrawal from the regular housing market. (Olsson and Nordfeldt, 2008: 163)

They argue that this means that the group of homeless people with the most complex needs are therefore often found within the tertiary housing system of emergency shelters provided by non-profit organisations, from which there is 'almost no possibility of re-entering the regular housing market' (Olsson and Nordfeldt, 2008: 163).

The exception to this general picture is housing for older people who do not qualify under the disability categories that make a distinction between disability and 'normal' ageing. The majority of older people are not segregated but participate in the primary housing system of owner-occupied, cooperative and rental housing, and some supported housing is available for them there. Nevertheless a secondary system exists for those with disabilities such as dementia.

The legal framework in Sweden for homelessness puts responsibility on municipal social services authorities and reserves the right to temporary and emergency shelter to those defined as needing social support under the social services assessment process. This process leaves a growing number of people with few rights in the current situation of housing shortage. It can be argued that a universal system was unnecessary when there was no shortage of housing and municipal housing companies helped those in need. However, both those requisites are no longer in existence and so homelessness is increasingly an issue. Sahlin (2010) argues that homelessness has been defined as a social services issue and central government intervention in homelessness is restricted to the propagation of a discourse defining the nature of the problem and the funding of innovative projects. In the prevailing discourse homelessness is defined as vulnerability due to drug abuse or mental health issues and attention is moved away from structural housing issues.

As a consequence there has been a growth in the secondary housing market, which is administered by the local social authorities for people who are homeless and who need support. This segment of the housing system consists of a variety of different kinds of transitional dwellings, such as shelters, monitored or supported housing, and 'contract housing' in the form of emergency housing, training flats and transitional contracts for people in rented housing where municipalities hold the contract, subleasing to residents. The terms used for these types of contract housing differ between different municipalities. This secondary housing market has clearly expanded within the Swedish municipalities in recent years. Research from the early 2000s shows an expansion by 58% during the 1990s (Sahlin, 2006).

The current Swedish housing system is far from the ideal of the social democratic model identified by Kemeny and others and it is doubtful whether it ever reflected this ideal model. Changes since the 1990s have resulted in substantial privatisation and a dilution of the universalist tradition. However, it is also not a completely liberalised system either, with considerable regulation of the private rented sector in particular which contrasts it with the British system. The resultant hybrid has left many problems that impact particularly on vulnerable people as we shall see in later chapters.

Conclusion

The chapter has shown the different contexts for supported housing in Britain and Sweden. The two countries' different welfare regimes have been described and there are clearly variations in their policies towards housing and support, although there are also similarities. Both countries have moved towards a more commodified housing system, with the role of local authorities and central government being reduced. However, Britain has moved further down this road than Sweden, and the market and individual choice elements of the British system are not replicated to the same degree in Sweden. Also, there are differences in discourses and policies towards issues such as homelessness as well as different institutional structures. For example, in Sweden responsibility for homeless people is largely the responsibility of local authority social services, whereas in Britain it is housing authorities that play the major role within a statutory framework. In both countries there is a quasi-market in the provision of support for vulnerable people, with statutory agencies, private organisations and the voluntary sector involved to varying degrees.

The Swedish housing system has been said to be a 'monstrous hybrid' in its mix of market and state institutions and processes. Despite its large public sector, Britain has the more commodified housing system, with a deregulated private rented sector and the dominance of owner occupation. However, Britain still has supply-side subsidies for social housing provided by housing associations and a housing allowance system for low-income households. The housing policy has an emphasis on providing access to rented housing for those in most housing need that is missing from Swedish policy. In Sweden the rented system has been reformed since the 1990s, with the dominance of the municipal housing companies challenged and their social mission diluted. Neither housing system fits closely to the neoliberal or social democratic models outlined earlier. In their own ways both are 'monstrous hybrids', with outcomes that can be criticised in terms of their value for vulnerable people.

Despite the similar policy rhetoric and moves in both countries in a neoliberal direction there are still major differences. Sweden is a much less unequal country in terms of incomes, and has much higher levels of general public expenditure and public social expenditure than Britain. Social support in Sweden is thus more extensive than in Britain, whereas the need for it is less because of the lower inequality. Britain has moved further in the establishment of quasi-markets of public and private provision, and in consumer rights through the personalisation programme.

In both countries there has been a rise in market relations in the fields of housing and support. Charging for services, with the resultant means testing to focus help on those unable to pay, has become ubiquitous. Coupled with increasing inequality, this has resulted in a growing differentiation in the experiences of people in need of support. Some people are dependent on state provided or funded services, whereas others have the resources to enter the increasingly large market sector.

This chapter has provided the context for our discussion of supported housing in the two countries and many of the themes introduced here will be taken up in further chapters. The key message of this chapter is that supported housing needs to be seen in the light of the discourses, policies and institutional practices that frame its use in these different contexts.

SIX

Supported housing for older people

The aim of this and the following two chapters is to illustrate the role of supported housing through the example of a particular 'category' of people. These examples enable a more detailed look at the specific models of supported housing available and their impact. The choice of examples has been made in order to show a wide spectrum of models and to illustrate the different factors that are at play. Each chapter begins with a discussion of the discourses that surround the 'category' in question and influence government policy as well as the behaviour and choices of individuals. This discussion will include mention of the factors that influence the identity, lifestyle and well-being of the individuals concerned. The chapters will continue with a description of policy towards the group in question in Britain and Sweden, and this forms the context for the discussion of the main models of supported accommodation available and their impact on the well-being of their residents. The conclusion will draw out the main implications of the discussion for our understanding of supported housing. Has the experience in the two countries shown us the factors important in influencing the type of provision made? Are there some models that seem to have a good impact on the well-being of residents in all contexts?

In this chapter the focus is on older people, who are by far the largest category in supported housing, and the older population is growing in most countries as people are living longer. The models they have access to are specific to this category and include examples from all the models discussed in Chapter One such as sheltered and extra-care housing, senior housing and retirement villages. Older people also make up a major group in institutional living and that experience was important in the general move towards community care. The size of the older population in general makes them an important group politically and it can be argued that their political power has resulted in them being well catered for compared with other groups we discuss in the book. This is helped by the high status that older people have in society compared to other groups. They have historically been categorised in the dominant discourse as the deserving poor because of their disengagement from the labour market. Good provision in old age can be an incentive for hard work in employment earlier in the life-course and older people have not been expected to engage in paid employment so there does not have to be consideration of work disincentive effects. Also, the social control elements of support discussed in the previous chapter are perceived as having little relevance for older people, which means that their well-being can be the sole objective of policy.

There is a considerable difference within the older population, as many older people have considerable wealth tied up in their housing and have reasonable pension incomes. The result is a desire from governments looking to reduce expenditure to use the stored wealth for funding through charges for care. It also means that some provision for more affluent older people has appeared in the market through retirement villages and retirement or senior housing. The provision of supported housing through private market mechanisms is therefore more widespread for older people than for other categories covered in this book, with the concomitant concerns about inequalities in provision.

The chapter begins with a discussion of the discourses that frame the category of old age and the societal expectations that surround it. This is followed by a general description of policy for housing and support for older people in Britain and Sweden. The models of provision for this group are then considered in the light of their impact on the well-being of older people. Finally, conclusions are drawn on the impact of supported housing for this category.

Discourses, identities and lifestyles

Our understanding of old age through the discourses of ageing has changed considerably over time. The predominant discourse used to be the concept of disengagement (Cumming and Henry, 1961), in which old age was seen as a gradual withdrawal from mainstream life in preparation for death. The basis for this was the empirical research showing that older people tended to have fewer social contacts and activities as they aged, but it was unclear whether this was desired or merely the unwanted outcome of growing frailty. Disengagement was based on a life-course concept of childhood, adulthood and old age, with the first and last being ages of dependence. Laslett (1989) drew attention to the growth of what he termed the 'third age' – of active old age, between adulthood and dependent old age. He argued that the longer an active third age could be prolonged the more likely that independence could be sustained well into later life. Laslett's analysis was based on observation of the growing number of affluent and active older people. Improvements in health led to increased longevity whereas the transition from work to retirement was becoming more 'blurred' for many people, with early retirement being mixed with some people staying in employment beyond retirement age.

For some, these trends led to an active and affluent stage in the life-course and attention became focused on 'woopies' (well-off older people), who had the resources and the health to be able to consume products and services, such as overseas holidays and consumer goods that increasingly became marketed specifically at them. Some chose to spend their money on exercise and cosmetic surgery to hide the signs of the ageing body that seemed to contradict the youth that many felt inside. In this and many other ways, older people were active agents in their own ageing, choosing the identity and lifestyle that suited them. Of course, not all older people had the health or the resources to join in this consumer lifestyle, and there was increasing awareness of the differences between older people. Many lived in poverty, dependent on state benefits and suffering from difficulties in heating their homes and coping with rising food prices. Others suffered from poor health that constrained what they could do. Therefore, there was increasing focus on difference in old age, with the recognition that identity and lifestyle, as well as needs and preferences, were not necessarily the product of an age category. Gilleard and Higgs (2000: 1) have referred to the fragmentation of ageing as a social attribute.

> It is increasingly meaningless to consider age as conferring some common social identity or to treat older people as a distinct social group acting out of shared concerns and common interests. The growing disparities of wealth within the retired population and the concomitant rise of lifestyle consumerism mean that more and more 'sites of distinction' are emerging which fragment and render less possible any common cultural position that can be represented as 'ageing'.... Ageing has become more complex, differentiated and ill-defined, experienced from a variety of perspectives and expressed in a variety of ways at different moments in people's lives.

One element of this difference is the expectations and family structures of older people from different ethnic backgrounds. For example, there may be different concepts of family with three- or four-generation households being more common in Indian families and the prevailing ethos that it is the duty of the family to cope with the accommodation and support needs of its members. Alternatively, migration at particular stages in the life-course may leave some older people with little in the way of family close to them.

Taylor and Ford (1981) identified 10 lifestyle types of older people, who they conceptualised as constantly struggling to maintain cherished lifestyles against the threats of internal changes and external events. The types were: taking life easy; gregarious; solitary; spouse-centred; invalid; altruist; hobbyist; family-centred; work-centred; and full-life. The key point from this is that older people are active agents in their own ageing and choose different paths in their attempts to achieve well-being.

In their study of what older people with high support needs value, Katz et al (2011) cite many of those factors that we have discussed as constituting well-being. Their categories are as follows:

> *Social well-being*; Meaningful relationships; social interaction; good relationships with formal carers based on respect for individuality, friendliness, continuity, reliability, kindness. Continuing to make a contribution and feeling valued as a result; participation in cultural activities.

> *Psychological well-being*; self-determination; personal identity and self-esteem; continuity and change/sense of self; humour and pleasure; mental health; stimulation and sense of purpose in life.

> *Physical well-being*; safety and security and a good living environment; familiarity with place; safety in the neighbourhood; ability to get out and about; physical activity; control and privacy of body functions; physical health.

There is a substantial literature to suggest that home is an important element in the well-being of older people and many of the elements highlighted above are related to the home environment (for a review see Wahl et al, 2012). A withdrawal from the labour market may mean that more time is spent in the home and this may be reinforced by any mobility problems. Privacy may also be important in old age, as body maintenance activities may result in feelings of shame or prurience given the problematic nature of the ageing body in popular culture. The emotional meaning of home may be especially important for some older people, particularly if the home has been the setting for major life events and a repository of memories of previous stages of life or of family members. Also, home is the setting for personal possessions that can be invested with considerable meaning. Some older people may take great pride in their home, which they may have paid for over many years and which they may have shaped to fit their lifestyle through DIY or other alterations or adaptations. A house is also a window on the neighbourhood for some, where they can observe the changing scene of the street or neighbourhood.

However, home may not have a completely positive meaning for all older people. Although older people tend to be more satisfied with their houses than people in other age groups, on average they tend to live in worse accommodation (see, for example, Heywood et al, 2002). Some older people who are more restricted to the home than others because of physical disabilities and mobility problems may, in Allan and Crow's (1989) terms, consider the home to be a cage rather than a castle. Also Percival (2002) shows the importance of housework to many older women for preserving feelings of self-determination and self-esteem. In addition, a clean and tidy home reinforces older people's identity in the community. Therefore, the compromising of control or standards brought about by physical incapacity can threaten feelings of being at home. As we shall see later, the provision of support in the home environment may also change the meaning of the home.

There has been much criticism of the inability to create the affordances of home in institutional settings (Willcocks et al, 1987) and this has applied particularly to older people. The difficulties of sustaining personal loving relationships in institutions, the inability to take in pets, the lack of meaningful activity, and the physical environment that falls short of the domestic ideal, may all make institutional care difficult to see as home. In addition, in this environment women may feel that their house-making and caring roles have been taken on by paid carers.

Croucher et al (2006) argue that the most intimate relationships (particularly marriage) are most important for older people in sustaining well-being. However, Evans (2009) argues that higher levels of social interaction are associated with improved health and well-being for older people, as well as lower rates of depression, decreased risk of dementia and lower mortality rates. The neighbourhood is therefore a key locale for many older people. Rowles (1983) notes that the current generation of older people are more likely to have spent most of their lives in the same neighbourhood than future generations are likely to have done, even if this is less than previous generations. Also, older people are more likely to spend more time in the neighbourhood than other age groups, and are therefore more likely to have a strong sense of emotional attachment to it. Social contact in the neighbourhood is higher for older people, who are more likely to cite their neighbours as also being their friends. For those with mobility difficulties it is important that the neighbourhood affords the basic requirements for shopping and for maintaining their lives as well as for social contacts and activities. Rowles (1983) argues that neighbourhoods come to represent a 'scrapbook', documenting the achievements of a lifetime. Any move from a neighbourhood that has been lived in for some time may threaten important social ties and emotional attachments that sustain well-being.

There is some debate about the desirability of age-segregated communities of older people that are often involved in supported housing models. It is often assumed by providers of some models, such as retirement villages, that this is what older people want, but the evidence for this is mixed. Many older people value security and some feel that an age-segregated environment achieves this. However, in a US study (Sherman, 1975) it was found that patterns of social contact were different in age-segregated and age-integrated environments, with residents in the former spending less time with grandchildren and family, but having more friends of their own age. Contact with grandchildren and a positive role in their care has been shown to contribute to older people's self-esteem and feeling of being valued, as well as offering an important contribution to society (Lee, 2006). In a study by Evans and Means (2007) some residents said that their retirement village could not be a community because it had no people of different ages, whereas others complained about the noise of children visiting residents in the village. It appears that there is no single answer as older people vary in their desired lifestyles.

For both home and neighbourhood reasons the predominant wisdom is that older people will choose to stay in their own home and this is the emphasis in public policy in most countries. However, it must be remembered that difference is a key feature of the lifestyles of older people and for some a move away from an unsatisfactory home may improve their well-being. Hillcoat-Nallétamby and Ogg (2014) examined the dislikes that older people in Wales had about their homes and neighbourhoods. Although most older people were satisfied with both and intended to stay put, a minority had dislikes, particularly about their house, that stimulated a desire to move. Foremost was the affordances of the house, that could change as people aged, particularly for those with long-term illnesses or disabilities. They found that not all older people had a strong attachment to place, particularly if they had little social contact in the neighbourhood and so became more likely to want to move to an environment that maximised security and safety.

Housing and support policies for older people in Britain and Sweden

Older people have generally been relatively well favoured by welfare states and some have been able to cope for themselves through recourse to market mechanisms. State involvement in welfare in many countries started with old age pensions and older people have generally been considered to be the deserving poor, who are given benefits that have been earned from a working life. As those over the retirement age are not expected to work, benefits are not constrained by the need to be below what people could earn in work. Indeed, the possible availability of good benefits in later life could be perceived as an incentive to work if they are linked to earnings in work. Increased longevity has led to a growing older population, which has been important in giving older people a strong political voice. However, it has also led to increasing calls for the reduction in benefits for older people. For example, the increasing longevity coupled with recent economic problems has led to pressure on private pension provision, with many schemes being reformed to decrease benefits. State pensions in both Britain and Sweden have also been under threat and the retirement age is being gradually increased. The retired population has been branded as a burden on the taxpayer in government rhetoric, and the country's economic fortunes are said to be dependent on reducing the benefits given to older people.

In Britain and Sweden there is a political awareness of the costs of coping with an ageing population and ways are being sought to shift the burden of paying for care in old age onto older people themselves. A key to this is the equity that many older people have tied up in their house through owner occupation. Ideas of asset-based welfare (see for example, Doling and Ronald, 2010) seek to enable or encourage older people to use house equity to fund care, as older people are among the most frequent users of domiciliary services, such as home help and the provision of meals, as well as domiciliary health services.

Sweden

Some 1.5 million Swedes are aged 65 or over (17% of the population), and 482,000 are aged 80 or over (5% of the population). Sweden has the 'oldest' population in the world in terms of the proportion over the age of 80 (Larsson, 2007). According to Szebehely and Tygard (2012) Sweden is probably one of the most generous countries in the world in terms of the public spending on care for older people, but expenditure has not kept pace with the growth of the older population. During the 1990s public expenditure for care for older people relative to the number of people over 80 reduced by 14%, and between 2000 and 2009 it declined in absolute terms by 6% (Szehebely and Tygard, 2012). Nevertheless, in 2007 only 29% of Swedes said they were worried about becoming dependent on the help of others some day (the lowest in the EU) compared to 59% in the UK (Eurobarometer, 2007), which must reflect to some degree the care provided to older people in the respective countries, although perceptions of the quality of home care services for dependent people were very similar in the two countries. Overall, 60% of Swedes said that professional care is available at home at an affordable cost compared to 26% in the UK (Eurobarometer, 2007). In the same survey, 84% of Swedes said they would be provided with appropriate long-term help and care if they needed it compared to 61% in the UK (the lowest in the EU).

Since legislation in 1990, municipalities have been given the statutory responsibility for all types of institutional housing and support facilities for older people including long-term hospitals (geriatric clinics are excluded), nursing homes, old age homes, service houses, group dwellings and day care facilities (Johansson, 1997). Thus the municipalities were given the statutory responsibility to provide health care to older residents within the institutional housing and care facilities mentioned above, although they were not responsible for medical care provided by doctors. Municipal authorities were also given responsibility for domiciliary support and for assistive aids for those at home or in other settings, as well as for medical home care other than by doctors.

From this time Swedish policy has been based on the assumption that older people will be able to live active lives and exert ongoing control over their general circumstances and their everyday lives. It is assumed that older people will live in their own homes with access to social and medical care, partly because it is assumed to be what older people themselves want, and partly in the belief that the costs to the public purse of an older person living in ordinary housing and receiving domiciliary support are half that of provision in an institution. Between 1992 and 2005, the number of hospital beds was reduced by almost 50% and, as a result, Sweden today has significantly fewer hospital beds and shorter lengths of stay than all other EU countries (OECD, 2009, pp. 94–98). Nevertheless, the move away from institutional living has been slow. By 2002 some 22% of all older people (aged 80+) were in institutional living, whereas 21% received home-based support services (Swedish Association for Local Authorities, 2002). According to Nord (2011), there are only about 100,000 older people in Sweden in 'assisted living' or residential care in 2010, with the average stay being two years and in most cases it being the last home for most residents, although people may move in earlier if they suffer from dementia or other severe needs. In other words, institutional living is largely for those for whom living at home with support is impossible because of the severity of their needs. Nevertheless, it must be borne in mind that the form of institutional living has changed considerably, with residents having their own apartment rather than an individual room and paying rent on the apartment. Also, older people who are assessed as needing 'assisted living' have a statutory right for it to be provided within three months and the local authority is fined if this need is not met. If people do not wish to move into 'assisted living' they have a right to home care.

Financial pressures have led to restrictions on access to public services and a greater reliance on informal care, thus creating incentives for some older people to have recourse to private providers. Although Sweden has been renowned for the extent of its domiciliary services, there has been increased targeting as financial restrictions have become more acute (Larsson, 2006). Under the Social Services Act 1980 and later legislation such as the Social Services Act (2001: 453), home-help services are provided to older people in their own homes to facilitate their everyday lives. Municipalities have adopted a purchaser–provider split, as in most British community care services, and so the actual provision may be by private or public agencies. Depending on the individual's needs, help can be given with personal care (for example, to go to or get up from bed, and with dressing, showers and toileting), and with domestic tasks (for example, shopping, cleaning, cooking and washing clothes). There are no mandatory rules about the level of the home-help entitlement by need or living arrangement, and there are considerable local variations in provision between different municipalities. Users are charged a fee for home-help services, and most municipalities vary these according to both the user's income and the extent of intervention. During the 1990s, about 10% of home-help recipients paid nothing at all, but the rest paid a fee. In 2002, a national regulation introduced an upper limit on user fees for public elderly care, after which one third of recipients paid no fee. Only 5% of expenditure on home help is funded by charges to the users (Szebehely and Trygard, 2012). The proportion of older people receiving home-help services has reduced and the amount of help given to individuals has increased as it is focused on those with more acute needs. In 2008, 22% of older people over 80 years of age (and 9% of those over 65) had home help compared with 34% (and 16% of those over 65) in 1980. At the same time, the percentage of older people living in supported housing had decreased from 28% to 17% (Szehebely and Tygard, 2012).

A fifth of those who received home help in 2005 were granted it for 50 hours or more per month, often both in the evenings and at weekends; most received less extensive assistance, however: two thirds were granted up to 25 hours per month (Larsson, 2006). People who only need help with household chores such as cleaning or shopping are increasingly receiving such assistance from relatives, or are buying private services for the purpose. In 2010, 19% of those receiving home care were buying it privately, whereas in 1993, 98% of care was publicly provided (Szehebely and Trygard, 2012). In 2007, a tax deduction on household services and personal care was introduced. Under this reform, taxpayers of all ages are entitled to deduct 50% of the price of household services up to SEK 100,000 (close to €11,000) per person, per year if the service company has a business tax certificate. The services may be carried out in the purchaser's own home or in a parent's home. These services are not needs assessed and they are not regulated by the state or local authority. Therefore the part of home care usually referred to as practical assistance – housecleaning, laundry and bringing home groceries and so on – is available privately, so some older people are choosing to pay private agencies to undertake these tasks for them and receive a public subsidy for doing so. If the publicly funded home care is provided by a private company, many of these offer a 'top-up' of extra services for those able and willing to pay. Family and friends have increased their help, not only to older persons with smaller needs outside the home care system, but also to those with more extensive needs who receive home care but seemingly not enough (Szehebely and Trygard, 2012). This is despite the fact that Swedes prefer to rely on public services rather than the family: only 17% would prefer family support rather than formal care for an older and frail parent, compared to an EU average of 54% (Eurobarometer, 2007: 67).

Gunnarsson (2009: 257) reports that the cutbacks and budget restrictions in the 1990s, which have meant that only older people with intensive support needs are now entitled to public home help, has influenced the perceptions of older people.

The informants are rather sceptical about home help, wondering whether the help will be there when needed and whether the quality of the help will be acceptable. Developments in public home help, which have led to many more care-demanding older people being taken care of in their own homes, have meant that providing help for everyday activities has, to a great extent, again become a responsibility for spouses and children, mainly daughters. This development has affected the concerns of older people regarding the sort of help they will be able to get when they eventually cannot manage their everyday tasks. First is the concern as to whether any help will be available. Second is whether the quality of the care and services will satisfy their needs and expectations. A third, if less obvious, concern is who will determine what are legitimate needs and how this determination will be made.

Nevertheless Swedish support services for older people are extensive by any international comparison, although the rise in private services runs the risk of turning the public services into a residual sector only for those who cannot afford private provision. It is clear that family provision is far more common among the lower income groups and that the purchase of private services more common among higher income groups (Szehebely and Trygard, 2012). Szehebley and Trygard (2012: 300) conclude that:

> The combination of income-related user fees, customer-choice models and the tax deduction has created an incentive for high-income older persons to turn to the market instead of using public home-care services. Thus, Swedish home care, as a universal welfare service, is now under threat and may become increasingly dominated by groups with less education and lower income which, in turn, could jeopardise the quality of care.

Every local authority in Sweden is obliged by law to provide a housing modification grant to people with disabilities who are in need of some adaptation or modification to their dwelling. Grants are not means tested and are available to people in all tenures. The most common modifications are minor in nature, such as levelling thresholds, adapting water taps or installing safety timers for cookers. Common extensive measures are rebuilding the bathroom and replacing the bathtub with a shower; installing automatic door openers; special toilets; levelling platforms, stair lifts and ramps; improving the lighting; changing the surface material on walls or floors; and modifying the kitchen (Lilja et al, 2003: 132). The need for these grants has been increasing over time and 85% of them go to older people (Lilja et al, 2003). Sweden has long-standing building regulations stating that everything being built or rebuilt should be accessible and usable for individuals with disabilities. The new provision of housing is therefore subject to building controls that ensure a minimum level of accessibility, but the cost of a new apartment can be prohibitive for some older people, meaning that many are living in older apartments not built to the latest access standards.

The emphasis on active ageing has meant that there has been a policy emphasis on older people staying at home. Following criticism of this approach, however, the government appointed a Senior Housing Commission in 2006 with the main task of recommending how new 'intermediate forms' of housing could be developed. In addition to creating new housing alternatives between ageing in place in ordinary housing and some form of institutional living, the Commission was asked to ensure that municipalities also created more places in institutional living meeting modern standards. The Commission argued that the dismantling of institutional living as a consequence of a dominant policy of ageing in place had gone too far, and that there were not enough places in supported housing for those who wanted and would need such an alternative. A further commission has been established in 2014 to consider the position of older people in the housing market and why older people cannot or do not wish to move into accessible housing. The commission is also considering the difficulties and possibilities of municipalities providing housing for older people, in the situation where municipal housing companies have to operate on a 'market basis'.

Following the 2006 Commission, a government grant was made available for new build or refurbishment of housing into sheltered or 'comfort' housing. This was meant for people over 70 years of age, and there were communal facilities such as meeting rooms and eating places, staffing during office hours but no onsite provision of support (although residents could receive domiciliary services if they were assessed as needing them) and entry is not dependent on a needs assessment. The costs of the communal facilities are borne either by the municipality or the housing provider (such as a municipal housing company), depending on negotiations between the parties involved. However, the central government grant was small (around 10% of costs) and there were some conditions, so not all developers took advantage of them, although some have proceeded with their own version of the model with numerous forms of 'branding'. Nevertheless, the pressures on local government finance and the growing philosophy of support at home meant that one consequence was that some service buildings were changed into sheltered housing. Service buildings are a form of sheltered housing (most akin to the British concept of extra-care housing), in which tenants have their own barrier-free apartments, usually one room and a kitchen, and where there are also premises for common activities as well as around-the-clock staff. A reserved space in a service building is allotted after needs assessment and tenants have all the usual tenancy rights.

Senior housing, on the other hand, is by definition a form of ordinary living into which you move as you wish without having to undergo needs assessment (the equivalent form in Britain would be 'retirement housing'. There is only minimal central direction in the form that senior housing should take and so forms have varied considerably in terms of the extent of communal provision. Senior housing can exist as rented or owner-occupied apartments, or as cooperative housing, although there can be a more communal management in the rental housing through the senior hostess (or warden, as in sheltered housing). There are sometimes premises for common activities and in provision by one company, Bovieran, there is a substantial, climatically controlled, indoor communal garden with different planting zones. There is not usually a round-the-clock staff service in senior housing (although staff may be present for some of the time), but the residents have access to domiciliary care on the same conditions as older people in other forms of ordinary housing. All apartments are barrier-free. One problem is that there is no rent pooling in Sweden between different developments and so new or refurbished dwellings can be very expensive compared to older apartments. This can create a dilemma for older people as to whether to stay in their inadequate apartment or move at much greater cost to a new senior apartment. However, those on housing allowances may be able to reclaim some of their costs.

As with retirement housing in Britain, the decision to move into senior housing is usually based on housing and location rather than any support or communal issues, although residents appreciate such support when they are there. The primary motivation seems to be to get away from worries about maintenance and the garden.

As in other countries, there was deemed to be a particular issue in Sweden concerning older people with dementia. One common approach is called group living. Patients with dementia requiring 24-hour supervision and support, but with only a limited need for assistance with personal activities of daily living (ADL) and able to fit into group treatment, were considered suitable for group living. Some older people with dementia are housed in 'assisted living', but it is perceived that specially designed dementia units are required to improve the well-being of the residents. Experiences from relocating nursing home patients with mild to moderate dementia into small, home-like environments such as group homes were considered successful. The housing and equipment in the group homes are adapted to the abilities of the residents, and the surroundings are made as home-like as possible to provide stimulation and the possibility for an interactive and therapeutic atmosphere. Group homes involve eight to nine residents living in one unit, consisting of a common area (kitchen, living room, dining room and a laundry room) and one private room for each, consisting of a combined living and bedroom, a shower and toilet. Each resident has a tenancy agreement for their own private quarters. The homes are usually staffed by registered nurses, trained and experienced in dementia care, and are usually on site around the clock to provide support, guidance and help to the residents.

An interesting form of provision for older people is co-housing, which involves a group of people taking responsibility for the running of their apartment block and providing support to each other. This is a small element of provision at the moment, but is growing among the middle classes as it is in Britain.

In summary, there has been a dominant discourse of support at home in Sweden that has resulted in fewer older people entering institutional living. The discourse has been partly based on a belief that staying at home is beneficial for the well-being of older people and is desired by them, but is also considered by government and municipalities to be less costly than institutional living. There have been positive alternatives through senior housing and through both public and private provision of home care services that have resulted in a reduced use of service houses. It is thought that the alternatives have not always prevented older people from entering institutional living, but have delayed it so that the average stay has reduced considerably. 'Assisted living' has become a form of 'end of life care', but it has been reformed so that it is qualitatively different from service houses or institutional living in Britain, with residents having their own apartments. Nevertheless, there is ambiguity in the policy in that some 'comfort' housing involves moving to an age-segregated environment in which there is support available (although to very different levels in different schemes). This seems to be a recognition that there is not enough accessible housing or home support services to prevent people moving into institutional living. Therefore, intermediate supported housing models, such as 'comfort' housing and senior housing, have been promoted as ways of delaying the move into institutional living.

Britain

Since the community care reforms of the 1990s the discourse in Britain has been about 'staying put' and receiving support in one's own home. The criticisms of the standard of care in nursing homes and other forms of institutional living, and the costs involved, both to the state and to individuals, have meant that institutions are regarded by most people as a last resort. As a consequence, state provision of institutional living has declined, although private provision has remained at a substantial level, often paid for in whole or part by the state. For individuals funding their own care, the costs are very high. State funding for private institutional living is available, although there are different arrangements in the different countries of Britain. In England, state financial support is subject to a needs assessment and a means test. The funding regime for private institutional living has been the subject of much political debate, with older people complaining about the high costs. There is a 'wealth trap', where people who have saved and have equity in their homes are being forced to pay for institutional living, often by selling their homes, whereas those with little wealth receive free provision. However, successive governments have failed to grasp this nettle, largely because of the constraints on public expenditure and concerns about the cost of caring for the growing older population. However, the Commission on Funding for Care and Support (2011) made recommendations for change in the funding for support, including capping the total amount that any individual should need to pay for support, and this was implemented in 2014.

The quality of life in institutions for older people has been widely criticised, but there is a regulatory regime designed to enforce physical and management standards that are based on the normalisation and well-being criteria such as: fulfilment through meaningful activity; dignity through personal space; autonomy through choice; the expression of individuality through personal taste; self-esteem; the meeting of emotional needs; risk taking in order to undertake normal activities such as shopping; and overall quality of experience. The value of personal clothing and possessions is stressed, as is the ability to form voluntary social relationships.

The key issues here are the extent to which these standards have been met in practice, and the extent to which they can be met in an institutional setting in which health and support needs can be extensive and take priority over other factors, and in a situation where cost is a constraining factor. The cost of institutional living is one of the major criticisms. Although governments and local authorities have attempted to keep costs low by constraining the funding available, the costs of alternative models of supported housing may be lower for particular individuals.

For older people living at home, pressures to reduce public expenditure have meant that domiciliary support has been reduced substantially and charges introduced for many services. As in Sweden, help is being concentrated increasingly on the most frail and those with less acute needs are receiving less support. For example, in 2008 there was a 5% increase in contact hours compared with the previous year, but the number of households receiving home help reduced by 2% (Health and Social Care Information Centre, 2009). Between 2008/9 and 2013/14, the number of contact hours for all forms of home care increased by 15% and the number of households receiving home care reduced by 7% (Health and Social Care Information Centre, 2014). Keeping the most frail out of institutional living seems to be the primary objective.

Other forms of supported housing in Britain, which house approximately 5% of the older population, have seen mixed fortunes. The most ubiquitous form is sheltered housing, which has reduced in scale, with an emerging problem during the past decade of difficult-to-let public sector sheltered schemes that did not meet modern standards of facilities (some consisted of just one room for sleeping and living) or were sited in inaccessible neighbourhoods. The decision of many local authorities to divert Supporting People funding away from warden support in sheltered housing also played its part, although there have been well publicised examples of residents fighting the perceived reductions in their provision (usually the withdrawal of a resident warden) through the legal system. The view of many local authorities is that Supporting People funding is better spent on domiciliary services that can be provided to people in many different settings, rather than be focused on a few residents in sheltered housing whose need for support may not be acute. The role of a sheltered housing warden is a rather ambiguous one because, although providing 'good neighbour' support, the warden did not carry out many of the tasks needed for frail older people to live independently, which needed to be provided by domiciliary services as they would if the residents were living at home. Thus it is easy to see why the warden's existence was increasingly questioned.

Two criticisms of sheltered housing schemes have been their isolation from the outside neighbourhood and the concentration of resources on a few residents at the expense of those living elsewhere. One reaction to these criticisms has been to open up the schemes to older people in the neighbourhood and to use the facilities as a base for support staff who meet needs in the neighbourhood as well as in the scheme. This 'community hub' is a form of the core and cluster model described in Chapter One and is becoming increasingly popular with commissioners and providers because of its flexibility and wider coverage. It has found particular favour with developers of extra-care housing, as well as being encapsulated in the form of retirement villages.

The rather unsuccessful history of sheltered housing has meant that little is currently being built. However, rather than use the experience to question the concept, the policy reaction was merely to upgrade the facilities to extra-care housing, which is sheltered housing with more in situ support services. One of the failings of sheltered housing was said to be its inability to enable residents to avoid institutional living. It was thought that increasing the support would overcome this. However, evaluations of extra-care housing have shown this belief to be misguided. In a review of extra-care housing in Wales, Burholt et al (2010) found that the support provided lacked both depth and breadth, and was particularly unsuitable for those with cognitive difficulties. Support was restricted either to emergency situations or to where there was a personal care plan, with support brought in from outside. Staff were particularly restricted by their lack of ability to offer any health care, which meant that they could not administer eye drops or pills, or touch residents if they fell. Burholt et al (2010) found that older people in extra-care schemes were less physically frail than those in their own homes, and less cognitively impaired than those in residential care. Although it was shown that extra-care housing took many different forms, it seemed that the same problem existed in all of them of residents having to leave when they became frailer. Extra-care housing may have delayed a move into institutional care for some residents, but it did not prevent it. In their survey of supported housing for older people, Pannell and Blood (2012) found that, in all forms of care, 34% of tenancies ended with a transfer to another form of accommodation, suggesting that there was a form of continuum of care along which people moved as their needs changed. Twenty-seven per cent of tenancies ended with the death of the tenant and 21% with a move to residential care. For extra-care housing, which could be considered to exist to cater for frailer people, approximately half of tenancies ended with death and a third with a move to residential care. So even this form of accommodation was not a final destination for a third of tenants (see also Croucher et al, 2006).

The growth of owner occupation and the reduction in public rented housing has resulted in a decline in the demand for traditional models of supported housing that were largely public sector oriented. Housing developers saw the growing potential and introduced models of owner-occupied retirement housing. However, this largely consisted of small apartments with caretaking facilities and did not offer any support. They did allow some older people to downsize and release equity, and to move to a modern apartment with few maintenance worries, but they came with the added burden of service charges, which could be higher than many households predicted.

The concept of a retirement village has received increasing attention in Britain and there are a number of examples that have been established (see Evans, 2009 for a review). They are usually privately developed, although there may be a partnership with a housing association or a local authority. The amount of support provision varies substantially.

> Retirement villages are usually self-contained developments that offer Housing, care and support in an environment that aims to promote independence and offers a range of social and leisure facilities. A range of tenures are [sic] commonly provided, including rental, outright purchase and shared ownership. Flexible care packages can be purchased by residents to meet their changing needs, and some retirement villages have onsite care homes. (Evans, 2009: 47)

There is a trend towards larger developments, with up to 600 homes. Evans (2009) identifies three forms of housing with support options that are usually provided:

- *Independent living* – where residents buy an apartment and pay a monthly service charge that covers maintenance and other property related costs. A range of personal support services can also be purchased flexibly as residents' needs change.
- *Fully serviced apartments* – where a higher level of charge is made for a hotel-style package that includes meals, laundry and visits from a carer, as well as access to personal support from an onsite team.
- *Nursing care home* – where there is full support and nursing care available.

In summary, policy in Britain has been relatively protective towards older people compared to other vulnerable groups, but this has not prevented cuts in service provision, such as for domiciliary care and for wardens in sheltered housing. New developments, such as retirement villages, have been largely driven by the voluntary and private sectors. There has been a wide variety of forms of supported housing and, even in a time of fiscal austerity, there has been publicly funded development of extra-care housing, which seems to be counterintuitive given the well documented limitations of sheltered housing and the overall policy of supporting older people at home. One explanation may be the importance given to keeping older people out of institutional living, both for financial reasons and for the perceived well-being of the older people themselves.

Well-being in supported housing models

The models of supported housing most often used by older people have been developed specifically with their needs in mind. In particular, sheltered housing and extra-care housing have been seen as the primary alternatives to institutional living in residential or nursing homes or service apartments. But older people are also major users of domiciliary services and so there is, both in Sweden and in Britain, a spectrum of supported housing options for older people. Chapter One outlined the main features of the different models. We will now examine the options for older people using the structure outlined in the first part of the book.

The affordances of home

In their study of the residential homes in Britain originally included in the Townsend (1962) study, Johnson et al (2010) found many improvements, although, in general the older residents were frailer than in Townsend's day. They found that, despite the improvements, the ideal of home was still difficult to achieve. 'There may be a decorative veneer of homeliness through, for example, the inclusion of potted plants, rugs, old fashioned furniture, ornaments and pictures in the public spaces of the home, but the accompanying homely lifestyle is more elusive' (Johnson et al, 2010: 123). They found that the 'homely' aesthetic of the home was controlled by the manager rather than the residents. 'Often it was not just the aesthetics of the home that belonged to the manager but also the arrangement of spaces, the routine, programme, culture and ethos of the home, all of which could be equally controlling'

(Johnson et al, 2010: 123–4). Some rooms visited had an institutional look and feel. 'Sometimes the more homely touches, such as flowers, plants, photographs or fluffy toys were to be found cheek by jowl with commodes, large plastic waste bins or hospital style large mobile bed-trays' (Johnson et al, 2010: 124). They found incontinence pads left in full view and lots of notices worded in a peremptory style.

Nord (2011) examined the strategies used by staff and residents to maintain privacy in 'assisted living' residential care in Sweden. She argued that privacy was an ambiguous issue that arose in spaces categorised both as private, such as the resident's apartment, and public areas such as dining rooms and corridors. In the scheme she examined, the staff had an ideology of individualised care according to the wishes of each resident. The staff were therefore very conscious of the privacy of residents and would knock before entering their room, and maintained distance and dignity as much as possible when performing personal tasks. Residents were expected to furnish their own rooms and to display personal objects, which created some feeling of home. However, the rooms were dominated by the 'hospital type' bed provided by the institution that was placed in a central position to better enable staff functions. In general, Nord (2011) shows how staff ideologies could lead to routines that could maximise control and feelings of home, even in the unhelpful surroundings of institutional living that constrained what could be achieved.

The symbolic element of an institution can be very important. In general, it is unlikely that an institution will have a high status. The usual symbolism is of separation from 'mainstream life', of difference, and of an inability to cope in a home setting. Some institutions may attract a stigma because of their function, for example, a hospital for people with mental health problems or for those with drug misuse problems, or older people suffering from dementia. In some institutions people may be held against their will, perhaps because of a mental health problem. Some institutions carry the stigma of being associated with places where people were taken for the protection of society. Even in Swedish 'assisted living', where conditions are different from institutional living in Britain in that residents have their own apartments, many of the schemes have been converted from previous service buildings and may carry some of the previous symbolism and stigma with them.

But despite this negative picture there are many developments in both Sweden and Britain for older people with dementia that have sought to make institutions more homely and have in practice made the provision more like an extra-care home. For example, individual space has been increased and can contain living, sleeping, cooking and bathing facilities, just as a sheltered apartment would. Practical aids and adaptations can be made to look good with high design standards that can avoid negative imagery. Communal areas can be made homely and sociable. But, as in many other forms of supported housing, older people have to move into the schemes to receive support. The move from a much loved home can be difficult for some older people, particularly if they have lived there for some time. Of course, for others it may be a relief to leave an old and unsuitable home for a newer and purpose-built home with facilities tailored to people with physical impairments, such as handrails, easy-to-use kitchens and toilet facilities, and so on.

In summary, there have been many attempts to make institutions as much like home as possible, in the physical surroundings, but also in the way that residents are treated. Privacy can be respected to a degree and personal choice and control maximised. Residents can be given apartments rather than just rooms. However, the physical and social settings restrict the degree to which institutions can be like homes. The instruments of support, such as hoists and bedpans, can make rooms look like a hospital rather than a home. Regulations for fire and safety can dictate the layout and look. Support routines can dictate the layout of rooms. For example, it is common in some institutions to find the seats in a sitting room arranged around the walls in a way that eases staff surveillance and support tasks, but makes social interaction between residents difficult. Much of a resident's life is lived out in a common space, such as a sitting room or dining room with many other people, which is, therefore, difficult to personalise or attach a personal meaning to. Private space is limited and, as a consequence, so is the ability to store personal memorabilia. The social practices in the home, prevalent in institutional living for older people, are clearly of a limited nature compared to independent living.

Both extra-care and sheltered housing in Britain include self-contained accommodation, as do forms of senior housing and comfort housing in Sweden (as well as 'assisted living'). In the 1960s in Britain this could include bedsit-type accommodation, but is now more usually a one- or two-bedroom flat. Each has its own front door and can provide privacy and security. So sheltered and extra-care housing can provide the physical aspects of home. For example, Pannell and Blood (2012) point to a generally good living environment with space for storage and the possibility of having visitors, although they report some problems of repair, poor views and lack of space. However, Barnes et al (2012) criticise the design of the four extra-care schemes in their study. They found that the physical design restricted accessibility and activities for residents who were disabled and so reduced their capacity for independence. They found that buildings were too brightly lit, too hot and badly ventilated, and the kitchen design was poor. They argue that the design was suitable for relatively healthy older people, but that those with disabilities or cognitive impairments could find the building restrictive leading to marginalisation.

Whether residents experience the emotional aspects of home will depend on how they react to its specific features, such as the age-segregated environment and the common room, usually with its organised activities. In their review of supported housing for older people in Britain, Pannell and Blood (2012) argue that sheltered housing gives residents privacy when compared with residential living and security when compared with mainstream housing, although the latter was reduced if there was not a resident warden.

Sheltered housing was popular because of its perceived positive symbolism as well as its perceived security and ease of everyday living. Although usually in a scheme separated from and different from surrounding houses, sheltered housing escaped the stigma of other forms of supported housing, probably because of its perceived deserving clientele. It was also perceived differently from institutional provision such as nursing homes. Extra-care homes have had a different symbolism, mainly because of their association with frailty, but the general perception of them has still been positive. Therefore, both sheltered and extra-care housing offer many affordances of home and the social practices within the home are similar to 'ordinary' housing. The problems of this kind of provision lie in the link between accommodation and support and not the accommodation itself.

Residents in core and cluster schemes (such as some retirement villages or community hubs) will have a wide variety of accommodation. For some it will be in purpose-built accommodation in the core, which may be in the form of sheltered or extra-care housing or an institution. For others it will be in their previous home or in a dwelling not physically attached to the scheme, although attached in the provision of support. This usually will involve a self-contained apartment in the local neighbourhood.

The ability in this model for residents to be able to have more control over where they live should enable them to enjoy more of the benefits of home. Some will be living in their long-standing homes and will not have had to move to receive support. Others will be in independent 'ordinary' housing while receiving support. Of course, there may be an issue about the quality or appropriateness of the houses, but any problems can be dealt with independently from issues of support. The detached nature of the link of accommodation to the support should also counteract any problems with low status or stigma. It need not be known that residents are part of any support arrangement. However, the lack of any real evaluation of core and cluster schemes means that these conclusions are theoretical and not grounded in empirical research, which is surprising given their popularity with policy-makers in Britain and which is, therefore, a priority to inform policy and the choices of individuals.

As argued in Chapter One, domiciliary care that provides support in one's own home seems to offer the advantages of allowing residents to enjoy the full benefits of home. Undoubtedly this is generally true for many older people who will not want to move home because of support needs. Perhaps more than any other category their homes may have strong links to their personal histories and form the basis of their family ties and social contacts. We showed above that older people tend to spend more time in their homes and are more attached to them than others. However, in Chapter One two main caveats were applied. The first is that the house itself needs to be appropriate for the changing needs and lifestyle of the resident. A home that is in poor repair and becomes a financial burden may not leave residents with a positive meaning. As also pointed out in Chapter One, the provision of support may lead to changes in the physical form of the house through aids and adaptations such as grab rails in bathrooms or ramps for outside doors that may signal to the resident infirmity and frailty. Alternatively, funds may not be available for needed adaptations and residents may be left in an inappropriate environment that may limit their access to parts of the house or make everyday activities difficult or impossible. Second, the support may be provided in such a way as to change perceptions of home. The example given in Chapter One was of support workers who enter the home, causing residents to feel a loss of privacy and control. If support is offered in a condescending or controlling way that does not respect the privacy, control, self-confidence or self-esteem of the resident, then this can impact on their sense of home, causing home to be associated with shame, dependence and lack of control, which may outweigh the positive elements. Aronson (2002) argued that older people differed in their reactions to the provision of support in their home. Some 'took charge' of the situation and asserted their views on the use of their home and the support provided. Others were 'pushed over the edge' and overwhelmed by the new situation they found themselves in, and demonstrated substantial distress and shame at their situation. Others 'restrained expectations' and resigned themselves to their new indignities. Clearly the well-being of older people will vary considerably depending on which of these reactions they have.

In their study of home adaptations in Sweden, Johansson et al (2009) noted that greater well-being was achieved if the creativity and views of residents themselves were included in the adaptation process. Residents actively sought to maximise their individual home affordances through the type and design of adaptations made. Resident involvement was an empowering process that reinforced the attachment to home and maximised affordances. If residents were excluded from the process, the adaptations could reduce affordances and the process could disempower and reduce the independence of residents. Petersson et al (2012) examined the impact of technologies and adaptations on improving the feelings of safety of older people living at home in Sweden. Their conclusion was that the technologies by themselves did not achieve the aim of increased feelings of safety unless three prerequisites were met. These were that residents were feeling healthy, had someone to rely on and felt at home, in that they felt that they were in control of their home and the activities within it, as well as feeling at home and supported in the neighbourhood environment. These two studies show the importance of the adaptation process in enabling older people to achieve high levels of well-being at home. As we argued in Chapter Three, affordances have emotional and symbolic elements as well as physical ones, and they have to be considered together if well-being is to be maximised. Just because older people are living at home and in adapted houses does not necessarily mean that their well-being is maximised.

Despite the problems that can be encountered, being at home offers older people more of the affordances of home and puts them in a more powerful position to influence the way that support is provided, and to enjoy social practices that increase their well-being.

The affordances of neighbourhood

In their study of residential care in Britain, Johnson et al (2010) commented on the lack of meaningful activity experienced by many older residents. They found a risk-averse management culture that curtailed the extent to which residents could help each other or undertake activities by themselves. Thus they were reliant on staff to form a bridge to the local neighbourhood. Excursions and activities were organised, but there were problems in catering for a wide range of interests among the residents. The result was increasing confinement.

Moving to receive support in any supported housing scheme can result in a loss of the affordances of neighbourhood and the personal satisfactions and benefits that they can bring. The loss can be avoided if the scheme is local to a previous dwelling and this may help people to retain social contacts and other neighbourhood affordances. For some people the move can mean losing contact with family and friends, and perhaps difficulty in accessing previous activities; research in US retirement communities reviewed by Croucher et al (2006) shows that the people who moved tended to have fewer social ties than others. Loss of contact with friends may particularly be the case if a move into supported housing is associated with mobility problems. Older people generally spend a lot of time in the local neighbourhood and so the affordances it offers – both practical and symbolic – are particularly important for them. Many but not all supported housing schemes are sited in areas where there is easy access to facilities such as shops, recreational and health facilities. Pannell and Blood (2012) argue that the location of a scheme is vital in enabling residents to feel part of a local community. Evans (2009) has shown how design of the communal elements of a retirement village, such as the 'indoor street' and the landscaped areas, as well as the social activities provided, can promote social interaction. A move of neighbourhood to access supported housing may result in the loss of the benefit of pursuing a favoured lifestyle through, for example, particular hobbies or social events. It also means moving into an age-segregated environment that may suit some older people but not others, depending on their lifestyle. Some schemes have developed a strong link with the neighbourhood, with the scheme being used as a base for domiciliary services in a community hub model. This moves the provision into the category of the core and cluster model.

For some people, however, a move into supported housing can be a move towards family and existing friends, as well as providing the opportunity to make new friends. Pannell and Blood (2012) report that 50% of residents of sheltered housing said that contact with family and friends had improved since they had moved in. There may be benefits of contact with other residents in the same situation and with staff. Pannell and Blood (2012) report that 75% of residents say that their sheltered housing scheme is a good place to make new friends. Evans (2009) argues that many older people are moving into supported housing settings in search of connectedness and community. Therefore they create shared narratives of belonging within the scheme, which, if successful, can create a secure and convincing narrative for identity in later life. Also they create a narrative of outsiders by believing in the inferior quality of life of those in ordinary neighbourhoods and nursing homes. However, Burholt et al (2010) found that the increased social contact between residents that occurred in extra-care schemes did not necessarily result in less loneliness and isolation, as it tended to consist of unplanned encounters in common areas that did not lead to high-quality and emotionally satisfying social relationships. In their study in Wales they found no difference in loneliness or isolation between older people at home, in extra-care housing or in residential care. Croucher et al (2006) conclude from their review of the evidence that most older people reported their most intimate friends as being family or long-standing friends from outside the supported housing setting. It is possible that residence in an institution or linked housing scheme can prevent social isolation and loneliness in some people who would be cut off in their own homes and do not have the physical or social abilities to pursue social relationships with neighbours and friends who live elsewhere. Schemes can foster 'communal support' for mutual benefit, whether this is in the form of practical help or a communal feeling in which problems are shared (Croucher et al, 2006). Nevertheless, schemes can hinder contact with people outside them and result in segregation from friends, family or from people of other ages or characteristics. Not all social interactions within schemes are harmonious and some people could be resented and excluded, while others may withdraw from social interaction in order to maintain their privacy. For some people, congregate living will be an advantage and, for others, a strong disadvantage. There is some evidence that men are more likely to be socially isolated than women, partly because of their lower numbers in most supported housing settings for older people (Evans, 2009).

Support in one's home should mean the preservation of existing neighbourhood affordances, including social contacts. However, if the existing neighbourhood is low on affordances and is either threatening or unpleasant, or of low status, then staying in that neighbourhood may not lead to high self-esteem or well-being. In ordinary neighbourhoods, fear of crime, inadequate transport, poor design, lack of disabled access and insufficient information may lead to feelings of social exclusion (Social Exclusion Unit, 2000). Some older people will favour a move away from an existing neighbourhood into, for example, an age-segregated retirement community or sheltered housing scheme, which could offer the perceived advantages of sociability with like-minded people. Some older people will move house and neighbourhood to locate in an area which offers better facilities for their changing lifestyle on retirement and which perhaps is more age segregated to avoid any problems arising from a clash of lifestyles with other residents.

The core and cluster model is predicated on a neighbourhood principle. The core is accessible to residents in the neighbourhood and so even people resident in the core will meet and share activities with others living nearby. If people have to move from scattered accommodation, for example an older person with increasing mobility or functional problems, it is likely that they will be able to continue existing neighbourhood activities and to maintain neighbourhood contacts. Croucher et al (2006) have argued that the larger retirement villages are in a good position to provide a wide range of facilities for residents and, as a consequence, social interaction is greater in these large schemes. 'Notwithstanding the importance of long-standing, intimate relationships, various studies reported larger social networks and more frequent social contacts following a move to a retirement community' (Croucher et al, 2006: 37). Those with residential care included accord with the core and cluster model, and can obviate the need for older people to move and cut their social ties when they become frailer.

In summary, neighbourhood affordances are higher for people in their own homes in appropriate neighbourhoods and for those in core and cluster schemes. In congregate living environments, such as sheltered or extra-care housing, the outcome can depend on their situation and lifestyle. For some people, a move into this form of accommodation can increase their social interaction, but for others it can result in a loss of previously enjoyed neighbourhood affordances.

Well-being, personal control, identity and self-esteem

In their analysis of research on living in supported housing for older people in Britain, Croucher et al (2006) comment on the lack of research that measures the impact on the quality of life or well-being of the residents. They concluded: 'Currently the evidence base lacks a robust assessment of quality of life for those living in housing and care schemes' (2006: 65). It is necessary, therefore, to piece together the picture from partial fragments on the individual elements of well-being.

The different supported housing options for older people offer different degrees of personal control. Pannell and Blood (2012) suggest that older people in supported accommodation have more control over their lives and are more able to do things for themselves, and have less routinised lives. Of course the control that can be exercised by individual older people may vary with their abilities. For example, people suffering from severe dementia may not be able to exert the same level of independent control as someone who does not. Individuals will vary in the extent to which they have exerted control during their lives and this may impact on their abilities. However, personal control is a subjective concept and it is the feeling of being in control that is important in sustaining well-being.

Percival (2001), in his study of residents of sheltered housing in Britain, said that the impact on self-esteem was mixed. Residents had three main techniques for maintaining self-esteem. These were: creative compensatory behaviour; use of self-deprecatory humour; and active involvement in local community activities. He argued that these strategies were strengthened in an age-segregated environment where there were peer role models and reference groups. This enabled self-appreciation and self-respect, as well as the accentuation of existing attributes, feelings of greater control and shared reminiscence.

However, Percival (2001) also found evidence of factors that reduced well-being. For example, he found that the environment could exacerbate loss and loneliness and alienation, with bereavement being more closely felt. Some people disliked the quietness of an age-segregated environment that could 'feel like a morgue', and some felt excluded from the communal activities. He found some frustration and intolerance towards some of the frailer residents, who could be excluded because they were slow or resented because they took up too much time of the warden or scheme manager. Percival (2001) argued that some residents were exhibiting distancing behaviour from the frailer residents to protect their own self-esteem.

In Sweden, some supported schemes for older people with dementia had made efforts to provide different facilities in schemes that reflected different identities and lifestyles. For example, one scheme may have opportunities for residents to take part in gardening, in another for dance or other artistic activities. Some schemes were in the middle of cities, whereas others made the most use of their country settings. In this way, residents could hold on to long-lasting lifestyles and identities, as well as having practical ways to spend their time that reflected their preferences.

In summary, there is little information on the well-being aspects of congregate living of older people and this should be an urgent focus for future research. But there is evidence of the impact of independent living and neighbourhood affordances on well-being for those in domiciliary and core and cluster forms of supported housing, as we discussed in previous sections. However, there is a lack of research that focuses on well-being and examines well-being as the important outcome.

Conclusion: well-being and supported housing for older people

Perhaps more than any other group considered in this book, older people have an array of different forms of supported housing to choose from or be assigned to. Why is this array available and is it appropriate? Are there some forms of supported housing that are better at achieving well-being than others?

The comparison of the provision in Britain and Sweden shows a similarity of policy and provision that is not present in other examples in this book. The array of supported housing options is similar in both countries and policy discourses have followed similar paths. In both countries the dominant discourse has been a very positive one, with a desire to prolong active old age through policies that promote independence and choice. There are differences in emphasis here and there, such as the greater visibility of co-housing in Sweden and retirement villages in Britain, as well as the better provision of domiciliary support and the better condition of the housing stock in Sweden. Institutional living is very different in the two countries because of the provision of apartments in assisted living in Sweden. However, there are enough similarities to make the analysis of the different models worthwhile across both countries.

In both countries, policy has been dominated by the move away from institutional living, largely because of the cost, as well as concerns about the quality of life for the residents. However, neither country has found alternatives that prevent many people from entering institutional living. For example, extra-care housing in Britain has been shown in some cases to delay entry to institutional living, but not to prevent it, and extra-care is also expensive to run. In Sweden, the move away from service houses and assisted living was hindered by the lack of other alternatives that would result in less use of institutional living. In both countries, the search for a model of supported housing that can avoid the need for institutional living has been a fruitless one. In Britain, extra-care schemes can delay admission to institutional living, as can good domiciliary provision, either in people's own homes or for those in senior or sheltered housing. However, the continuing need for institutional living means that it should not be regarded as a last resort and more effort needs to be spent on ensuring an appropriate standard of care, particularly in Britain.

The analysis of well-being in the previous section shows the limited affordances of institutional forms of provision. It is more difficult for residents to enjoy the affordances of home and neighbourhood, and their control and self-esteem as well as their lifestyle and identity may be more difficult to maintain. It seems clear that the policy to prevent unnecessary residence in institutions is a correct one. However, for those who are very frail and for whom living at home is difficult, institutions may still be necessary. There are many attempts in both countries to make institutional life as good as possible for the residents by providing the forms of accommodation and the support practices that maximise well-being. The most flexible forms of provision are those that attempt to break down the barriers between institutional living and the local neighbourhood through, for example, the core and cluster models of retirement villages or community hubs. These maximise the interaction between residents in the institutions and those outside, as well as delaying the transition to institutional living by making its facilities more widely available and by making the transition easier for those forced or choosing to move.

The search for a generic model of supported housing for older people has been made more difficult by the lifestyle differences inherent in the choice of an age category. As we saw earlier, older people do not constitute a meaningful category in lifestyle terms. For example, some older people like living in an age-segregated environment whereas others do not. This diversity in preferences would make the pursuit of any one model futile, as it would only be appropriate for a fraction of the population. It is clear that older people differ in their wish to live in a segregated or integrated environment. Some supported housing models, such as extra-care housing and retirement villages, may provide for those who prefer segregation, but community hubs and domiciliary care are more appropriate for those who wish for a more integrated environment.

Ideas of a continuum of care, with older people moving along a ladder of different forms of supported housing as they become frailer, also have limited application, as older people are reluctant to make the succession of moves that would be necessary for them to receive the appropriate level of support at different stages and older people do not necessarily follow a set pattern of stages. So it is difficult to justify the development of new models of supported housing, such as extra-care, which is prevalent in Britain. Extra-care is expensive to develop and run, and offers only a limited delay in any move to institutional care, while involving a move out of the independent home for the resident. There will continue to be a limited role of this form of care for some older people who wish to move, but it is unlikely this will be extensive if the emphasis is placed on the provision of adequate housing and domiciliary services, which offer most for the well-being of many older people who want to remain in their own homes, but to be warm and comfortable and receive (and have control over) the appropriate services for them to live an independent life. Extra-care housing offers fewer affordances of home and neighbourhood than other forms of provision, and is less flexible in meeting different and changing needs and lifestyles. In its current form, extra-care housing in Britain falls between many roles. It was shown earlier that it is appropriate for those with few health problems but can lead to restricted activities and isolation for those with disabilities. The solution would seem to be to follow the Swedish model of assisted living as the appropriate form of institutional living that can cope with the more disabled residents while offering individual homes in its apartments and the conversion of extra-care schemes to this model.

There does seem to be some justification for the use of the core and cluster model, however, whether in the form of the retirement village or the community hub in Britain. This form offers flexibility and enables residents to change their housing and support situation while retaining neighbourhood and social ties by staying in the same home or location. Retirement villages are more appropriate for those who prefer a segregated environment in the countryside, but community hubs are more relevant for provision in existing urban neighbourhoods, and where people wish to remain in integrated neighbourhoods. The community hub model is the only real justification for the continuance of extra-care housing in Britain, and even here it could be argued that residential care is a more appropriate core or hub than extra-care housing.

So why has extra-care housing been promoted by governments in Britain at the expense of further improving domiciliary provision, despite its drawbacks? It may be that successive governments have believed that it is an appropriate way to reduce reliance on institutional living, in which case we should expect to see a reduction in provision once the evidence that it does not do this is known. But extra-care housing also has a strong lobby among pressure groups and providers of supported housing for older people that have been pushing the idea hard. We have become used to the concept of the poverty industry to describe the organisations that have a vested interest in the provision of schemes to help the poor. The concept of a supported housing industry may be important in a similar way and this is a point to which we will return in the following chapters.

Sweden has focused more than Britain on domiciliary models of supported housing through its provision of senior housing, comfort housing and co-housing, as well as its emphasis on domiciliary services. The better housing conditions in Sweden, including its better design standards for new housing, make this more possible, as does its wider provision of home help and other domiciliary support services. In Britain, it is hard not to conclude that public funds should be devoted to the improvement of general housing standards in the manner of lifetime homes and more extensive domiciliary services rather than building more extra-care schemes. Domiciliary and core and cluster models offer more of the affordances of home and neighbourhood, while being flexible enough to meet different and changing preferences and lifestyles.

The non-emergence of retirement villages in Sweden may reflect the make up and objectives of the house building industry, but it may also be because of the stronger domiciliary care system that means that older people can receive support without having to move into a retirement village, through the use of private provision if they do not qualify for state aid. In addition, older people in Sweden are more likely to live in accessible apartments because of the impact of mainstream housing policies. Retirement villages seem to be most prevalent in countries such as the US and Britain, where universal, mainstream housing and support policies are less developed than in Sweden.

The differing financial situation of older people and the desire of governments in both countries to reduce public expenditure have meant that a market for practical support services has developed in both countries. This is coupled with the widespread market provision of housing to comprise a substantial sector where older people are paying for their own support and housing. Models such as retirement villages in Britain are one example of this. However, the assessment procedures in both countries ensure that those in particular need receive support, although charges mean that resources are clawed back from those judged to be able to afford it. In Sweden, charges for those on higher incomes are equivalent to the private market price and tax reliefs are greater the higher the income. Those paying for themselves may have more choice of supported housing and of domiciliary services, and may demand higher standards than those dependent on state financial aid. There is a risk in this situation that public provision may become stigmatised and a second-rate service, and there are a few signs that this beginning to occur at the moment in both countries. The extent of public financing and provision has helped to offset the inequalities that have built up over the lifetimes of older people. However, the financial differences between older people, and the large market sector, mean that supported housing has the potential to mirror inequality in a way that is not reflected in other categories considered in this book.

SEVEN

Supported housing for homeless people

Homelessness is a continuing phenomenon in all western countries and in Britain it has been particularly visible among young people (but to a lesser extent in Sweden). In Britain, the number of homeless people rose substantially during the 1980s and 1990s. While the numbers fell in the early part of the present century, they started to increase again after the financial crash in 2007, in line with the growing unemployment. In Sweden, homelessness has been less of a problem and has received less political or media attention than in Britain (Nordfeldt, 2012). However, problems in accessing affordable housing in the 1990s and in recent years, particularly for immigrants and for single parent families and others on benefits, have raised the political profile of the issue and there are moves to change the predominant approach to embrace the 'Housing First' model pioneered in the US.

There are many discourses surrounding the definition of homelessness, its perceived causes and the appropriate ways of dealing with it. As we shall see in the chapter, these discourses have varied between Britain and Sweden, and this has led to very different policies and practical approaches in the two countries. However, in both countries, models of supported housing are seen as part of the solution to the homelessness problem, although the models used and their objectives are different. The comparison between the experience in the two countries provides insight into the different roles that supported housing can play in response to the different objectives sought and the impact this has on the types of supported housing provided.

The homeless category hides a wide variety of needs and problems, and attributes such as age and ethnicity. Some people may just lack housing, but others may have other problems, such as drug abuse or mental ill-health. Some may be young people who have just left home and have problems in accessing appropriate housing, while others may be older people who have been homeless for some time, and yet others families with children. As we shall see, discourses and policy can vary between these different categories. However, unlike the example of older people in the previous chapter, homeless people in general do not have the same high political priority, and they may be subject to discourses that prioritise the primacy of employment and the achievement of sanctioned norms of personal behaviour regarding issues such as drug and alcohol use, criminality and financial independence. The result is that policy towards homeless people in general, and young homeless people in particular, often incorporates a social control element, in that it is designed to reward or to discourage certain forms of behaviour. This means that, sometimes, support for the homeless person may be conditional on the performance of particular forms of behaviour, such as abstinence from drug use. As we shall see, the dominant policy discourses in both countries emphasise the desirability of the independence of people and their participation in the labour market.

The chapter begins with an analysis of the discourses of homelessness that forms the background to a description of the policies towards homeless people in Sweden and Britain. This is followed by an analysis of the impact of different models of supported housing used in the two countries using the framework described earlier in the book. Finally, some conclusions are drawn on the impact of supported housing on the well-being of the homeless residents.

Discourses, identities and lifestyles

Jacobs et al (1999) have divided the discourses surrounding homelessness into minimalist and maximalist conceptions. The minimalist discourse roots homelessness in the pathologies of the individuals concerned, whereas the maximalist discourse places emphasis on the contextual factors, such as lack of employment or housing opportunities, that influence the likelihood of homelessness. As we shall see, discourses and policy in both Britain and Sweden tend to be a mix of these two elements, in varying degrees for different people. For example, in Britain there is a distinction between those deserving of the right to permanent housing (primarily families with children) and those, such as young single people without children, who are given advice, but are deemed to be independent and not to be deserving of priority for permanent housing. In Sweden, there is tension between the predominant 'staircase model' that is based on the assumption that homelessness is caused by individual failings that need to be corrected, and the 'Housing First' approach that assumes that everyone deserves permanent housing who lacks it and that it is the base for enabling the person to deal with any other problems they have.

Much research on homelessness has followed this distinction by taking either an individualist or a structuralist approach to the study of the phenomenon. However, there have been many attempts to overcome this crude dualism. Fitzpatrick (2005) sums up what she terms a 'new orthodoxy' as being made up of three factors: (1) structural factors create the conditions under which homelessness can occur; (2) people with personal problems are more vulnerable to these structural factors; (3) therefore the high concentration of people with personal problems in homeless populations can be explained by structural rather than personal factors. Fitzpatrick herself takes a critical realist view of homelessness that sees the different levels of causation as being nested systems with relationships between them. The current author has attempted to overcome the dualism between structural and personal factors through the concept of a housing pathway that includes episodes of homelessness (see Clapham, 2003).

In both Britain and Sweden, there is a different discourse for young homeless people compared to other age groups that reflects societal attitudes to work and predominant discourses of youth. Youth can be regarded as a transition from childhood to adulthood that has a number of elements (Coles, 1995). Three important transitions are from school to further education and employment; from the family home to independent living; and from the family of origin to the family of destination. These three dimensions may or may not take place at the same time, but they are interrelated because experiences in one will have implications for the others. The transition process is situated within societal norms and expectations that vary between countries and that have changed over time (see Jones, 1995). During the 1950s and 1960s, young people generally left home, married and started families within a short space of time. The average age of marriage declined during this period and the general availability of employment and relative affluence meant that financial independence was possible at an earlier age than previously. In Sweden, the increase in housing supply in the 1970s also aided this process. This 'golden age' of the 'traditional family' has left a mark on popular discourses of the family and of the appropriate way to leave home. However, since this time the transition to independence for young people has been extended and fractured. The need for more complex skills in employment has meant that time in education has increased and financial independence has therefore been delayed. The average age of marriage has increased and uncertainty in the employment and housing fields, especially since the financial crisis of 2007 (and to a lesser extent in Sweden the economic crisis of the early 1990s), has meant that young people are delaying the exit from the family home and, after leaving, are more likely to return, leading to the popular label of the 'boomerang generation'. Also, the generally high level of unemployment among young people since 2007, and the barriers in Britain and Sweden to gaining entry to owner occupation, have increased the difficulties that young people experience in gaining independence (Clapham et al, 2014), and in Sweden young people have also had problems in accessing rental tenures (Knutagård and Boustedt Hedvall, 2013). All these factors have meant that the transition from childhood to adulthood has become more complex, more ambiguous and longer, and the period of semi-dependency on parents and the state has become more protracted.

The dominant discourses that have framed policy in both Britain and Sweden have stressed the need for young people to manage the changing transition process in a way that minimises impact on the state. The family is held to be the place for young people unless they have the economic independence to be able to live on their own. State help for those who have problematic transitions is usually conditioned by the perceived imperative to reinforce the need for independence, particularly economic independence. In other words, an overriding importance is attached to the work incentives that public policies should not undermine. In addition, the primary responsibility for young people is held to be their family, with the state only intervening when the family cannot take responsibility.

The transition from the family home to independent living can be difficult for some young people. In general, the earlier they leave home and the more that the exit is due to 'push' rather than 'pull' factors, the more likely that there will be a period of homelessness. The pull factors are the socially sanctioned ones of leaving to set up home with a partner, taking up employment, or taking up training or education. The 'push' factors are the non-socially sanctioned ones, such as family conflict or overcrowded conditions. Also the speed in leaving home can be important, with those leaving suddenly more likely to lack the skills and resources necessary to sustain independent living.

Housing and support policies for homeless people

Sweden

Previous chapters have documented the gradual withdrawal from housing policy by the central state in Sweden from the 1990s onwards, but a continuing element of policy during this time has been the definition of homelessness as a social services rather than a housing problem. This means it is held to be the responsibility of local social services authorities and the central state has only been involved in homelessness through the propagation of a particular discourse and the funding of demonstration projects that reinforced this discourse (Sahlin, 2010). The statutory homelessness framework in Sweden (and the right to permanent housing) is largely restricted to those who are assessed as needing social support under the Act of Support and Services for People with Certain Functional Impairments (LSS) system for people with disabilities, administered by social services departments of the municipal authorities. It is not surprising, therefore, that supported housing features strongly in the processes used to counteract homelessness defined in this way.

In the predominant discourse in Sweden, homelessness has been defined as vulnerability due to drug abuse or mental health, and the focus has been away from structural housing issues. In the categorisation used by Jacobs et al (1999) government has adopted a minimalist discourse of homelessness. Sahlin (2010) comments on local homelessness projects funded by central government:

> Through their choice of purposes and objects for change, local homelessness projects, as well as the central state directives and instructions that influence them implicitly state that the causes of homelessness are to be found within the homeless individuals, not in their counterparts on the housing market (landlords and housing companies), nor in the structures of society (laws, institutions, unequal economic resources or the working of the market). (Sahlin, 2010: 361)

Aside from the LSS, the legal obligations on municipal authorities with regard to homelessness are limited. Under the Social Services Act municipal authorities have the ultimate responsibility to see that those who are staying in the municipality get the help and support they need. However, this applies largely to emergency provision and so it has led to the provision of emergency shelters for homeless people. Even here, once the initial support is provided, conditions can be applied to further help (such as being drug free) and if these conditions are not met, then the obligation does not apply. In addition, under the Act, the authority is required to provide housing with special services for people who require it, which has led to the secondary housing market (Sahlin, 1999).

At first glance it may seem strange that a country in the social democratic regime category holds this minimalist discourse. However, the discourse flows from a time when the universal welfare state in Sweden, which included extensive housing and social services provision, meant that affordable housing was within the reach of almost all citizens. So it was understandable that those left out would be those who were vulnerable at an individual level. However, the homelessness discourse has not kept up with the changes in the welfare state since the 1990s, and the increasing difficulty of some people in accessing affordable housing, particularly in the major cities. There is a general housing shortage in almost half of Sweden's nearly 300 municipalities, and the shortage is most acute in the rental market and particularly impacts on young people (Knutagård and Boustedt Hedvall, 2013). Also, the universalist housing model and the recent 'marketisation' of the municipal housing sector has meant that low-income people, or those without permanent housing, do not get priority access to the sector. Nordfeldt (2012) has highlighted the weak position of immigrants in the housing market in Sweden. Immigrants have lower incomes than people born in Sweden and have little or no capital, but they also face discrimination on the part of landlords and housing enterprises. Nordfeldt (2012) also argues that economically disadvantaged households do not have a sufficiently high income to access owner occupation and face increasing barriers to gaining a rental contract. For example, the demand by both private landlords and municipal housing companies for personal references from previous accommodation, an absence of unpaid debts and a guaranteed income from employment, disdvantages many low-income and immigrant households, who are therefore being forced to rely on the secondary housing market.

Given the minimalist definition of homelessness in Sweden, it is not surprising that the majority of homeless people, as shown in national statistics, show evidence of drug abuse or mental health problems. Despite the narrow definition of homelessness, the number of homeless people has increased. In 2005 there were approximately 17,800 homeless persons in Sweden (21 per 10,000 inhabitants at the national level), 74% of them male and 26% female. A majority (62%) of the homeless people had problems with drug abuse and about 40% are considered to have psychiatric problems (a large proportion have a so-called 'dual diagnosis'). In 2011, there were 34,000 people deemed to be homeless: 13,900 were in the municipal secondary housing market (for example in training flats or apartments with sub-leases); 6,800 were in insecure short-term accommodation, for example with friends or in overcrowded flats; 5,600 were in institutional care or category housing; and 4,500 were deemed to be in 'acute homelessness', such as in shelters or hostels, with 280 of these said to be sleeping rough

(Socialstyrelsen, 2012). Over a third (34%) of the homeless people had children under the age of 18 and 46% of these were born abroad. Of these families, 50% were in the secondary housing market and about 20% were lodging with relatives and friends, or in forms of temporary housing. Comparison between the two dates is difficult because of changes in definition. Nevertheless it is clear that there has been a large increase in the number of homeless people recorded. It must be borne in mind that the statistics only cover those who are considered to have problems recognised by the social services. There are many people who have only a need for housing and are on waiting lists for accommodation, often for a long time, and these may not be recorded.

In Chapter Five, reference was made to the supported housing sector run by municipal social services departments as a 'secondary housing market'. This secondary housing market has clearly expanded within the Swedish municipalities in recent years. Research from the early 2000s shows an expansion by 58% during the 1990s (Sahlin, 2010) and the increase has continued. This segment of the housing system consists of a variety of different kinds of transitional dwellings. Examples include emergency housing or shelters, forms of linked housing such as training flats and transitional contracts (where the lease is held by the social services authority and the apartment is sub-let to the resident on reduced terms), although the terms used for these types of housing differ between different municipalities. In addition there are various forms of housing provision based around the model of apartments contracted to social services authorities and sub-let to homeless people. This may be a form of core and cluster or domiciliary provision in the categorisation used in this book. The re-emergence of shelters can be seen as a particularly noteworthy development. During most of the 20th century, emergency shelters were criticised for their low standards and were deemed unworthy to be human lodgings. During the 1960s and 1970s most of the shelters in Sweden were shut down and replaced by other forms of accommodation. The 'new' shelters are in many ways based on the same ideas and are spatially designed in much the same way as the old traditional 19th-century shelters. They cover basic needs, have strict rules and there is little or no 'home' furnishing (Knutagård and Nordfeldt, 2007).

The different kinds of shelters and supported accommodation in the secondary housing market are often organised in a so-called 'staircase of transition'. This staircase approach has become common practice among local social services authorities with respect to supported housing. The basic idea behind the staircase model is that:

homeless people are supposed to ascend step by step from the streets to a regular dwelling of their own via low-standard shelters, category housing (i.e., houses for specific categories, such as homeless male alcoholics), training flats and transitional flats. The higher they climb, the better their conditions in terms of physical standards and space, integrity, freedom, and security of tenure. Meanwhile, social workers monitor their efforts and progress in resolving 'underlying' problems (like debts, substance abuse, unemployment, etc.), and provide 'training in independent living'. (Sahlin, 2005: 117)

There are rewards for good behaviour and eviction for those who do not conform to the norms.

The terms for the different stages included in the housing staircase model have varied. An example sees the transition as advancing from the 'emergency and short-term living units' through the 'assessment and training units' (for improving the residents' capacity for independent living) to the 'reference units' (for verification of the resident's preparedness for their own tenancy) and, finally, the 'retention' units (for nurturing and maintaining the residents' acquired capabilities). The clients categorised as capable of independent living were placed in reference units, while those deemed never to be capable of independent living were placed in retention units. This highlights the major problem with the staircase model which is that the move out of the system into the regular housing market has proved to be very problematic, with few individuals making this transition and many staying in the retention units.

In a similar manner, the predominant model combating long-term homelessness in the United States, known broadly as the continuum of care model, emphasises the need to enhance the 'housing readiness' of homeless people. This is achieved by encouraging sobriety and demanding compliance with treatment, deemed as 'essential for successful transition to permanent housing' (Tsemberis et al., 2004: 651). The basic assumption here is that homeless people are incapable of maintaining independent housing, and that 'the skills a client needs for independent living can be learned in transitional congregate living' (Tsemberis et al., 2004: 651). Furthermore, again like the staircase model, the approach categorises supported housing schemes as 'rungs on a ladder, beginning with a shelter' and ending with an apartment of one's own. Homeless individuals are, ideally, to move steadily upwards on this ladder, which of course involves moving accommodation, and eviction is used as a punishment for residents who relapse into alcohol use. The staircase model in Sweden has been based on abstinence being a precondition of a place in supported housing, although there has been some acceptance of 'symptom tolerance' in relation to those considered to be incurable and therefore must remain in the supported housing staircase, as well as for those on the early rungs of the ladder, such as in a hostel. But often the outcome of tests for alcohol or drug use can result in staying in or leaving a particular scheme.

The staircase model has now largely been abandoned in principle in Sweden, reflecting its failure in practice. Instead of climbing up the staircase, homeless people moved horizontally between different supported housing schemes, staying on the same level of the 'staircase' or moving temporarily up or down, with periods in between of staying on the streets. A more accurate term would be the 'pinball' model. It has now been accepted in many local authorities and by central government that many homeless people will not in practice make the transition to independent living through the current staircase system and so a plethora of different types of supported housing is needed as a form of permanent housing. Municipal supported housing is not seen as a pathway to regular housing in practice, but as a permanent solution for the individual as well as for the municipality. At the rhetorical level, the metaphor of the staircase is now replaced with that of the 'elevator' in which people can get off and remain at particular levels (Lofstrand, 2010). Therefore, in many places supported housing is now presented as the permanent solution it has always tended to be in practice and there has been a proliferation of these forms.

In addition to category housing meant to serve a particular category or group, which has proved inflexible in practice, many municipalities are moving to a system based on sub-leases to homeless people in ordinary houses leased in the first instance by the municipality from a municipal housing company or private landlord. However, the homeless person has to meet various criteria to gain the sub-lease, such as accepting treatment or abstaining from alcohol or drugs. This form of housing is often seen as the final step of the housing staircase and makes up about half of the total of the secondary housing market.

The continuum of care approach or staircase model present in Stockholm, Malmo and Gothenburg has been largely superseded in the US, where the influential Housing First concept has taken root and this is now happening both in cities and in many other places in Sweden (Knutagård and Kristiansen, 2013). The basic principles of the (Housing First) model are the following: (1) homelessness should first and foremost be considered as a housing problem; (2) homeless

171

people should be re-established in the regular housing market as quickly as possible; (3) access to housing of one's own forms an important precondition for subsequently solving other problems; (4) permanent and safe housing is to be considered a basic human right that belongs to everyone (Lofstrand, 2012).

In 2012 the government set up a Housing Commission to examine homelessness and they have supported experiments with the Housing First model. There are now a number of such projects in Sweden that involve a very different philosophy than the staircase, but so far no city has used this model for more than a limited number of individuals. The philosophy of Housing First is that homelessness is both a housing and a support problem, and that if the housing issue is solved first, then the person has the security and self-esteem to cope with any personal issues that they may have, such as substance abuse. This is in direct contradiction to the staircase approach, which is based on the view that homeless people need to show that they deserve their own housing by demonstrating adherence to certain behavioural norms. Therefore the staircase system is based more on social control, whereas the Housing First model is based more on the improvement of self-esteem and confidence, leading to person-initiated change. In other words, the model creates the conditions through the provision of support and accommodation in which people can initiate their own change. Sahlin (2005) has suggested that supported housing is a favoured solution for those kinds of people whom the state wants to monitor and control – such as foreigners without residence permits and potentially disorderly homeless people – but not for those who need support and services, such as older people. This is an interesting point that will be considered further.

Malmo is an example of a local authority trying to break out of the staircase model. In Malmo there is a substantial and increasing shortage of affordable rented housing that impacts particularly on immigrants and low-income families. Between 2006 and 2012 the number of rented dwellings decreased by 10% and the number of people in the social services secondary housing market almost doubled. In a survey of homeless people in 2013, two thirds were men and 54% were born outside Sweden, with 39% holding citizenship of another country, showing the difficulty of access to rented housing allocated by means of a queue based on the time spent waiting. Forty per cent were diagnosed as having drink, drug or mental health problems, but this means that 60% were just short of housing and over two thirds of these were not born in Sweden. Unlike the situation in Britain, only about 15% of the homeless were under the age of 25 (personal correspondence).

Provision in Malmo consists of emergency shelters run by private organisations but with places funded by the social services department. People cannot book places and stays are limited to one night. Homeless people are then encouraged to move on to one of a number of longer-stay hostels, with stays of up to a couple of months. These hostels can be described as 'prison-like but friendly'. Drug taking on the premises is not allowed, but residents may take their drugs outside and enter under the influence. Residents have their own small room and have food and laundry services provided. The next step in the 'staircase' is an apartment leased by the municipal social services that is offered on a licence for one to two years. The intention is that this provides time with support to deal with problems of debt or addiction so that residents can take up the lease themselves. Also part of provision is hotel and bed and breakfast accommodation leased by the department that is mainly used for those without problems and families.

Malmo has introduced a 'Housing First' project that takes people from a waiting list of those applying without any assessment and provides rented accommodation in a number of apartments owned by the municipal housing company and a number of private landlords. In 2014 there were 16 apartments. Residents were supported by two staff who provided a wide range of support services, including training in housekeeping skills and acted as brokers with other services. Residents received a home visit every month to assessed and dealt with any problems. The scheme has been considered a great success and the aim is to expand it in the future by increasing the number of apartments available.

Gothenburg has had a basic philosophy since 2011 that people should be helped wherever possible in their own home and people should not have to move house to access support. This has led the authority to introduce a Housing First initiative that is different from that in Malmo. In Gothenberg applicants for Housing First are nominated by the social work department and are usually those with mental health, alcohol or drug problems for whom existing approaches have failed. In other words, the project is dealing with the most difficult cases, unlike Malmo, which has a mix of people with very different needs. The extent of needs in the Gothenberg scheme is reflected in the support staff, who have skills in psychiatric social work. The project has 10 apartments from the municipal housing companies in 2014, with a further 10 in the pipeline. The first lease is held by the municipal property department rather than the social work department to avoid the conditions attached to staircase housing, and residents are offered a sub-lease for 18 months and can take over the full lease after that time if this is considered appropriate. The philosophy is that the self-esteem of people is improved by being given a nice apartment in a 'good' neighbourhood, by being taken away from an environment in which drug and alcohol use is prevalent, and by being given social support from psychiatric social work staff. It is believed that this will create the conditions for residents to change and be able to take control of their own lives. The project is at an early stage and it is not possible to evaluate it at the time of writing. However, it is estimated that the cost of the project per resident is half that of staircase housing schemes.

While the Housing First programme is taking off, Gothenburg also has a staircase model. The lowest level consists of emergency hostels (about 75 places) and a hostel with 25 places in which access is through the social services outreach team. This hostel is in an industrial part of the town, away from neighbours, but is like an ordinary housing block from the outside and has a well-kept and pleasant internal appearance, apart from the security guards at the door. Local authorities have the legal duty to provide a roof over the head and food for a day for those who apply for it and the hostel has generously sized individual rooms for residents, and provides food, showers and a washing service as well as clothes for those who need them. People have to leave in the morning, but will be accepted the following night if they turn up. The hostel also has a medically supervised 'drying out room' where police or outreach workers can take people who are profoundly under the influence of alcohol.

Different floors of the hostel are reserved for longer-stay residents who have particular issues or fall into particular 'categories'. The rule is that stays are restricted to three months, but some residents are evicted before this for breaking the rules and others end up staying for years. Drugs are not allowed in the hostel in principle, but the rules are difficult to enforce and residents can take drugs or drink nearby and enter under the influence either of drugs or alcohol. In addition, there are a number of supported schemes for particular categories, such as women, older people with an alcohol problem, people with drug problems and so on, as well as 'training flats', usually in blocks, where residents have a sub-lease from the social services and receive support with the aim of them moving to their own tenancy, although the overall shortage of rental housing makes this difficult. It is estimated that out of the 1,100 people in the system, about 10% will achieve the ultimate goal of their own tenancy in a year, which means that the average stay in the staircase is about 10 years.

It is worth emphasising here that many people are excluded from the scope of municipal supported housing services (examples include immigrant families without residence permits, homeless families and single people without 'social problems' but who became homeless due to financial difficulties and economic hardship). Also excluded are homeless people placed in supported housing but evicted from it (on the grounds of rule-breaking, of being under the influence of alcohol, of allowing partners, friends, or others to stay in the room/ apartment, of failing to return home for the night, etc.). These two categories then form the 'tertiary market' that serves people who have fallen through the safety net and are excluded from both the primary and secondary systems. The tertiary system consists mainly of non-profit organisations working beyond the public sphere but at the same time very much dependent on financing from the local public authorities. The plight of the homeless has historically been, and still is, a niche occupied by non-profit organisations and charities; a system in existence long before Swedish modern welfare began to take shape around the Second World War. At that time the welfare state took over tasks from the non-profit sector and became the dominant producer of social welfare services (Olsson and Nordfeldt, 2008). By tradition, non-profit organisations working with the homeless are often related to the churches. Having worked with the issue of homelessness for over a hundred years, these organisations have developed knowledge, established practices and so secured legitimacy. Although formed to meet the social problems brought about by 19th-century urbanisation, they nevertheless continue to fit quite well into the individualistic homelessness paradigm because their focus is on the individual.

Britain

Homelessness in Britain has been a recurring problem that has received much attention from the media and politicians. The extent of homelessness has varied over time with a peak in 2003 of over 180,000 people being accepted as homeless by local authorities in Britain and reducing to half that level in 2009, before increasing again following the financial crash and government austerity programmes (Wilcox and Perry, 2014). Young people have been at particular risk of homelessness and Johnsen and Quilgars (2009) estimated the number of homeless young people between the ages of 16 and 24 to be 75,000 in 2006/7. Jacobs et al (1999) have charted how government policy in Britain has moved between the two maximalist and minimalist constructions over time, although it has rarely accepted either one completely. A good example of the equivocal nature of policy is the 1977 Homeless Persons

Act, which has formed the basis of statutory homelessness provision in Britain since its enactment (although amended and changed).

The 1977 legislation is based on a maximalist conception of homelessness and accepts that it is the role of the state, through municipal authorities, to prevent homelessness and deal with homeless people through the provision of permanent housing. However, the role is circumscribed because of the concern not to reward feckless behaviour. Therefore, to be able to take advantage of the statutory provision for permanent housing, individuals must be categorised as homeless and being in priority need, not intentionally homeless, and have a local connection to the area where they are applying. The original priority needs groups included households with dependent children, adults who are vulnerable due to old age, mental illness, disability or other 'special reason'. Sixteen and 17 year olds were included in the early 2000s in England, Scotland and Wales. Local authorities have the duty to those who fall into these priority categories of finding temporary accommodation and to provide settled housing when this is available. Therefore, homeless people can spend time in temporary accommodation that can include bed and breakfast hotels and hostels as well as self-contained accommodation in social or private rented stock. For those who do not fall into the priority groups, the local authority has a duty to provide advice and information, but does not have a duty to provide accommodation. Therefore, there is a key distinction in treatment between those who fall into the priority needs categories and those who don't. In general, young people fall into the non-priority category unless they are 16 or 17 or unless they qualify under the other categories by having dependent children or mental health problems. A young male over 17 leaving home generally is not in the priority categories and it is this group that is over-represented in those who sleep rough because of increasing problems in accessing affordable housing.

Since the 1977 legislation, homelessness has become a devolved function and so legislation and practice is now different across the different countries of Britain (for a review see Fitzpatrick et al., 2009). Scotland has developed a particular approach to homelessness within Britain following the recommendations of a Homelessness Task Force that provided a final report in 2002. In 2003 the government started a process of implementation of the major recommendation of the Task Force, which was to abolish the distinction between priority and non-priority groups, as well as abolishing the local connection requirement and requiring local authorities to provide temporary accommodation and support to those categorised as intentionally homeless. Although it was not expressed in those terms at the time, the proposals essentially create a right to permanent housing for homeless people and is the nearest to a universal right to housing of any country in the world. It was recognised that implementation of the proposals would take time and so the date of 2012 was set as the target date for full implementation, with a monitoring group established to oversee the implementation process, which has been largely successful (see Fitzpatrick et al, 2012).

Throughout Britain, there has been an increasing emphasis on dealing with street homelessness. For example, a 'Rough Sleepers Initiative' was launched in 1990 in London and 1996 elsewhere in England, which funded outreach and resettlement services, specialist support, and temporary and permanent housing. From the 1980s onwards there has also been an emphasis on preventing homelessness by providing information and advice and resettlement services to avoid homelessness in the first place and to prevent its recurrence. Despite these initiatives homelessness has remained a major problem and, following the economic crisis of 2007 and the subsequent recession, numbers have grown substantially, especially among young people.

Many young homeless people have experienced a breakdown in the relationship with their parents, which in almost half of cases is accompanied by violence (Johnsen and Quilgars, 2009). Also, some young homeless people have a wide range of complex support needs that may include drug or alcohol abuse, as well as work, education and money problems, a fracturing of social relationships and low self-esteem. Homelessness is associated with mental health problems of depression and anxiety, with young homeless people experiencing these at a rate of three times that of the general population of the same age (Pleace et al, 2008).

Following the general adoption of the prevention approach, much effort has been made to deal with homeless people's problems outside what has become known as the 'homelessness route'. Advice and support services have been made available, either to resettle young people in the family home or to enable homeless people to cope with their problems and to make a planned move into settled accommodation (Johnsen and Quilgars, 2009). However, this approach is not appropriate for many young people, who are not able or willing to return home or cope immediately with independent living.

There is a wide range of supported accommodation available for homeless people, such as hostels, bed and breakfast hotels, and supported lodging schemes. Many people, and especially young people, often report feeling unsafe in all-age hostels and bed and breakfast accommodation, where there is a mix of people of different ages and where they may be confronted with drug and alcohol abuse and the support facilities may not be specifically geared for them. Much temporary provision is in shared accommodation and homeless people differ in their response to this, with some finding it challenging, whereas others enjoy the company of others. The growth of foyers as a response to the accommodation and support needs of young people is significant, with the provision of around 10,000 places per year.

There has been a move away from the provision of large-scale hostels for homeless people and the example of Glasgow is apposite, where four large, male hostels housing nearly 240 people were closed in the early 2000s (Fitzpatrick et al, 2010). The closure was supported by the Scottish government through the provision of a Hostel Decommissioning Grant. The hostels were originally designed to provide basic short-term accommodation for as many people as possible and were ill-equipped to provide the intensive support and supervision required by the large concentrations of people with complex health and support needs who came to be accommodated within them, often on a long-term or recurring basis. Widespread drug use and drug dealing, money lending and violence made these hostels difficult and volatile places to live and work in. Many of those sleeping rough in the city were barred from the hostels because of their behaviour or rent arrears, and many others preferred to sleep rough rather than stay in such intimidating places, particularly if they were trying to recover from drug or alcohol problems (Fitzpatrick, 2000).

The aim of the closure programme was to move existing residents of the hostels into more appropriate long-term accommodation, whether this was in mainstream housing with appropriate support or in an appropriate supported housing scheme. New hostel admissions were to be avoided through a unified assessment tool used by all agencies to select appropriate forms of housing and support. There was a centre (Hamish Allen Centre) and eight locality teams for homeless presentations and for the arrangement of emergency accommodation, as well as the Clyde Place accommodation and assessment centre which provided emergency accommodation, support and assessment. This had self-contained bedsit accommodation with their own shower and cooking facilities. Accommodation was meant to be for 28 days but the lack of move-on accommodation means that it has been silted up (Quilgars and Bretherton, 2009). In addition, there was the use of bed and breakfast accommodation, which was being reduced, and temporary furnished flats (1,800 in 2009) which were also becoming silted up due to the lack of move-on accommodation and so were difficult to access by new homeless people. Also some were unpopular because they were sited in 'bad' areas.

There were still some hostels, largely run by voluntary and commercial organisations. These were difficult to access due to move-on problems, but were unpopular with many homeless people because they were considered to be unsafe and to be full of drugs, alcohol and vice. In the hostels, homeless people were 'warehoused' and received little input from support staff.

Other forms of help were specialist supported accommodation, which was considered difficult to access because of strict entry criteria – the person was required to fit the scheme rather than the other way round – and permanent accommodation through referrals to housing associations. This was perceived as difficult and slow, with long waits for some homeless people, who also had problems in acquiring furniture.

In England, the Hostel Capital Improvement Programme was launched in 2005 with £90 million (CLG, 2006). In *Places of change: Tackling homelessness through the Hostels Capital Improvement Programme*, hostels and day centres were to become 'centres of excellence that change lives'. The aim was to move people on to settled housing and training or jobs. This was to be achieved through: engaging residents in meaningful activity in the community; involving residents in the development of services; developing well trained, motivated and supported staff; and providing a quality physical environment.

In their review of provision for single homeless people, Jones and Pleace (2010) identified a number of trends in homelessness provision. These included the closure of large hostels and the growth of smaller supported schemes with more support geared to resettlement (with a two-year limit on residence); more move-on through resettlement programmes in hostels; more direct placement of homeless people in mainstream tenancies with floating support, in addition to a growth of tenancy support services to prevent homelessness and support those resettled. Also they noted the use of fixed site 'move-on projects', also called dispersed hostels, where staff are linked to the housing and in which residents have to move on to settled housing within a specified time period. Also there has been more specific supported housing (shared housing for particular groups) and more mixed schemes, such as core and cluster involving specific shared housing with outreach to dispersed accommodation or floating support. Emergency and direct access accommodation represented 30% of provision; supported housing schemes 37%; floating support 22%; outreach services 4%; and foyers 2%. In England 48% of provision was by the voluntary sector and 37% by housing associations.

Homeless people are likely to be badly hit by the public expenditure cuts that have taken place since 2009. Reductions in expenditure on the Supporting People programme, particularly in England, will hit support services for homeless people hard. This makes it more difficult to fund the support services that some homeless people need to be able to deal with their social problems and restricts the amount of supported housing that is available. In addition, the government has reduced housing benefit payments for many young people through the expansion of the single room rent and general reductions in housing allowances. Young people under 25 were only eligible for an allowance for a single room rather than for self-contained accommodation and this has now been extended to all those under 35, and the coalition government in 2014 has expressed its intent to remove all housing benefit payments for young people. This policy makes it more difficult for unemployed young people to find and keep accommodation in the increasingly competitive private rented sector when social renting is in such short supply.

Well-being in supported housing models

The affordances of home

The major form of shared housing in both Britain and Sweden is the hostel, which in both countries has often been of a basic physical standard. Older hostels had dormitory type sleeping arrangements and, although this has largely died out, the individual accommodation is often small and spartan. Usually, hostels are viewed by the providers as temporary accommodation and residents themselves may feel this, making it difficult for them to experience some of the emotional attachments of home. There is evidence (Hutson, 1999) that some residents in Britain have found hostels to be threatening environments in which they fear for their physical and emotional safety. It is difficult to see how residents can form an emotional attachment to home in these circumstances. However, it is also reported that hostels suited some older men, who reported a 'good social life' and who were able to participate in activities of their choice which were sometimes illegal (Hutson, 1999).

Many of the older hostels in Britain are in rather dilapidated old buildings. Some were built as hostels, but others were converted from downmarket hotels or sometimes from institutions or hospitals. Other buildings are newer and one objective of the move to foyers in Britain was to use new purpose-built accommodation to break the perceived low symbolic status of the older hostels. In many ways this has succeeded, with many foyers delivering well-designed and modern environments. However, both hostels and foyers are in schemes that are separate from other forms of residence and signal the difference of the residents. Hostels are therefore generally perceived as offering few of the affordances of home, and policy in both countries is to use them only as a last resort and for temporary accommodation.

Other forms of shared housing, such as group homes, can be purpose-built or in existing large houses. In both examples there has been an effort to try to make the accommodation look like an ordinary house from the outside to minimise signals of difference. However, this has its limits and it is usually possible to see that the house is not inhabited by an 'ordinary' family, even though it may be on a domestic scale. The model of group housing is an attempt to create a household on the scale of a family. Of course it differs from a family in many respects and residents will often be of similar age and perhaps gender. Attempts may be made to match people so that there is a mix of abilities in the scheme in order to foster collective self-help and minimise formal support. Living in group housing outside the family is not common in Britain or Sweden. The most usual example is students sharing a house or flat when at university or college. This may be followed by periods of sharing in the private rented sector as a young professional when income is low and flexibility prized. However, most people's aim is to live either alone or in a couple or family household. Sharing is unpopular among many young people on low incomes who have not had the student experience (Clapham et al, 2014). In a recent research study, some vulnerable young people expressed dissatisfaction with sharing when it could mean living with someone who exhibited challenging behaviour or who one just did not get on with (Clapham et al, 2014). The attitude seemed to be that they had enough to do dealing with their own problems without having to cope with the problems of others. So sharing is not necessarily a desired or a high-status way of living.

Residents in group schemes will usually have their own bedroom, but may have to share other facilities. Thus they have a degree of privacy, but the existence of other residents and support workers inevitably constrains this when living space is shared. If residents 'get on' there may be a sociable spirit in the scheme and a shared sense of home. However, this may not always be the case, and the control residents have over who they will be sharing with may be constrained. In the evaluation report of the Glasgow hostel closure programme (Fitzpatrick et al, 2010) most residents said that supported housing (in the form of group housing or core and cluster schemes) was better than the hostel. They had more freedom to come and go as they pleased, and enjoyed the use of their own bathroom and kitchen facilities. In general, there were no problems from fellow residents. Of the residents in supported schemes, half had to share a living room, but the other half had flats or scatter flats. Sixty per cent made all their own meals and 60% did their own laundry. Twenty per cent said noise from others was a problem and 18% said that there were general behavioural problems in the scheme. Not everyone felt settled in supported accommodation because of the temporary nature of the accommodation. Sixty per cent of residents living in their own home said that they found it easy, with no problems, but 2% said it was very difficult with lots of problems and 38% said it was ok in general but they did have some problems. The main problems cited were lack of money or difficulty managing bills. Some people did find it difficult to live on their own (Fitzpatrick et al, 2010).

In summary, shared housing in the form of group homes is less popular with homeless people than living in their own home, although it is preferable to hostel living. Most people do not find that living with others improves their well-being. A major gap in our knowledge is of the impact of foyers in Britain on the well-being of residents. There has been no systematic evaluation of this form of supported housing that focuses on well-being of the residents.

Blid and Gerdner (2006) studied homeless people with substance abuse problems in two cities in Sweden who had been placed in category housing, which consisted of one-room furnished flats with a bathroom and kitchenette and, in one scheme, communal facilities. Residents had sub-leases rather than their own tenancy and could be (and some were) evicted if they breached the scheme rules. The study found that residents did consider their housing situation to be better than before (when they were homeless) and they felt more stable and secure in their housing and also in their general lives. However, these effects did not seem to be long-term and residents made little progress in dealing with their substance abuse problems. The authors concluded, therefore, that this form of supported housing reinforced the social isolation of the residents and did little to promote independent living.

It is increasingly common in Britain for homeless people to be rehoused in the private rented sector by homeless agencies rather than in the public rented sector. This would seem at first thought to offer people the promise of their own home with all the benefits this entails and this was the expectation of many homeless people in this situation. However, a report from Crisis and Shelter (Smith et al, 2014) showed that usually these early expectations were dashed. At first, people appreciated the warmth of their new home, and the control that they could exert over their everyday life compared with being homeless, which they thought disrupted their everyday life, with profound implications for their mental and physical health and their general well-being. People were looking to rebuild their lives and gain some stability, and they perceived their home as being the foundation for this. They thought it would allow them to gain more control over their lives and to plan for issues such as child care, returning to work and dealing with drug or mental health problems. Some people made efforts to improve their home and exert control over it by decorating and making little improvements with the approval of the landlord. However, after 19 months, two thirds of people in the survey were unhappy in their tenancies and wanted to move out. The poor conditions, lack of repairs, hostile attitudes of some landlords and instability, because of the short duration of tenancies, had undermined and prevented people from realising their ambitions for home.

In summary, most homeless people in hostels or other forms of shared housing find that they are unable to experience many of the affordances of home and wish to have their own accommodation. However, the experience of those housed in the private rented sector discussed above shows that the hopes of a decent independent home can be difficult to achieve in a housing system where quality of the stock and management practices are poor. This example shows the challenges that confront policy makers in catering for homeless people in a flawed housing system. It also shows where the policy priority must lie. A focus on the housing system as a whole would not only prevent homelessness, but also make dealing with it easier.

The affordances of neighbourhood

Many hostel residents suffer from a range of problems such as alcohol or drug abuse that may sometimes manifest in challenging behaviour. Even if this is not the actual situation, it is often the perception among those who plan hostel provision and those who may find one planned for their neighbourhood. As a consequence many hostels are in city centre locations, in industrial locations or in deprived neighbourhoods, and few are sited in affluent residential neighbourhoods. There are few links between the hostels and their neighbourhoods and residents are unlikely either to find many affordances in the area or to form an attachment to it. Residents in the Glasgow study said that contact with other people in the hostel was difficult because of the rules and the stigma that they felt in inviting friends into the place. Most reported an increase in contact with friends and relatives on leaving the hostel (Fitzpatrick et al, 2010).

Group housing schemes vary in their neighbourhood affordances. Residents may be part of low-status groups, such as those with mental health or drug abuse problems that may be seen as bringing down neighbourhood house prices or creating safety problems for neighbours. The development of new schemes has been sometimes made difficult through local opposition. As a consequence, some group housing schemes are cut off from ordinary residential streets on parts of the grounds of old institutions.

Of residents in the Glasgow study who had left a hostel, 73% said they got on with the neighbours, although 18% said they never had contact (Fitzpatrick et al, 2010). Ninety-eight per cent felt safe in their homes at night, but 11% reported being a bit unsafe walking after dark and 13% felt very unsafe. However, these results are in line with responses from the general population. Seventy-five per cent said that they felt safer than living in the hostel.

In summary, there does not seem to be a priority given to neighbourhood affordances in provision for homeless people. Hostels and other forms of shared housing do not seem to prioritise this aspect and there is little research focusing on this issue. In Sweden, Blid (2008: 142) is moved to comment that:

> One may question to what extent policies are formulated primarily to assist homeless individuals in securing adequate housing and to provide support for them to be re-integrated into the community, or if the policies are primarily formulated in order to protect the community from homeless individuals

The comment is based on the number of service options that are not based on ordinary, integrated housing with full tenancy rights, but rather on category housing or other forms within the secondary housing market, with little seeming effort at integration or on individual development. It can be argued that services can be characterised as 'warehousing' homeless individuals in segregated environments.

Well-being, personal control, identity and self-esteem

In the Glasgow hostel closure study (Fitzpatrick et al, 2010), many homeless people who had left the hostel reported problems with employment, skills and training, and few received any help. Some also reported a lack of meaningful activity, particularly when they felt they suffered from a lack of social interaction. Many young homeless people reported being able to manage their money better because they felt more in control in their own home and reported fewer problems with drugs or alcohol. Those reporting that they felt extremely anxious or depressed went down from 33% to 17% after leaving the hostel. Where problems existed they were mainly associated with boredom and the lack of meaningful activity. The proportion of people who reported that they had access to emotional support was higher after leaving the hostel, but was lower than the population at large.

Eighty-one per cent in permanent housing reported being happy compared to only 58% in supported projects. The authors of the study attributed this difference to the supported housing group experiencing worse health and less contact with family and friends. Overall, 60% of homeless people said that life was much better than in the hostel. However, 98% of those in mainstream housing said it was much better, compared to 71% in supported accommodation. The authors report one homeless person as saying: 'You are a human being when you have a house. I have got my credibility back now.' These findings show the impact that independent living can have on the overall well-being of residents. Hostels and shared living are not conducive to the well-being of residents and most of them value independent living, which has been shown to increase their well-being.

Conclusions

The provision for homelessness in Britain and Sweden differs substantially. Sweden is undergoing a transition in the predominant discourse, as the traditional staircase model is being slowly replaced, in principle, by the Housing First model, even if the number of homeless people who enter Housing First projects is small. The traditional model is a more paternalist one, imbued with a philosophy of social control and requiring the performance of accepted behavioural norms. Housing First is a more person–centred approach that is based on the improvement of self-esteem and confidence through the provision of housing, and agreed and voluntarily received support for self-defined needs in order to initiate person-driven change. The Housing First project in Gothenburg is a brave example of the approach because it is housing those failed by the traditional approach and those with high support needs. Housing First is an example of a domiciliary approach in which the housing accommodation is separate from the support, which can be varied according to individual preferences, circumstances and changing needs. People need to move to enter the projects, but as they are mostly homeless or in supported housing the move represents a forward trajectory in their housing circumstances, and one that is desired. The domiciliary approach enables the affordances of home to residents who have their own home, and the control and self-esteem that goes with this. Also, apartments have been largely in high-status neighbourhoods, where the affordances are probably greater than in others. The scattered location of the flats reduces the impact of stigma, although the location can also create problems of a clash of lifestyles with neighbours, and there may be problems of isolation in unknown neighbourhoods. The initial experience of the Gothenburg project is heartening in this respect, with only minor problems experienced. If the Gothenburg project succeeds in its objectives it opens the possibility for the widespread adoption of the domiciliary model.

The staircase model in Sweden is steeped in the discourse of social control and segregation. Residents are usually in temporary accommodation in which they do not have a full tenancy. Although the accommodation can be self-contained, the residents lack some of the affordances of home, such as control and sometimes security. At the lower steps of the staircase, residents are in shared accommodation such as hostels. Higher up the staircase, residents have their own apartments (but without full tenancy rights), which are usually grouped together in an apartment block or category house, and residents are segregated into enclaves of those in the same position, opening possibilities of stigma and resultant low self-esteem. In this model, there are also inflexibilities in the support arrangements where they are attached to particular schemes or blocks. This is not always the case, however, and sometimes support is flexible and related to individuals rather than schemes or projects, particularly where residents are in scatter apartments. The many drawbacks of the staircase approach have been discussed in the chapter, but the overall impact of these problems is to create a system that does not improve the well-being of most of its inhabitants as they are trapped in a segregated and stigmatised environment that does little to increase independence and high self-esteem. The failings of the 'staircase' model in Sweden show the limitations of the conditional approach to supported housing and the early success of the Housing First pilots shows the worth of putting well-being at the centre of provision.

The British system involves a mix of social control and independence in a wide range of different forms of accommodation and support. The Glasgow experience of hostel closure offers a way forward that maximises well-being with its move towards the core and cluster model and the use of mainstream accommodation as scatter flats. Glasgow has the advantage that there is a greater availability of rented housing than in many other cities in Britain. Therefore there are fewer restrictions on its ability to implement these kinds of flexible solutions. In London, for example, it is unlikely that enough housing would be available to meet needs. Nevertheless, the lessons of the Glasgow experience offer support for a flexible approach, like Housing First in Sweden, that separates housing and support and provides residents with all the affordances of home and neighbourhood.

Hostels and foyers are forms of supported housing that are often associated with conditional welfare and they offer their residents very little chance of an attachment to home or neighbourhood. They signal difference to others and have low symbolic status, although foyers were a conscious effort to break from the existing view of hostels and to reduce the stigma associated with them. On the basis of the evaluation here, there is little justification for the pursuance of these models and the policy focus needs to be shifted to more flexible support arrangements servicing mainstream accommodation in the core and cluster or domiciliary models. However, the experience of homeless people rehoused in the private rented sector in Britain (Smith et al, 2014) shows that the success of the domiciliary-based models is dependent on the housing circumstances that people experience. Poor physical conditions, insecurity, unsafe neighbourhoods and poor landlord services can prevent residents from experiencing the benefits of home. Because of the better mainstream housing conditions and support services associated with the universalist model, Sweden would be in a better position to operationalise the domiciliary approach successfully if homeless people were able to access the mainstream housing system. The absence in Sweden of a mechanism to enable priority access to mainstream housing is a major drawback for homeless people. Housing First projects are small scale, mainly because they need access to ordinary apartments and therefore need municipal housing companies and private landlords to make properties available voluntarily. It is easy to see how this could be problematic for commercially minded organisations that may consider the letting of accommodation to homeless people to be a higher-risk activity than their normal commercial operations. The lack of access not only restricts the scope of Housing First projects and domiciliary forms of supported housing but also contributes to the lack of progress up the housing staircase by restricting possibilities of exit at the top. This is an important point that we will return to in Chapter Nine.

Britain, with its poorer condition housing stock and reducing support services is in a much worse situation in the implementation of domiciliary models, despite its social priority in access to social housing. If social housing is in very short supply then opportunities are still limited and the experience of housing homeless people in the private rented sector has not been satisfactory for the homeless people concerned. However, diversion of funding away from particular supported housing models, such as foyers and the remaining hostels, and towards core and cluster and domiciliary forms of provision would be a step in the right direction. The Glasgow hostel closure programme shows what can be achieved with the appropriate approach and resources.

EIGHT

Supported housing for disabled people

Introduction

This chapter is concerned with supported housing options for people with disabilities. A broad scope of issues is covered by the heading of disability, including both mental and physical health and illness, learning disability, physical impairment and disability. The categories used in policy making have varied over time. In Britain, the community care legislation was couched in terms of people with a physical disability; people with a learning difficulty; and people with a mental health problem (as well as frail older people who were covered in Chapter Six). The key legislation in Sweden is the Act Concerning Support and Service Provision for Persons with Certain Functional Impairments 1993, which covers three groups of people: people with an intellectual disability, autism or condition resembling autism; people with a significant and permanent intellectual impairment after brain damage in adulthood; people who have other major and permanent physical and mental impairments which are clearly not due to normal ageing and which cause considerable difficulties in daily life and consequently an extensive need of support and service.

The rationale for covering these diverse categories in just one chapter is partly one of space, but it also registers a concern that the usual categories are restrictive and hide similarities in the needs and characteristics of the individuals concerned. Also, the categories hide the overlaps that often occur. For example, many people with learning difficulties may also have physical impairments, and many older people with dementia or other chronic diseases may have physical and mental health and disability issues. In addition, the categories themselves are contentious. For example, the definition of learning disability in Britain is laid down in the government document *Valuing people* in 2001 (Department of Health, 2001) and includes a significantly reduced capacity to learn new information or skills, or to live independently, and which started before adulthood. This definition emphasises the functional capacity of the individual and relates this to permanent brain dysfunction rather than to the societal barriers that may hinder independence or functional capacity. The overlaps between the needs and attributes of disabled people and others means that some of the relevant issues have been covered in previous chapters (such as Chapters Six and Seven). For example, some older people have physical disabilities as well as dementia and so the provision for them may not differ much from disabled people of other ages. Also, some homeless people have problems with drug or alcohol addiction and have physical and mental health problems. Nevertheless, the consideration of disability as a topic in its own right serves to highlight some important issues not covered elsewhere in the book.

For some people who have physical impairments (whichever category they may be ascribed to), the overriding need is for housing that enables them to undertake the activities of daily living. However, an appropriate physical home environment may not always be sufficient and residents may need help to live a full life, as well as support and training to use aids if that is necessary. There is substantial evidence that people with physical impairments suffer numerous barriers in their quest for an independent life and that the home and neighbourhood environment is one contributing factor to the disabilities they face (Hemingway, 2011). Other factors include financial and communication barriers that can lead to inability to access the desired housing. For example, people may have difficulty in physically accessing properties they may consider buying, or the information on the property may not be in an accessible form for them, or financial institutions may impose additional financial costs because of the perception of the risk attached to their particular condition (Hemingway, 2011). As a consequence of these barriers, disabled people may find themselves in housing situations that they would not choose and that are neither appropriate for, nor conducive to their well-being, which may include forms of supported housing or institutional living.

For people with mental health problems, supported housing in the form of group homes or apartment blocks has been used as an alternative to institutional living in order to provide independence and a supportive, therapeutic community that helps healing. In provision for people with mental health problems, perhaps more so than in other official categories, there can sometimes be an element in support designed to control or change behaviour. In Britain, following the community care policies of the 1970s, a number of scandals emerged in the popular press about people with mental health problems committing violent crimes, despite being under outpatient care at a hospital. There was a concern that the taking of prescribed medication was not being monitored actively enough, which led to a move away from community care for that group, and a greater use of hospitalisation and of supported housing. As we shall see later, government concern about the risks posed by people with mental health problems has had an important impact on public policies towards this group, particularly in Britain.

For people with learning difficulties, there has been a policy priority in both Britain and Sweden to promote independent living. The challenge for policy has been to provide a homely setting for people unable or not wanting to live in a family environment. This may be because parents become frail as they age or are unable or unwilling to cope. The closure of mental institutions in both Britain and Sweden has led to the establishment of supported housing schemes for those leaving the institutions, and these have often taken the form of group homes or other congregate living models, as well as support for residents living in their own homes.

The chapter will follow a similar structure to the previous two, with a focus on policy discourses followed by a description of policy in Britain and Sweden. There follows an evaluation of the forms of supported housing most used for disabled people.

Discourses, lifestyles and identities

A continuing theme in the debate on the appropriate discourse for all of the groups considered here is the respective merits of the medical and the social model of disability (see, for example, Oliver, 1990; Morris, 1993; Barnes and Mercer, 2003). In particular, there is a substantial body of argument against the medical model and putting forward the social model, much of it written by disabled people themselves. The medical model can be summarised as the view that physical disability is a personal problem that is a product of the physical 'abnormalities' of the individual. Therefore, the focus is on treating or alleviating these physical problems by the medical or associated professions. In contrast, advocates of the social model have sought to draw a distinction between impairment and disability. Impairment is seen as the physical limitations of an individual such as the inability to walk. A disability is, for example, the inability to enter a building. In other words, an impairment is a characteristic of the individual body, whereas a disability is a product of the interaction between the body and the physical and social environment. This distinction enables advocates of the social model to focus on the social and economic factors that impact on disability. For example, there has been a structuralist criticism of the primacy of paid work in the capitalist system that disadvantages and stigmatises physically disabled people. The social forces that disadvantage physically disabled people can be thought to constitute oppression through disablism.

A focus in the social model of disability that is particularly relevant to our discussion here is on the physical environment and the way that it can create barriers for some people. Examples may be steps leading into houses or inadequate circulation room inside the house, creating problems for people who need to use a wheelchair. Imrie (1996) argues that 'modern' architecture had a model of an 'ideal man' who was six foot tall, muscular and healthy, around whom buildings were designed. Such a model had no room for people who did not conform to this ideal and led to the creation of rigid and inflexible buildings that excluded or disadvantaged many people. Imrie (1996) also draws attention to the overriding emphasis given to aesthetic considerations in the design of buildings that can background the functional aspects that may be particularly important for disabled people. The importance given to the nature of the physical environment in the social model of disability has had an impact on public policy in Britain and Sweden as we shall see later.

The social model of disability, with its distinction between impairment and disability and its almost total preoccupation with the latter, has been criticised for neglecting the physical body. Indeed, this emphasis has been in direct contrast to the trend in sociology to incorporate concepts of embodiment into sociological analysis. Imrie (1996: 44) poses the question, 'even if the oppressive social relations of disablism were to be transformed, would that necessarily remove the physicality (the reality) of the body?' He argues that there is a false dichotomy between impairment and disability that has led to a neglect of the bodily state of impairment that 'has the capacity to create (physical) pain and discomfort which need not be socially and/ or culturally reproduced or ascribed' (Imrie, 1996: 43). Also:

> surely the socio-political model must recognise that there is a physical state, a physiological status, which really negates any possibility of people with disabilities being afforded equal opportunities and treatment in that their very (physical) differences demand a difference in the way society responds to them and their social, human and physical needs. Indeed, the physicality of the body is too often ignored in such perspectives. (Imrie, 1996: 43)

What is needed is for 'the body to be situated and interpreted as a socio-cultural and biological construction, neither fixed nor unchanging, thus interconnecting social and medical conceptions of disability' (1996: 46).

A model based on the social model of disability that was particularly important in shaping policy towards physically disabled people was the concept of independent living. Originally developed in the US in the 1970s, what became known as the Independent Living Movement was taken up in the 1980s in Britain (Oliver and Barnes, 1998) and was the source of numerous community independent living centres. These centres provided advocacy and peer and other support to disabled people, as well as lobbying for policies such as the Independent Living Fund and, later, direct payments and personal budgets as part of the personalisation agenda. Although it is argued (Glasby, 2012) that the Independent Living Movement and the social model of disability that underpins its beliefs are relevant to people other than those with a physical disability, there has tended to be a reluctance to join forces with groups advocating for people with a learning disability and many older people do not identify with the social model of disability, despite their impairments (Means et al, 2008).

As well as the discourse of disability, the normalisation discourse has been influential in shaping policy for the people considered in this chapter. The concept of normalisation has a complex history. It was first developed in Scandinavia (Nirje, 1969; Bank-Mikkelsen, 1980), where it was defined as 'creating an existence for the mentally retarded as close to normal living conditions as possible' (Bank-Mikkelsen, 1980: 56). This early formulation of the concept was based on the rights of service users and focused on equality in terms of an individual's quality of life. It was based on 'a humanistic and egalitarian value base, emphasising freedom of choice and the right to self-determination' (Perrin and Nirje, 1985: 71). Interestingly, this formulation of the concept did not necessarily challenge the segregation of disabled citizens. Integration was not an end in itself, but only justified if it served as a means of achieving normalisation.

The concept was redefined in North America in the 1970s (Wolfensberger, 1972). This later formulation was not based in notions of human rights, but on a sociological theory of the nature of disadvantage. Normalisation was defined as:

> [the] utilization of means which are as culturally normative as possible, in order to establish and/or maintain personal behaviours and characteristics which are as culturally normative as possible. (Wolfensberger, 1972: 28)

The emphasis on cultural norms, or the later reconceptualisation as socially valued norms and lifestyles, follow from Wolfensberger's adoption of labelling theory to explain disadvantage. The assumption was that the characteristics and behaviour of members of deviant groups are largely determined by the way that society responds to them. In other words, if a person adopts a social role (whether by choice or constraint), it inevitably results in them fulfilling the expectations associated with the role. If the role is not socially valued then nor is the person inhabiting it. Therefore, the aim was to change the label to a more socially valued one, which would alter the characteristics and behaviour of the person.

This formulation of the concept does directly challenge segregation, as without integration individuals cannot be valued as full members of the society. Interestingly, the concept is not based on the human rights or indeed the well-being or freedom of choice of the individual. Wolfensberger was prepared to force integration and socially valued lifestyles on individuals for their own good. Normalisation was defined by those working with disabled people and not those people themselves.

The concept of normalisation was actively promoted by pressure groups associated with people with learning difficulties in Britain in the 1970s and early 1980s and it fitted well with the community care and anti-institution emphasis of the time. The following definition of the concept by Tyne (1982: 151) shows the links with concepts of identity and lifestyle:

> First, helping handicapped people to gain skills and characteristics, and to experience a lifestyle which is valued in our society and to have opportunities for using skills and expressing individuality in choice; secondly, regardless of people's handicaps, providing services in settings and in ways which are valued in our society and supporting people to participate genuinely in the mainstream of life.

One important element of this definition is the social value which is deemed necessary for people to have a positive self-identity and to express this in a lifestyle that is valued and 'mainstream'.

Normalisation was an influential, but strongly contested, concept that held sway for a limited period of time. It was criticised by advocates of the social model of disability, who argued that it overplayed the necessity of impaired people to fit into 'mainstream' life, without placing emphasis on the changes necessary in society to reduce the barriers that led to their disability and reinforced their exclusion. The concept was also criticised for being too vague and difficult to use in practice. What exactly is 'mainstream' or 'normal' life? However, despite the controversy, the essential features of normalisation were incorporated into policy and practice in both Britain and Sweden. This was helped by the existence of tools that provided a rating scale for judging the extent to which a particular service promoted social image and personal competency. This was the forerunner of many different lists of service requirements that have formed the basis of service planning and evaluations of service delivery that were discussed in Chapter Two. There has been little dispute around the issues included in these lists of important principles of policy and practice. However, divorced from their normalisation roots, the concepts chosen seem to lack a unifying rationale. Why these factors and not others?

In the field of mental illness, Maycraft Kall (2010) has identified three important policy discourses in Britain and Sweden. Two of these are the medical and social models of disability outlined above. In mental health policy, the medical model has had more of a lasting impact than in physical disability, and has been the dominant discourse in Britain and Sweden. However, there have been moves in both countries to move towards a social model but movement in practice has been slow. A third discourse that Maycraft Kall (2010) labels the risk discourse has risen in importance, particularly in Britain. This discourse focuses on the risk that people with a mental illness are said to pose to the general population and so places emphasis on the control of behaviour and risk management practices, as well as the exercise of coercion or compulsion towards the mentally ill person in order to reduce perceived risk. In Britain, responsibility for care for people with mental health problems was given to health services rather than social services because of the primary role given to the medical profession in treating illness and concerns over the importance of control of behaviour through medication. Adoption of the medical model did not mean, in practice, that there was no role for other medical professions, such as counsellors, in care for people with mental health problems, particularly in fields such as alcohol and drug abuse. Maycraft Kall (2010) argues that elements of each of the three policy discourses can be found in British government rhetoric. She argues that there was never a clear social disability discourse and there was a marked shift towards the risk discourse over time.

In Sweden, Maycraft Kall (2010) argues that inquiries on mental health policy in 1992 and 2006 both adopted a social disability discourse in framing the problem as being a lack of rights and service entitlements for mentally ill people, but government consistently rejected this approach. Therefore there was no break from the grip of the medical model. Despite the responsibility for mental health issues being transferred from health to social services authorities, the responsibility for psychiatric health care remained with health authorities and this area of responsibility was the one emphasised by governments. Despite this medical emphasis, there was an aim to close existing institutions and to provide services more in keeping with the ethos of normalisation. However, the risk discourse has not achieved the same standing in Sweden as it did in Britain, despite examples of violence highlighted in the media, and the approach was not reflected in government rhetoric, or policy and practice, to the extent that it was in Britain. Therefore Maycraft Kall (2010) characterises the approach in Sweden as following a medical discourse with the social model not being implemented by government in this field.

Housing and support policies for disabled people

Sweden

Since the 1960s, there has been a strong emphasis on closing the larger mental hospitals, as in Britain and other western countries. In 1967, there were nearly 5 psychiatric hospital beds per 1,000 inhabitants, alternative psychiatric treatment was rare and there was little care outside of institutions. Policy was changed in order to reduce the use of hospitals for people with mental health problems and to increase the use and improve the composition of outpatient psychiatric services, as well as increasing the role of social services and health para-professionals such as nurses and psychologists. Nevertheless, community provision of social support did not improve until the responsibility was given to the municipal social services in 1982 and taken from county councils that ran the health services. However, a parliamentary commission of 1992, the Committee on Psychiatric Care, concluded that the efforts of social services were still largely inadequate and were not being provided in a satisfactory manner. The responsibility of municipal social services was clarified through the Mental Health Care Reform, which came into effect in January 1995. The reform was directed towards individuals suffering from severe and long-standing mental illness. The objective was social integration and the best life possible for people with mental health problems on equal terms with the rest of the population. The aim was to bring home to the community the 3,000 people who were in psychiatric hospitals and nursing homes. By 2007 there were no mental hospitals left in Sweden, although there are psychiatric wards in general hospitals that have the capacity to receive about 5,000 patients.

The Independent Living Movement has had a large influence on disability policy in Sweden, which therefore has a strong rights basis. Swedish disability policy is based on the principle of universal equality of dignity and rights. The disability policy aims to achieve full participation and equality. The major legislation that became operative in 1994 was based on several projects in Gothenberg and Stockholm instituted by the Independent Living Movement (Askheim et al, 2014). The objective of the Swedish Act of Support and Services For Persons with Certain Functional Impairments (1993: 387) on support and services to people with certain functional impairments (LSS), and the Assistance Compensation Act (LASS) (1993: 389) (which provides the framework for meeting the costs of personal assistance for certain disabled people) is for people with physical or mental impairments to be able to live like everyone else, mirroring the normalisation discourse. The categories covered by the legislation include: (1) people with learning disabilities, people with autism or conditions similar to autism; (2) people with considerable intellectual disabilities/learning disabilities as a result of a brain injury as adults (acquired brain injury); and (3) people with other durable physical or mental disabilities that are evidently not caused by normal ageing. People over the age of 65 do not qualify for this support unless they were receiving it before they reached this age, in which case support can continue. However, the omission of older people in general is an important difference from the position in Britain, where older people qualify on the same basis as other disabled people through the community care system.

The legislation in Sweden specifies a number of specific forms of assistance that disabled people have a right to receive, including counselling and support, personal assistance, housing with special services, and contact people and companions. There is an independent assessment process that has to adhere to national guidelines and which can be challenged in a court of law. Once assessed as needing specific help, a person has a right to receive this from their local authority which has a duty to provide it whatever the resource constraints (unlike in Britain). Personal assistance is free to the user and since 1997 the costs of up to 20 hours per week are paid for by the municipal authorities and central government pays for any additional hours. Failure to provide the support that is assessed as needed can give rise to fines from central government on the municipal authorities and legal challenges from the individuals concerned. This strong system of legal rights is allied to an important role for user groups in policy formation at both national and local levels and in the design and running of service provision.

An important element of the legal rights given to disabled people is the right to personal assistance, if they are not in supported housing where support is provided as part of the scheme. The majority of people receiving this support in 2010 (60%) came under category 3 above and 38% in category 1 (Askheim et al, 2014). Personal assistance could either be organised by the municipality or as direct payments to the user. The latter could then either retain the responsibility for employing the relevant assistance (hiring and managing the employment themselves) or could hand it over to a cooperative, a private company or another organisation. This means that disabled people in Sweden do have choice over their personal assistants and can directly employ them and control what they do, as in Britain through the direct payments system. However, the choice of direct employment is not taken up by many individuals (only 2.5% in 2010), with 44% using assistants employed by the municipality and 40% 'other service organisations' that can include private companies (Askheim et al, 2014). Since the establishment of the scheme, the number of people receiving personal assistance and the average amount of help received has increased considerably, thus impacting on costs (Clevnert and Johansson, 2007). The government has therefore been examining ways of regulating the system with a view to keeping costs down (Askheim et al, 2014).

A survey of users of personal services was instituted by a government commission in 2005. The results showed that most users had the opportunity to choose their provider from among alternatives as well as to choose the individual assistant, and many had changed their provider at least once (Clevnert and Johansson, 2007). Almost two thirds of respondents said that they could decide which tasks the personal assistant undertook, although this was more common when assistance was provided by a cooperative rather than in provision by the municipality. Clevnert and Johansson (2014: 76) conclude:

> Almost 60% confirmed that the assistance was tailored to their personal needs. More than half of those participating in the study confirmed that they themselves had the 'final say' regarding the help and services they received. There is a pattern throughout the study indicating a higher degree of satisfaction among those using private or cooperative providers, compared to those using public providers. However, on the whole, nearly 90% of the recipients were 'very satisfied' or 'rather satisfied' with the personal assistance

Clevnert and Johansson (2007: 77) argue that personal assistance is very popular in Sweden and has achieved its objectives.

> The reform has increased the opportunity for people with severe disabilities to choose their own way of living, that is, 'to live a life as anybody else,' as it is phrased in the Swedish disability policy. Personal assistance secures rights and equal opportunities for care recipients to make choices concerning their own lives and to have their wishes respected. With a personal assistant, recipients have the right to decide what the assistant will do, when he or she will do it, and how it will be done, as well as from whom the recipients choose to have the assistance. It has increased opportunities for care recipients to live on their own or with family, to study, to work, and to participate in community life. Overall, personal assistance has enhanced the quality of life for people with severe disabilities as well as for their families.

One of the aims of giving municipal authorities the responsibility for disabled people was to further reduce the number of people living in institutions and provide alternative forms of housing and support. As a consequence of these changes, in 1998, only 8% of people with mental health problems lived in an institution, 72% lived in their own homes with support from social services, and 10% lived in supported housing that was the responsibility of municipal social services, usually under the LSS system, which gives people assessed as being in need the right to appropriate accommodation and support, and specifies the forms it should take. For example, shared housing should consist of a maximum of six places per scheme, although some schemes have exceeded this limit in practice. For people with learning disabilities, Sweden has led the world in deinstitutionalisation, with the result that traditional institutions no longer exist and the law enshrines the right to community services (Mansell, 2006). The early alternatives to institutions were large residential homes, but these gave way to group homes of 3–8 people with high support needs living with staff. More recently, there has been a move towards supporting people in individual apartments, with the support separated from the housing accommodation.

Debate in disability policy has been around the idea of a continuum of care, in which people are placed in different settings according to their condition and their changing needs. In some cases this has meant in practice people moving their residential setting as their needs change, for better or worse. In others it just refers to the need for an array of services to meet different needs. As well as hospitals and other institutions such as hostels for drug users, the continuum can include training flats and group homes with 24-hour care, as well as an array of domiciliary social and health services. In group homes, each individual has their own apartment and holds their own lease but has access to a service base, usually in their own building. In training flats the lease is held by the municipal authorities and residents are expected to show they can live independently before being given their own lease. The continuum of care requires the effective matching of patients to the appropriate treatments (as in the staircase model of homelessness provision). Critics of the continuum of care approach argue that it is unnecessary and disruptive for individuals to move through the system from setting to setting. Instead they propose a system of supportive services provided to individuals living in normal residential settings in the community. They disapprove of the idea of an array of residential 'settings' or 'services' offering 'beds' for individuals for whom the goal is normalised life in the community as 'normal' citizens. They argue for support for people in their own homes.

In practice, a number of forms of accommodation and support are available in different municipal areas. For example, in Malmo there are shared houses primarily for those with learning disabilities and mental health problems. Some are in the form of grouped bungalows and others are in blocks of flats. The provision includes individual bedrooms coupled with common leisure, eating and cooking areas. The aim has been to make these look like ordinary housing, but this has been difficult in some cases where they have been created by reshaping old nursing homes and have retained an institutional feel and look. Each shared scheme has 24-hour support and does not preclude people because of drug or alcohol problems. The alternative that is being increasingly pursued is for satellite apartments in mainstream housing, owned by the municipal housing company, private landlords or cooperatives, and leased to the social services department, which then offers a licence to the resident. Apartments have an alarm system and appropriate support is provided in the person's own home according to an individual personal support plan. The key to this provision is said to be building trust between the support workers, the resident, the landlords and the neighbours, but neighbour problems have been few. Malmo also has a programme to increase the occupation of disabled people by working with the aspirations of people towards work and hobbies with the aim of promoting integration through purposeful activity and work as an alternative to traditional day centres.

In Gothenburg, there are several supported living environments for people with mental health or alcohol or drug problems, many associated with the homelessness services reviewed in the previous chapter, including the Housing First team. Most forms of accommodation fit into the staircase model discussed in the Chapter Seven. Other forms of supported housing included block schemes, where a number of apartment blocks were dedicated to people with a mental health problem. As an illustration, one scheme started as a perceived need for an alternative to provision in a nearby psychiatric clinic 30 years ago. In 2014 it consisted of 108 flats of between 50 and 60 square metres, with two rooms and a kitchen and bathroom. There was also a communal flat, used as a base by the eight support workers, who were largely trained as psychiatric nurses or social workers. The ethos of the scheme was the idea of a therapeutic community and residents receive counselling as well as practical help and training with living skills. There are many occupational activities and clubs, and organised outings. The apartments are unfurnished, allowing residents to bring their own furnishings, and residents pay rent for the accommodation, although they may receive a housing allowance. Food is provided for those who want it and residents can drop in to the communal flat at any time. Residents either arrive from the psychiatric clinic or through the homelessness system. It is hoped and expected that residents will move on into a sub-leased mainstream apartment, and about 10% do each year, with about half of these continuing to receive support for a transitional period. It is estimated that 20% of the residents who have been in the scheme a long time will not leave, and a number of people have been in the scheme for over 20 years. The scheme is physically isolated from other residential properties and has few links with local people. Volunteering is not a feature of the scheme and services are not provided to others living nearby.

In summary, provision in Sweden is based on a strong base of individual rights, is not resource constrained and has a clear normalisation discourse at its heart. User groups are given a prominent position in policy and service provision. Provision has been moved out of institutions and into linked homes and training flats where residents have their own apartments, but there is a service area and communal facilities, as well as into people's own homes.

Britain

In 1976 there were 50,000 people with learning disabilities in institutions in Britain and this had been reduced to 4,000 25 years later. The reasons for this reduction included the rise of disability rights as part of the human rights agenda, increasing liberality and economic growth; scandals concerning conditions in long-stay institutions; an increased focus on the learning possibilities for individuals; and the availability of smaller shared housing models. Deinstitutionalisation was a major national programme, but it was implemented locally by health and social services agencies, so there was considerable variation in the type and extent of services provided. The government document *Better services for the mentally handicapped*, published in 1971, (Department of Health and Social security, 1971) set the vision for the deinstitutionalisation and the direction of policy. Nevertheless the vision was criticised as being essentially negative in the sense that there was a clear idea of the desire to move away from institutional care, but no clear idea of the alternative. During the 1970s, most people with mild learning disabilities were placed into existing services such as hostels, bed and breakfast accommodation, group supported accommodation, and independent living and family placement schemes. People with severe learning difficulties usually found themselves in community health hospitals, which had between 12 and 30 spaces. This form of health provision was increasingly challenged during the 1980s, with the growth in influence of the normalisation discourse. By the end of the 1980s, the dominant model was of group, staffed homes in a domestic setting, but cluster or campus housing also existed (that is, accommodation clustered together, often in the grounds of a hospital, with a hospital emphasis) as well as the remaining large institutions. According to Emerson et al (2005) in England in 2001, 6% of people with severe learning disabilities were in National Health Service long-stay institutions and a further 6% were in campus or cluster homes. Ten per cent were in local authority homes, but this was reducing because of the quasi-market reforms introduced in the 1990s. Fifty-seven per cent were in the independent sector, mostly in group homes of four people upwards, with the average size of home being 9.5 people per home. This picture had not changed much by 2004/5, with only 18% of people with learning difficulties living alone or with a partner or in 'supported living' (Emerson et al, 2005). A review by Mencap in 2011 found that 38% of people with a learning disability lived with family or friends, 22% in a registered care home, 16% in supported accommodation, 12% in social housing, and 3% in private renting (Mencap, 2012).

During the early 2000s, the policy focus in Britain has been on the personalisation agenda, which is based on the idea that all service users should be able to exert choice and control over their services and their lives. It is built on the former direct payments system instituted in 1996 and 'is driven by the need to progress independent living outcomes for all disabled people' (Williams, 2013: 21). The major operational tool in personalisation is the 'personal budget', that is, the resources that can be managed on a personal basis and that are set according to the assessed needs of the individual. Disabled people can get help from family and from organisations established in order to support disabled people in planning for their own social support. However, there have been continuing doubts among some people about the capacity of people with learning difficulties to make these decisions for themselves and concerns about the risk of independent living for this group of people. These doubts have found their way into policy and practice with the result that they have often been the ones left out in the move to independent living (Williams, 2013). The 2001 learning disability strategy, *Valuing people* (Department of Health, 2001) laid out four key principles of provision, namely: rights, independence, choice and control. However Williams (2013) argues that it did not take a very strong line on housing, although it did stress the need to close the remaining long-stay care hospitals, mentioned joint working between housing and social services at a local level, and prioritised 'supported living'. In the revised strategy of 2009, *Valuing people now* (Department of Health, 2010), however, housing was identified as a priority action.

There is little agreement about the appropriate models of living for people with learning difficulties. Williams (2013) discusses the model of 'intentional communities', which are 'places set apart from mainstream society for people with learning difficulties to have a home suited to their own needs', which could be in a 'village community', mirroring the retirement villages for older people. This model of segregation is controversial. On the one hand it is argued that living with people with similar skills and abilities enables closer social ties between like-minded friends, and can provide an appropriate learning environment in which the residents are sheltered from what can be hostile forces in the 'mainstream' world. On the other hand, there is a distrust of segregated settings because of the history of the old isolated asylums, and it is argued that the ethos of normalisation can only be achieved through integrated settings.

Thus the alternative to intentional communities is reflected in the growing trend to 'supported living', where the concept is based on detaching the type and level of support provided from dependence on where someone lives. In other words, the appropriate support should be assessed and provided in whichever setting an individual chooses to live.

An interesting model of supported housing for disabled people is the 'KeyRing' concept of small networks of residents (usually of 10 people) living in independent housing within walking distance of each other. The housing can be rented from the council or a housing association, or in some instances is owned by the resident (perhaps bought for them by parents) or is shared ownership. In one of these houses is a volunteer support worker who lives rent free and who has experience of interacting with vulnerable people and can offer informal support and advice and bring the residents in the network together to maximise peer support. A key role of the volunteer is to mobilise community resources and to link residents with their local neighbourhood. In addition, each resident usually has a support plan, often through a personal budget, and individualised support is offered by the professional support team from KeyRing, who also work to mobilise community resources where possible. KeyRing was initially formulated for people with learning disabilities, but now has networks for people with mental health problems, drug and alcohol abuse, and even for people with autism. Residents do not always have to move to join a network as networks are created around existing accommodation wherever possible. Where moves are made, care is taken to ensure that the resident is not giving up vital social networks and community ties. Networks are usually commissioned by health or social services authorities who usually provide some financial support. KeyRing has over a hundred networks operating in about fifty local authority areas. This innovative and (as we shall see) successful model seems to be a kind of domiciliary provision, although it has some similarities to the core and cluster model (see Chapter One).

The ability to live at home is dependent on many things, but, as we shall see in the later discussion of 'home' the condition and facilities of the property are crucial for disabled people, many of whom are on low incomes and so may have problems in affording improvements or repairs and may lack the experience or training to be able to manage the improvement process. There have been two major areas of policy to deal with this. The first is regulation to enforce standards in new-build property. Means et al (2008) discuss the difference between lifetime standards and visitability. The former, which was devised and publicised by the Joseph Rowntree Foundation, is an attempt to stipulate standards that make access to and use of new property suitable for disabled people, based on principles of sustainability, flexibility and adaptability of design that caters for changing needs over the life course (see Cobbold, 1997). But, as Means et al (2008) point out, the standards do not allow wheelchair users to access all the areas of their accommodation and so would not meet the needs of all people without further modifications. The alternative approach was based on the concept of visitability, in order to make properties accessible for disabled people. The government did not accept the lifetime homes approach, largely because of arguments from housebuilders about the additional costs involved. Instead they implemented changes to building regulations, largely along visitability lines, although only 3.4% of homes surveyed in the 2007 *English house condition survey* met visitability standards and only 0.5% met the lifetime homes standards (CLG, 2009b). More recently, with the low rate of housebuilding and the desire to reduce regulation, further progress in meeting these standards has come under threat.

Hence the predominant emphasis is still on the adaptation of individual properties to meet the needs of individual disabled people. The major policy instrument to deal with this in Britain has been the means-tested Disabled Facilities Grant (DFG). In a review of this programme, Heywood (2001) showed how minor adaptations such as grab rails were appreciated by disabled people and had an impact on different elements of their lives, but major alterations (such as the provision of stairlifts or accessible bathrooms) were life-changing for many people. Despite this proven impact, the DFG programme has been underfunded and remains complex and subject to delays in assessment and provision. A review by Heywood (2005) drew attention to the difficulties caused by the means test and the restrictive maximum grant level. As a consequence, many people who would benefit from adaptations do not have them (Hemingway, 2011).

Well-being in supported housing models

The affordances of home

The deinstitutionalisation policy has not always resulted in bringing to an end the worst aspects of institutional living. As Emerson et al (2005: 40) point out:

> Closure of large institutions has not therefore resulted in the end of institutional life. Aspects of institutional living

that still persist in residential homes have been flagged up in robust quantitative studies, and include a life dominated by staff rotas, lack of choice over who you live with. (Emerson et al, 2005: 40)

There are said to be fewer opportunities for community contacts and activities, and a sense that the house belongs to the staff, not to the people who live there. Bigby et al (2012) examined the culture in group homes and found a clear difference from institutions, although they still found examples of rigidity of routine, block treatment of residents, depersonalisation, and social difference between staff and residents that characterised institutional life.

In a study by Agneta Kanold of group homes for people with a learning disability in Sweden noted by Sahlin (1999), it was found that the provision of individual apartments rather than just rooms meant that less support was needed. This was partly because residents learned to cope by themselves and so developed their own abilities, and also because residents could retreat for privacy and were less likely to experience friction with other residents over the use of space or facilities.

Borg et al (2006: 252) point out the value of home for people with severe mental illnesses and its value in helping recovery. For those with severe mental illness, having a home – either temporary or permanent – may take on special significance through reminding the homemaker of who s/he was prior to the illness, the freedom to establish fulfilling routines based on who one feels her/ himself to be currently, and the excitement of pursuing dreams and goals for the future.

> although informants in this study did not always feel appreciated or even recognized within their communities, they affirmed that managing the 'little things' in everyday life – such as walking one's dog, writing emails, or daily prayer – often proffered the faith and energy to move on in life. As a stage for such activities, having a home may be critical for maintaining a sense of personal and life continuity while living among 'normal' others in the community. This is, of course, distinct from the imposed continuity of institutional life. (Borg et al, 2006: 253)

Home was seen as a place of personal growth and development, a place of control, a place to balance privacy and social life, and a place to long for and dream about.

In a review of studies of congregate living arrangements in different countries for people with a mental illness, Nelson et al (2007: 91) concluded: 'The results of these studies suggest that residents who live in supported housing, particularly in their own apartments, report more choice, control, and privacy compared with those in group living arrangements.' In their own study in Canada, they found that being supported in their own apartments gave people with mental illness more choice and control over their housing and support situation, and that this had an impact on their overall subjective quality of life. They conclude:

> Our findings suggest that how we deliver housing services and the type of housing that is provided are both important. By promoting choice over where and with whom people live, both subjective quality of life and community functioning can be improved. (Nelson et al, 2007 p.98)

In their study of young people with mental health problems in Sweden, Olin et al (2011) found that there was a real appreciation of home as a sanctuary and a place of control. For some people, home could also be experienced as a lonely and isolated place and the young people varied in the extent to which they used their home for socialising, depending on their lifestyles, and some used places such as the day centre to interact with others.

Hemingway (2011) points to the importance of home to many disabled people because of the large amount of time spent there, as accessing employment can be difficult and mobility outside of the home may be restricted. A house with an appropriate physical layout and facilities can enable a disabled person to live independently by reducing the need for support and offering the person control over their daily life. Hemingway (2011) cites examples of the way that inappropriate housing can make sustaining employment difficult by hindering necessary daily activities such as dressing and washing, and can create a lack of privacy for intimate activities such as using the toilet and bathing. Some adaptations can give an institutional feel to a home and can signal difference and dependence even if they do allow practical activities. The conclusion for disabled people is that a suitably equipped house with a layout that affords necessary activities for the individual concerned and does not stigmatise or brand them as different is the foundation of the well-being of the resident.

Home is associated with having one's own private place, somewhere to call one's own, including stability and the ability to choose and put your own stamp on the place you live. But Williams argues:

These notions of home are often totally left out of the equation for people with learning disabilities, and privacy is very hard to maintain. Other people, especially support workers are likely to have their own key to the front door, or to intrude without invitation into people's own private rooms (14% recorded this happening in Emerson et al, 2005). (2013: 141)

In the KeyRing project, where residents lived in ordinary housing in a local network including a community-living volunteer, there is evidence that the opportunity to live in their own home was one of the key attractions for residents. In an evaluation of a number of networks in Walsall for people who previously had been in residential care (Alder, 2012), residents valued the increased freedom, control and independence that they achieved. Their own house was considered to be better than residential living in terms of space, safety, quietness, nicer neighbourhood and the ability to escape from fellow residents.

In summary, there is substantial evidence that the affordances of home are much greater for people living in their own home than for those in institutions or in shared housing, where some of the features of institutional living persist.

Affordances of neighbourhood

Emerson et al (2001) argue that there is consistent evidence that greater choice and self-determination is available in smaller and less institutional settings. Residents in such settings have larger and more active social networks, and more engagement in community based activities (see for example Walsh et al, 2010). Residents in group homes or other non-domiciliary environments were more likely to have a greater number of community activities; they were also more likely to have had their home vandalised, however, and to be thought at risk (Emerson et al, 2001).

Olin and Ringsby Jansson (2008) studied the design and use of communal facilities in three group homes in Sweden for people with learning disabilities. In each scheme residents had their own apartment but the communal facilities had very different uses. In one they were used just for group activities organised by staff and this they called 'the restrictive room'. In the second, called 'the familiar room', residents were encouraged to use the room for informal activities and socialising. In the third scheme the room (called 'the neutral room') was slightly differentiated spatially from the individual apartments and was visible from the outside, which meant that it was used more by people from outside and so encouraged more integration. The study shows the importance of the design of individual schemes as well as the attitudes of the staff in influencing the extent of integration within the scheme and with the local neighbourhood.

In a reflection of the debate on integration or segregation Emerson (2004) argues that 'intentional communities' can deliver gains from segregation, enabling residents to make more like-minded friends, and this can be supportive and meaningful for some people. Emerson (2004) shows that people with a learning difficulty living on their own or with their family are much more likely to live in areas classified as 'hard pressed' or 'of moderate means' in the ACORN categorisation than the population as a whole. Thus it is likely that they will live in poorer neighbourhoods with fewer facilities and are likely to feel less safe. Nevertheless, only 17% said that they felt unsafe at night, although 54% of those who were unhappy with where they lived said that they did not like the area. People with learning difficulty in supported accommodation were much more likely to live in prosperous areas, but generally were found in all kinds of different types of area. Despite this, the proportion not liking the local area was only slightly less than for those not in supported housing.

In a study of young people recovering from mental health problems in Australia, Duff et al (2012: 2) concluded that:

> the lived experience of housing security for youth in recovery is as much a function of one's community attachments – the sense that one belongs in a community, and has a range of connections to local people and places to sustain this belonging – as it is a product of the tenure and/or amenity of one's home.

They highlighted the social, material and affective links with the neighbourhood that reinforced the feeling of security in the home and was critical to recovery.

Olin et al. (2011) found that young people with mental health problems in their research in Sweden enjoyed the local neighbourhood, where they felt they could blend in and meet others, both acquaintances and strangers. Different types of contacts were made, such as acknowledging contacts, greeting contacts and helping contacts, and sometimes these contacts developed into strong ties.

In the KeyRing scheme, residents who had been in residential care reported greater contact with family and the local neighbourhood

(Alder, 2012). A previous evaluation noted in Department of Health (2009) notes that KeyRing residents had strong links in their local neighbourhoods and used community facilities.

Well-being, personal control, identity and self-esteem

In a study by Emerson et al (2005) of those in supported housing, two thirds said they had no choice over who they lived with and 54% said they had no choice over where they lived. However, 93% said they were happy with where they lived.

Emerson et al (2005) found little evidence that what he labelled as 'community settings' (which meant non–institutional living) resulted in improvements in challenging behaviour, or that residents were more likely to gain friends, or get a paid job. They had more personal possessions, however, used less medication, expressed greater satisfaction about their home, enjoyed greater choice over everyday matters and used community facilities more. Williams (2013) argues that many communal living settings are hardly distinguishable from residential care, and that residents still only had control over small everyday choices and not over major decisions 'in some cases residential homes have transformed into supported living arrangements with very few noticeable changes for residents themselves' (Williams, 2013: 143).

One argument put forward by Emerson et al (2005) and Mansell (2006) is that there needs to be a greater focus on the support arrangements than on where they are delivered. Mansell (2006) points to the variability of community settings in terms of their success in improving well-being and argues that the attitude of staff is the key feature in success. We will return to this in the conclusion.

In the KeyRing project, residents who were living in their own homes reported greater control over their lives and a growing ability, with support, to undertake everyday activities. Staff reported personal outcomes being almost universally achieved and even people with high support needs could live independently in this setting, with growing independence and a consequent reduction in support. It was reported that residents felt ownership over their lives and the support available to them (Alder, 2012).

Conclusion

Policies for disabled people in Britain and Sweden have followed similar paths, although there have been differences of degree. Sweden has been more rigorous in closing the old institutions, but, as in Britain, has created some new forms of supported housing in the form of congregate living environments that have some similarities with the institutions they have replaced. In both countries there have been recent moves towards independent living and this is now the major focus. In Sweden, user groups have a substantial influence over policy and provision, and disabled people have the opportunity to choose their personal assistant, employ them and control their work, although few disabled people actually employ the assistant directly themselves. Britain has taken a consumerist approach through the personalisation agenda. In Britain, personalisation has been an important policy that has given many disabled people more control over their support arrangements and, therefore, makes independent living easier to accomplish. However, there are many barriers to independent living in both countries, but Sweden has the advantage of the better condition and design of its housing stock and its more extensive domiciliary services.

The evidence cited in the chapter shows that, for people with disabilities, the affordances of home and neighbourhood are crucial for their well-being. For example, it was found that a feeling of a secure home and neighbourhood was crucial to the recovery of young people with mental health problems. In most cases (the exception being in learning disability, which we will return to shortly) it is clear that well-being is improved in home-like settings, such as an apartment, rather than in group or congregate living. In the mental health field, for example, there is considerable evidence that living in one's own apartment results in a better subjective quality of life. In group settings there is evidence that some elements of institutionalised living are still prevalent, even though in a watered-down form, and this form of supported housing is more closely linked to a social control agenda and conditionality.

In the field of learning disability, some reviews have found mixed evidence of the impact of differences in the forms of community living on the well-being of the residents. Emerson et al (2005) and Mansell (2006) argue that the ethos and culture of the support may be more crucial to well-being outcomes than the particular setting. The evidence from the KeyRing scheme in Britain, however, seems to show that this particular setting, which exemplifies the best aspects of the domiciliary model, does have an impact on the well-being of residents. The Emerson finding is a useful reminder that inappropriate support can undermine the best of settings, especially for those who are most in need, and so the primary focus should be on the way that this support is provided. However, the argument of this book is that, if the setting is right (in the sense of providing the affordances of home and neighbourhood) and is detached from the support, which therefore can be personalised, changed and controlled without changing the setting, then the focus does fall on the elements of support that aid or hinder well-being. Of course, attention is also focused on the factors that can prevent the setting from being appropriate, such as inadequate housing or unsafe neighbourhoods. The key point is that these are mainstream issues that depend on mainstream health, care and housing policies.

The KeyRing project in Britain seems to incorporate all that is best about models of supported housing. It provides residents with their own home, and with informal and formal neighbourhood support as well as professional support for those who want it. This form of supported housing puts the resident in control of their situation while providing the support needed to live a full life.

NINE

Conclusion

The book has described the main models of supported housing in Britain and Sweden for the groups taken as examples, and has evaluated these models using a framework built on concepts of well-being and the affordances of home and neighbourhood. Some conclusions that relate to older people, homeless people, and people with disabilities have been reached in the individual chapters. The aim in this final chapter is to draw some general conclusions on the wider issues. The chapter begins with a comparison of Britain and Sweden. The comparative part of the book started in Chapter Five with a discussion of welfare regimes and the position of the two countries in this categorisation. This section will reflect on the welfare regimes approach and comment on the position and trajectories of the two countries in the light of the evidence presented in the book.

The chapter continues with a discussion of the discourses that are associated with policy and provision, and will reflect on similarities and differences between the two countries. Also, the chapter will focus on examples showing the impact of discourse in shaping policy and provision, and the agents that attempt to influence this. The section will attempt to answer some questions on the existence of particular forms of provision. For example, why have extra-care housing and foyers been adopted in Britain, despite being expensive forms of provision that do not maximise the well-being of residents? In Sweden, the continuance of the staircase model as the cornerstone of provision for homeless people is discussed. Although it is under threat from the Housing First approach, it is still the predominant form of supported housing provision for homeless people.

The focus of the chapter then moves on to the well-being framework that is used in the book to evaluate forms of supported housing. This section will reflect on the usefulness of this framework and its future application.

The penultimate section reflects on the evaluation of the different models of supported housing. In the individual chapters, conclusions have been reached on appropriate forms of supported housing for the people considered there. In this section, the focus is on consideration of the value of the general models. It is concluded that some models are better than others at increasing the well-being of the residents.

This discussion leads to a final consideration of the future of supported housing. Based on the findings here, what should it look like in the future and are there general philosophies that should underpin policy and provision?

Welfare regimes in Britain and Sweden

In Chapter Five the concept of welfare regimes was introduced based on the work of Esping-Andersen (1990). The underlying assumption was that countries made political choices that determined the relationship between state, market and family, and that these choices varied between countries or groups of countries. Britain and Sweden are usually categorised as being in different groups, with Sweden being in the social democratic category and Britain in the liberal category. The analysis of housing and support in the two countries shows that this general picture needs to be modified in a number of ways.

The welfare regimes are ideal types and so do not reflect the position in any one country (or even any particular country). We have seen that Sweden never has been the epitome of the social democratic approach and Britain seems to defy simple characterisation in its mix of universal state provision of some public services within a neoliberal economy. In addition, one of the criticisms of the welfare regimes approach is that it minimises the differences between countries in the same category. The strength of the approach is that it highlights the influence of political choice and political ideologies in shaping public policies. Nevertheless, it can only be used as a starting point in the study of individual countries.

Another criticism of the welfare regimes approach has been that is lacks a dynamic dimension. In other words, it freezes the situation in time. As we have seen in the field of housing and support, the situation in both countries is changing rapidly. In general, both countries are becoming more unequal in the distribution of incomes, although from very different bases. Housing systems in both countries are becoming more individualised and market based. In Sweden there is an ongoing debate about provision for homeless people as reflected in the staircase and the Housing First models that have very different underpinning philosophies and discourses. In Britain, the political project of 'austerity' has resulted in substantial cuts to public services in general and support services in particular. The key point is that the states are continually changing over time in their mix of market, state and family, and that the welfare regime approach tends to overlook this.

It can be argued that both states are moving in a similar direction, towards a more market- oriented system. However, the changes are not the same and the starting points are very different. For example, the analysis of the housing systems characterised both countries as having 'monstrous hybrids' of state and market that had emerged over time because of the path dependent nature of change. In other words, existing social institutions and cultures have shaped both the nature of current provision and also the nature of change. Although housing systems in both countries are becoming more market oriented, they still have unique institutions that mean that the situation in each country is different. This is not to say that common problems do not exist as both countries have problems of affordability and housing shortage, particularly in the rented sectors. There is also substantial variation between different sectors and forms of provision. For example, the housing field has been pushed towards the market faster than support services, and provision for older people faster than homelessness services. The lessons for future research using the welfare regimes approach are the need to take into account path dependence and the direction of travel of the different countries.

What can we say about Britain and Sweden? Sweden clearly has some of the legacies of a social democratic welfare state. It stands out from Britain in the extent of its basic health and social services and, as we shall see later, this makes it more possible to pursue flexible home-based services when this universal provision is in place. Nevertheless, the remnants of the social democratic welfare state are shown by the paternalism and social control in the 'staircase model' and in the relative lack of the individualisation of service planning and provision. Disabled people have the right to choose their personal assistant and to employ them and control their work. Nevertheless, this mechanism deserves to be expanded to encompass the idea of personal budgets and to be offered to other categories such as older people, as it is in Britain.

The major criticism of the Swedish housing system is the lack of priority given to vulnerable people. The universalist system worked well in a situation like in the 1970s when the supply of housing was plentiful and there was a tenure–neutral subsidy system. However, the withdrawal of the supply side subsidies and the increasing bias towards owner occupation has left problems of affordability and of access for vulnerable households. The increasing commercialisation of municipal housing companies has added to these problems. In addition, income inequality has risen recently in Sweden, which will make access for low-income people more difficult unless they are given priority. For people unable to wait for rented accommodation, such as immigrants and homeless people, as well as many other vulnerable people, there are few housing options unless they can gain access to the 'secondary housing system' run by municipal social services authorities. The existence of this secondary system is fundamentally problematic. It is partial in scope, only covering some vulnerable people and leaving others without help. It encourages the special needs discourse that all people with support needs have needs that are different or 'special' and so is segregationist and potentially stigmatising. The system drives the use of inappropriate models of supported housing that do not maximise the well-being of the residents. An example here is the assumption in the system that all homeless people have support needs (as we saw in Chapter Seven). An urgent need in Sweden is to find a way to enable access to mainstream rented sectors for vulnerable people that are not segregationist and stigmatising. At present the lack of this access mechanism leads to constraints on the Housing First response to homelessness and the silting up of the 'staircase', resulting in few vulnerable people making it into the mainstream housing sectors.

In Britain, the personalisation agenda, including the use of personal budgets, could be interpreted as a move towards neoliberalism or, alternatively, as a core element of a welfare state that improves the well-being of its citizens, or a mixture of both. Whatever the interpretation, the evidence is that it does increase the control that people in need of support can exert over their lives. Sweden has been slower to adopt this approach and this has reduced the flexibility of its housing and support options.

In Britain, there are mechanisms for the integration of vulnerable people into the mainstream housing system, such as through the homelessness mechanisms or the priority given to housing need in the allocation processes of social landlords. However, the same 'special needs' discourse exists, and the general failures of housing policy to provide enough affordable and quality housing in the right places to meet need is reflected in the problems that many vulnerable people have in accessing appropriate housing, as was evident in the preceding chapters. Britain is characterised by a housing stock that is older and of a smaller size, a shortage of new housing and relatively poor accessibility, and other physical conditions compared with Sweden. In particular, the private rented sector provides poor conditions, at high rents, and insecurity, with short leases and few enforceable rights for tenants or landlords. Homeless people who have been housed by local authorities in this sector have found it difficult to enjoy the affordances of home, as was shown in Chapter Seven. In addition, Britain suffers from a higher level of income inequality that makes access more difficult for low-income people. In support services, the availability of domiciliary services has been declining with the imposition of substantial financial cutbacks following the government adoption of the discourse of 'austerity'. In Britain, therefore, vulnerable people can be forced into supported housing in order to receive support services, when it would be cheaper and more conducive to their well-being to provide these services in their own homes.

The discourses of supported housing

The examples of supported housing from Britain and Sweden described in the book show how discourses shape the nature of the solutions to the problems faced by vulnerable people. An interesting example is the contrast between the staircase and Housing First models of accommodation and support for homeless people. The staircase model is based on a view of homeless people as dependent and undeserving. People have to demonstrate their capacity to live independently and to show that they are deserving of a place in mainstream society by conforming to rules of behaviour such as abstinence from drugs. This does not mean that people are not treated with dignity and respect and, in many cases, love, but that the initial assumption is that people have failings that have to be remedied through support and training from others. In this model, power resides predominantly with those who plan and provide the support, as they are the ones who have to be satisfied that a move up the staircase is appropriate and deserved. Hence, the model tends to be associated with lower-status service users, where there is deemed to be a societal interest in controlling their behaviour. In turn, this discourse tends to be associated with models of supported housing that are segregated (particularly on the bottom rungs of the ladder) and give fewer accommodation rights to the residents. Examples are congregate, group housing or supported housing that is based on apartment blocks with support on site and some communal facilities, as described in Chapters Seven and Eight. An example in Britain of such an approach is that of foyers, where young homeless people live in a shared scheme and receive training in independent living and support to overcome their problems in order to earn a mainstream tenancy. These models of supported housing tend to afford fewer of the affordances of home and neighbourhood than others, and have a tendency to get 'silted up' as residents find it difficult to move out and on to mainstream living.

The competing approach is that epitomised by Housing First. In this model, it is assumed that homeless people have the right and the ability to live in ordinary housing, and this is always the first priority. The philosophy of support is to enable people to take control of their own lives and to offer help and support when and in the form requested by the resident, in the belief that effective change has to come from the person themselves and cannot be enforced from the outside, and that being treated well will reinforce the self-esteem and self-confidence that is needed for change to take place. Hence this discourse empowers residents rather than service providers. Housing First uses domiciliary or core and cluster models of supported housing that offer greater affordances of home and neighbourhood.

In Britain, the two competing discourses are not so clear cut and tend to be mixed in practice, reflecting the mix in the legislation between the maximalist and minimalist discourses. For some homeless people with a right to permanent housing (the deserving), the domiciliary models are the ones used, even if the short-term outcome may be a stay in bed and breakfast accommodation or, long-term, in unsatisfactory private rented housing. For those who do not have the legal right to permanent housing (the undeserving), other forms of supported housing are brought into play, including foyers, hostels and shared living schemes that form the British equivalent of the staircase.

For other service users, such as disabled and older people, the British concept of personalisation is a contrast to the staircase approach. The aims of personalisation are to put the service user in control of their own support and enable them to organise the support in a way that fits in with their own lifestyles and priorities. Personalisation of support enables people to choose housing options that maximise their well-being and offer more affordances of home and neighbourhood. It enables people to stay in their homes or to move on the basis of their housing situation, rather than having to move in order to receive adequate support. Of course, the actual impact of the personalisation discourse and policy depend on the context of implementation, which includes factors such as the housing options available. We will consider this in more detail later.

The main point of this section is to show the force of discourses of supported housing and their impact on the lives of people, through the options that are made available to them and the way they are treated. Well-being is not maximised in situations where people are not in control of their own housing and support situations and, in some discourses, this control is moderated by the belief that the state has an interest in exerting control to ensure adherence to expected modes of behaviour. This applies to some labelled categories more than others, with young people and those with mental health problems being most often included because of their closeness to the labour market and the perception that they may present a risk to others. It is interesting that examples of this kind of discourse and policy are found in both Sweden and Britain, but in different situations. In Britain, young people are a category subject to substantial control, but the personalisation agenda has enabled many older and disabled people to control their circumstances to an extent that is not common for their counterparts in Sweden. The individualism of the neoliberal paradigm can have advantages for vulnerable people in this situation, although this is of course substantially offset by the inequality that besets neoliberal regimes.

It is interesting and illuminating that in the field of supported housing for older people, where the policy discourses in Britain and Sweden are very similar, so are the supported housing options available. In both countries there is a move away from institutional living and a policy priority to allow older people to remain in their own homes. In terms of supported housing options, there are three major differences. The first is the growth of retirement villages in the British context, which have not emerged in Sweden. The second is the different circumstances facing older people living in their own homes, with the greater availability of domiciliary services and the more widespread adoption of higher quality housing standards in Sweden being reflected in the experience of residents. Third, the popularity among policy makers of the extra-care model in Britain is not shared in Sweden, where similar models have been shunned and, where they exist, have been largely reserved for older people with dementia.

The case of extra-care housing is an interesting and enlightening one. Its evolution from the recently unpopular (with policy makers) model of sheltered housing was described in Chapter Six. Its roots signal the similarities of the critiques of both forms of provision. Both have been considered inflexible, to be poor value for money and unclear in their objectives and in who they are meant for in terms of the different needs and lifestyles of older people. So why was extra-care housing developed and why has it received strong government backing? It could be argued that it was considered to be part of the desire to avoid the expense of institutional living. But the evidence is that, at best, it only delays the need for institutional living and is a very expensive way of doing this. An additional explanation lies in the interests of the providers of supported housing. Faced with a move away from the model of sheltered housing, providers such as housing associations and other voluntary bodies could see their role diminishing and so adopted the extra-care model to sustain their businesses. Another example of this may be the provision of foyers for young people that have been pushed hard by providers and their joint body, the Foyer Federation. This interpretation illustrates the strength of the path dependence theory of housing development mentioned in Chapter Five. It also draws attention to the fact that that policy discourses are created and sustained through the political process on the basis of political ideologies and party interests, and also that the policy process includes other actors, such as the providers, who may be acting according to their own perceived beliefs and interests. It is perhaps not a coincidence that the models of supported housing that seem to be most subject to the provider interest are ones close to the institutional end of the spectrum, tend to be inflexible in terms of the services provided and, as a consequence, are more likely to fit residents to the provision rather than changing the provision to suit the needs, lifestyles and preferences of the residents. An example of this is the allocation policies of sheltered and extra-care housing that have been built around the idea of a 'balance' between so-called fit and frail older people in order to avoid too much pressure on the support staff. Another example is the choice of young people to enter foyers on the basis of their perceived readiness to benefit from the services on offer.

The impact of social control discourses and policies on the housing and support options available to vulnerable people merits an important political discussion of the need for such control. Is it necessary? Exactly what needs to be controlled and why? Is it possible to minimise the extent of control or the number of people subject to it? Can discourses such as personalisation and Housing First be extended in their scope to a wider number of people and maybe to labelled categories such as young people? The restriction of social control discourses would change the pattern of supported housing options available, as it is clear that general policy discourses set the context for the supported housing picture.

These discourses not only have an impact on the models of provision but also on the philosophies embedded in the way that the schemes are run and, consequently, on outcomes. For example, it was argued in Chapter Eight that the regime or philosophy of care and support, based on discourse and power relations, has an important impact on outcomes for people with learning disabilities, whatever the supported housing setting.

Well-being as an evaluation criterion

Before looking at the results of the evaluation of different forms of provision it is worthwhile reflecting on the use of the framework of well-being used in the book and its value in offering insight into the choices between different models of provision. The framework was chosen because of its focus on the impact of supported housing on the people living in it. It is a value judgement that this is the most appropriate factor and we have seen above that some discourses emphasise the control that is imposed on the residents. It is a foundation of the approach used here that the aim of supported housing is to improve or sustain the subjective well-being of individual residents. In order to achieve this it is necessary to be flexible to meet the many different identities and lifestyles of the people concerned.

Clearly there may be a conflict with an emphasis on well-being if policy and provision is intended to serve the defined interests of the society rather than of the individual. The discussion in the last section emphasised the desire to restrict the social control aspects of supported housing provision. An emphasis on subjective well-being will highlight aspects of social control that limit its achievement and put pressure on providers to justify the reasons for limiting well-being.

The evaluation framework devised and used in the book has a number of important features. The first is the focus on home and neighbourhood as important factors that impact on general well-being and so it has been argued that they should be separated out from the overall analysis to ensure that their importance is recognised. The second is the use of the concept of affordances to provide a holistic analysis of the relationship between people and their environment that includes the practical uses to which a setting can be put as well as the symbolic and meaning elements of activities. The two main elements are combined in the concept of social practices that encapsulates the everyday practices that people undertake in specific settings. In the supported housing context, these practices are influenced by the physical environment that may enable or prevent particular activities, but also by the practices that surround the provision of support. Even if the physical environment affords a particular activity it may not be possible for residents to undertake it if support staff give it low importance or the rules of a supported housing setting prohibit it. As was argued in Chapter Eight regarding the field of learning disability, the outcomes achieved in any physical setting may be crucially dependent on the type and philosophy of support provided. Nevertheless, the physical setting may make particular philosophies more or less difficult to sustain. For example, it would be difficult or impossible to enforce an institutional regime in an independent living context. The key point is the need to take a holistic view of social practices and to examine the interactions between the physical and social setting and the support.

The framework used in this book can be used at the level of individual choice or of policy planning and evaluation. The latter has been the focus here, but it is possible to use the factors identified as a tool to provide the information needed by residents, with support from their family and carers, to make a decision about an appropriate model of accommodation for them as well as the precise details of individual location or scheme. Of course this is dependent on the relevant information being available, and one of the lessons of this study has been the lack of information on key issues. There is a pressing need for more information at the policy level to guide policy decisions and the allocation of resources. The framework used here draws attention to the key factors that need to be examined and provides a literature background of existing knowledge and measurement techniques that can be supplemented.

Models of provision

The previous chapters have shown that there is evidence from the limited number of evaluation studies undertaken that there are considerable differences in outcomes between different forms of supported housing. In this section we will review briefly the findings and draw out their implications for policy and practice for supported housing.

It was emphasised at the outset that the differences between the needs, abilities, desires and lifestyles of individuals mean that it is unlikely that one model of provision will suit all people. There need to be different models available to enable choice and to meet the wide variety of difference in residents as well as a flexibility of provision that can be adapted to meet the different identities and lifestyles of the residents. It is clear from the analysis in the book, however, that some models of provision are more flexible than others and give more power to the residents, and can therefore meet a wider range of needs and change when needs and lifestyles change. Such models are likely to be better value for money than others because of the flexibility inherent in them. The most flexible models were those where a specific level of support was not tied to a specific housing location and where the support could be varied. One example is the domiciliary model where, in theory at least, a wide range of support can be made available to someone in their own home, assuming of course that the home itself is, or can be made, appropriate. Another example is the core and cluster model as exemplified by retirement villages, some models of support for homeless people, and community hubs. The key to the flexibility here is the ability to provide support to people, and change or withdraw it, where they are living, even if they have to move to access the model. If needs or preferences change and more intensive support is needed, such as institutional living, this can be accessed without too much change in terms of social contacts and other locational affordances. Therefore, flexibility in the model of provision in order to meet different and changing needs and lifestyles is an important element of the impact and desirability of different models.

At one extreme of provision, institutional living is less likely to achieve the benefits identified and so the policy priority in both countries examined here to rely on it as little as possible is a correct one. For some people, however, institutional living may be necessary and perceived to be desirable by the residents themselves. Examples may be older people with severe dementia or disabled people who need 24-hour support. So, despite the policy focus on other models, it is vitally important for the residents that this form of provision is built and run in a way that maximises the benefits to the residents. The Swedish policy of providing self-contained apartments even in institutional environments is a good one that is worth following in other countries. There are good examples in both Britain and Sweden of accommodation that is self-contained and looks like an ordinary apartment, but has design features that afford practical daily living and a positive symbolism. The affordances of neighbourhood can be maximised through appropriate location and links with the surroundings. Self-esteem and control can be bolstered by appropriate management styles and by fostering activity and achievement.

It is clear from the analysis in the preceding chapters that more flexible and home-based models are better at maximising the affordances of home and neighbourhood and the benefits of improved subjective well-being. The domiciliary model is at the opposite extreme to institutional living and the analysis shows that it can deliver substantial affordances of home and neighbourhood, and benefits of well-being, for many people. There are conditions that have to be met though. The most obvious is that the home has to deliver the appropriate affordances, which may often mean that it has to be in an appropriate physical condition and may have to cater for people with physical impairments. This also applies to the affordances of the neighbourhood, which needs to offer safety, status and access to social relationships as well as physical facilities. In addition, support needs to be provided in an appropriate and flexible form that respects the control, dignity and well-being of the resident. For some people these conditions are not met and a move into another model of supported housing may be appropriate.

For the conditions to be met in general there need to be comprehensive housing and support policies that enable appropriate housing and support to be available. In both these areas, Sweden is superior to Britain. It has gone further in the pursuit of the accessibility standards for new properties, which, combined with the increased incidence of apartment living and the lower average age of the housing stock, provides a better context for the domiciliary model. In addition, Sweden has a better standard of domiciliary support services than Britain because of its relatively well-funded social services. Unfortunately, at the time of writing Britain was moving backwards in relative terms. Government financial cuts have reduced the availability of domiciliary support services and the perceived need to increase housing production has resulted in a dilution of the standards applied to new construction. The paradox is that the failure to enable people to access the domiciliary model will not only result in lower well-being for those people, but could also increase the cost of service provision for those helped. The pattern is for help to be concentrated on fewer people, but through the provision of expensive models such as residential care or extra-care housing. Unfortunately, the same trends are observable in Sweden, but the extent of change is less and the pre-existing base of service provision is greater. The major problem in Sweden is the lack of access of some low-income people to the primary housing system because of the universalist policies and structures of the past, combined with the growing commercialisation of the municipal housing companies. There is an urgent need for an access mechanism that takes into account the housing and social needs of residents.

The more that universal domiciliary services are restricted to those in most need, the more space is created for market mechanisms to emerge in supported housing. At the moment these are largely restricted to private provision of supported housing procured by the state. However, market provision has emerged more for older people than in other fields, largely because of the higher income and wealth that some in this group possess. In Sweden, the market provision is primarily in personal and practical support, repairs and adaptations for which residents can claim tax relief, in addition to the provision of private housing options including 'senior housing'. In Britain, the market has expanded to cover retirement villages, private retirement housing as well as private health and domiciliary provision. One implication of this rise in market provision is the scope to reproduce existing income and wealth inequalities at a time when they are rising in both Britain and Sweden, as well as the danger of reducing state provision to a residual service. At present this may seem some distance away in both countries, but the first signs of a growing distinction between public and private provision are becoming visible, and the danger is there if current trends continue, especially in housing and support for older people, where market mechanisms are more developed than in other areas.

Rising inequality is likely to impact profoundly on the vulnerable people who are the focus of this book, who are largely low-income people, many of whom are dependent on welfare benefits. Reductions in these benefits make it harder to provide the housing and support that improves their well-being and disadvantages them in the competition for good housing in particular. The higher level of inequality in Britain makes it a particular problem in this country, as neighbourhoods and regions of the country become difficult for vulnerable people to access or survive in. Inequality makes it both more likely that vulnerable people will have housing problems and more difficult to solve their problems through domiciliary or other home-based solutions. The role of inequality in the creation of homelessness is clear, but in other cases, such as disabled people, living in inappropriate housing or neighbourhoods can increase problems and make it more likely that people have to resort to shared living or institutional forms of supported housing. Inequality also makes it more difficult to achieve the conditions needed to deliver domiciliary solutions that improve the well-being of residents. The example of homeless people in Britain housed in the private sector (see Chapter Seven) shows the dangers of pursuing domiciliary solutions when the housing and neighbourhood conditions are not appropriate. A basic condition of this approach is decent housing and neighbourhoods that are accessible to vulnerable people as well as the rest of the population.

If Sweden is superior to Britain in the extent of resources committed to domiciliary services and the extent of coverage, it lags behind in the personalisation of support and the provision of personal budgets. The analysis showed the impact of personal budgets on the well-being of residents, and the flexibility it gives them to take control of their own situation and to maximise the affordances of home and neighbourhood. A combination of the resource availability of Swedish policy and the personalisation of British policy would make the most of existing resources to increase subjective well-being. It is through personalisation that difference can be accommodated within supported housing, and the needs and lifestyles of individuals met in a way that maximises subjective well-being. Personalisation ensures that models of provision and services are appropriate and flexibly tuned in to the changing needs and preferences of individuals.

Of the models of supported housing in between the two extremes, those at the domiciliary end delivered the most favourable outcomes. Particularly important were core and cluster models, such as retirement villages, community hubs and other examples, such as core and cluster schemes for homeless people and the KeyRing scheme for people with learning difficulties. This model provided the affordances of home and neighbourhood and exhibited the flexibility identified above.

Less successful were other models at the more institutional end of the spectrum, such as group homes, extra-care housing, and hostels and foyers. These models were inflexible and struggled to offer the affordances of home and neighbourhood or the benefits of well-being. They were also models associated with social control, as identified earlier, and ones often with a fixed level of support attached to the scheme which reduced flexibility.

The way forward for policy

The data from the evaluation of the different models of supported housing offer clear directions for future policy at national and local level. The clear priority is to expand the use of domiciliary provision while continuing to foster core and cluster models.

The evaluation here provides added weight to the oft-repeated and long-standing calls to expand domiciliary forms of supported housing. So why does this call still need to be made? A clue lies in the relative success in Sweden in pursuing the domiciliary model because of its more comprehensive and well-funded social care systems and its stricter regulations on the standards of new-build housing. In Britain, the public funding has never been in place to provide the comprehensive domiciliary support necessary, and resources have been increasingly concentrated on a few individuals in acute need at the expense of offering support to others with currently less need. The pressure to keep those with acute needs out of institutional living has stifled any attempts to implement a preventative agenda where people are supported to stay active and remain in their own homes for as long as possible and thus delaying the need for institutional living. Also, the pressures for more new-build housing have resulted in a dilution of the building standards that could enable more people to stay at home. This is coupled with a funding shortage in the provision of aids and adaptations to existing housing. The result is a greater call on institutional living and other forms of supported housing, as well as on health and other services.

But the overall shortage of public funding is not the complete picture, because resources have been spent on supported housing options such as extra-care housing, group homes and foyers where there has been little evidence of their efficacy. We have commented previously on the power of the provider lobby in steering resources, but another factor here is the pressure on limited resources created by the overwhelming desire to avoid the costs of institutional living. This has meant that there has been an overriding emphasis on forms of provision perceived as doing this at the expense of the wider and longer-term preventative agenda. Thus, a change of emphasis is needed, with different funding priorities and a more long-term perspective.

As well as the domiciliary model, the analysis has shown the value of core and cluster models of supported housing such as retirement villages, community hubs, the KeyRing scheme and other forms of provision for other groups. The philosophy of the core and cluster is applicable in a wide range of different circumstances in terms of needs met and the mix of segregation and integration contexts. The model is flexible and is cheaper than many less flexible forms of provision. The model can be applied to people living in their existing home or to those who desire or need to move because of the inadequacy of their existing accommodation. Clearly this form of provision should be extended and it is where resources for it should be prioritised (in addition to the domiciliary model). Innovation is necessary in new applications of the model to different groups of people. The possibility of the model in preventing unwanted entry into institutional living is at least as great as that of other less flexible and more expensive options that have been popular in the past.

For other models of supported housing, such as hostels and group homes, as well as for institutional living, the analysis shows the directions in which policy and practice should move. More affordances of home and neighbourhood can be provided by incorporating self-contained accommodation and fostering integration with neighbours and family and friends. Provision can be 'opened out' to become the core element of core and cluster models. Flexibility of support arrangements can be prioritised and regimes instituted that put residents at the core of the provision and promote subjective well-being.

Judt (2010) has commented on the waning of the welfare state in Britain and other countries, and the lack of political and consumer support for welfare services. He argues that some features of these services have undermined their popularity, most notably the uniformity of provision and the powerlessness of those receiving the services. Examples of these drawbacks are evident in the supported housing models discussed in the previous chapters. The adoption of the concept of well-being as the cornerstone of policy helps to avoid these problems.

Well-being is promoted through increasing the self-esteem, control and efficacy of residents of supported housing. Services that achieve this are likely to be popular and to deserve and receive popular and, therefore, political support. Supported housing that does not take the well-being of its residents as the paramount aim is unlikely to be successful in changing behaviour, or in providing people with the self-esteem and efficacy that is necessary for them to take control of their lives and to increase their well-being by having an identity and lifestyle that they value and enjoy.

References

Alder (2012) *Evaluations of the KeyRing Networks Plus in Walsall*, London: KeyRing

Allan G and Crow G (eds) (1989) *Home and family: Creating the domestic sphere*, Basingstoke: Macmillan

Allen C (2008) *Housing market renewal and social class*, London: Routledge

Anderson K and Smith SJ (2001) Emotional geographies, *Transactions of the Institute of British Geographers* 26(1), 7–10

Antonovsky A (1974) Conceptual and methodological problems in the study of resistance resources and stressful life events, in BS Dohrenwend and BP Dohrenwend (eds) *Stressful life events: Their nature and effect*, New York: Wiley

Aronson J (2002) Elderly people's account of home care rationing: Missing voices in long-term care policy debates, *Ageing & Society* 22, 399–418

Askheim OP, Bengtsson H and Bjelke BR (2014) Personal assistance in a Scandinavian context: Similarities, differences and developmental traits, *Scandinavian Journal of Disability Research* 16 (supp1.), 3–18

Atkinson R and Kintrea K (2002) Area effects: What do they mean for British housing and regeneration policy? *European Journal of Housing Policy* 2(2), 147–66

Ball M (2006) *Buy to let: The revolution – 10 years on. Assessment and prospects*, Report, Amersham: Association of Residental Letting Agents

Bank-Mikkelson N (1980) Denmark, in RJ Flynn and KE Nitsch (eds) *Normalisation, social integration and community services*, Austin, TX: Pro-Ed

Barnes C and Mercer G (2003) *Disability*, Cambridge: Polity Press

Barnes S, Torrington J, Darton R, Holder J, Lewis A, McKee K, Netton A and Orrell A (2012) Does the design of extra-care housing meet the needs of residents? A focus group study, *Ageing & Society* 32, 1193–214

Bartley M, Blane D and Davey Smith G (1998) Introduction: Beyond the Black Report, in M Bartley, D Blane and G Davey Smith (eds) *The sociology of health inequalities*, Oxford: Blackwell, 1–18

Beck U (1992) *Risk society: Towards a new modernity*, London: Sage

Bengtsson B (2013) Housing and housing policy in Sweden, in JM Lundstrom, C Friedrikson and J Witsell (eds) *Planning and sustainable urban development in Sweden*, Stockholm: Swedish Society for Town and Country Planning

Bengtsson B and Ruonavara H (2010) Path dependence in housing: Introduction to the special issue, *Housing, Theory and Society* 27(3), 193–203

Bigby C, Knox M, Beadle-Brown J, Clement T and Mansell J (2012) Uncovering dimensions of culture in underperforming group homes for people with severe intellectual disability, *Intellectual and Developmental Disabilities* 50(6), 452–67

Blid M (2008) Normality or care: An inventory of Swedish municipalities' responses to unstable accommodation for vulnerable groups, *European Journal of Social Work* 11(4), 397–413

Blid M and Gerdner A (2006) Socially excluding housing support to homeless substance misusers: Two Swedish case studies of special category housing, *International Journal of Social Welfare* 15, 162–71

Blomqvist P (2004) The choice revolution: Privatization of Swedish welfare services in the 1990s, *Social Policy and Administration* 38(2), 139–55

Blunt A and Dowling R (2006) *Home*, London: Routledge

Borg M, Sells D, Topor A, Mezzina R, Marin I and Davidson L (2006) What makes a house a home: The role of material resources in recovery from severe mental illness, *American Journal of Psychiatric Rehabilitation* 8(3), 243–56

Brown T and King P (2005) The power to choose: Effective choice and housing policy, *European Journal of Housing Policy* 5(1), 59–76

Burholt V, Nash P, Doheny S, Dobbs C and Phillips C (2010) *Extra care: Meeting the needs of fit or frail older people*, Swansea: Centre for Innovative Ageing

Butler J (1993) *Bodies that matter: On the discursive limits of 'sex'*, London: Routledge

Christian J, Clapham D and Abrams D (2011) Exploring homeless people's use of outreach services: Applying a social psychological perspective, *Housing Studies* 26(5), 681–99

Christian J, Clapham D, Thomas S and Abrams D (2012) The relationship between well-being, future planning and intentions to utilise intervention programmes: What can be learned from homeless service users? *International Journal of Housing Policy* 12(2), 159–82

Christophers B (2013) A monstrous hybrid: The political economy of housing in early 21st-century Sweden, *New Political Economy* 18(6), 885–911

Clapham D (1995) Privatisation and the East European housing model, *Urban Studies* 32(4/5), 679–94

Clapham D (2003) A pathways approach to homelessness research, *Journal of Community and Applied Social Psychology* 13, 1–9

Clapham D (2005) *The meaning of home*, Bristol: Policy Press

Clapham D (2006) Housing policy and the discourse of globalization, *European Journal of Housing Policy* 6(1), 55–76

Clapham D and Franklin B (1994) *Community care, housing management and competitive tendering*, Coventry: Chartered Institute of Housing

Clapham D and Munro M (1990) Ambiguities and contradictions in the provision of sheltered housing for older people, *Journal of Social Policy* 19, 27–45

Clapham D and Smith S (1990) Housing policy and special needs, *Policy and Politics* 19, 193–205

Clapham D, Kay H and Munro M (1994) *A wider choice: Revenue funding mechanisms for housing and community care*, York: Joseph Rowntree Foundation

Clapham D, Mackie P, Orford S, Thomas I and Buckley K (2014) The housing pathways of young people in the UK, *Environment and Planning A* 46(8), 2016–31

Clark W (2009) Changing residential preferences across income, education and age: Findings from the multi-city study of urban inequality, *Urban Affairs Review* 44(3), 334–355

Clevnert U and Johansson L (2007) Personal assistance in Sweden, *Journal of Aging and Social Policy* 19(3), 65–80

CLG Communities and Local Government) (2006) *Places of change: Tackling homelessness through the Hostels Capital Improvement Programme*, London: CLG

CLG (2009a) *The private rented sector: Professionalism and quality*, London: CLG

CLG (2009b) *English house condition survey 2007: Annual report*, London: CLG

CLG (2012) *English housing survey*, London: CLG

Cobbold C (1997) *A cost benefit analysis of lifetime homes*, York: Joseph Rowntree Foundation.

Cole I and Furbey C (1994) *The eclipse of council housing*, London: Routledge

Coles B (1995) *Youth and social policy: Youth citizenship and young careers*, London: UCL Press

Commission on Funding for Care and Support (2011) *Fairer care funding*, http://webarchive.nationalarchives.gov.uk/20130221130239/http://dilnotcommission.dh.gov.uk/files/2011/07/Fairer-Care-Funding-Report.pdf

Coolen H (2006) The meaning of dwellings: An ecological perspective, *Housing, Theory and Society* 23(4), 185–201

Crook A and Kemp P (2011) *Transforming private landlords*, Oxford: Wiley Blackwell

Croucher K, Hicks L and Jackson K (2006) *Housing with care for later life: A literature review*, York: Joseph Rowntree Foundation

Cumming E and Henry W (1961) *Growing old*, New York: Basic Books

Davidson J, Bondi L and Smith M (eds) (2005) *Emotional geographies*, Aldershot: Ashgate

Dean J and Hastings A (2000) *Challenging images: Housing estates, stigma and regeneration*, Bristol: Policy Press

Department of Health (1989) *Caring for people: Community care in the next decade and beyond*, London: HMSO

Department of Health (2001) *Valuing people: A new strategy for learning disability for the 21st century*, London: Department of Health

Department of Health (2009) *Care services efficiency delivery case study: KeyRing living support networks*, www.keyring.org/site/KEYR/Templates/Generic3col.aspx?pageid=222&cc=GB

Department of Health (2010) *Valuing people now*, London: Department of Health

Department of Health (2012) *Caring for our future: Reforming care and support*, London: Department of Health

Department of Health and Social Security (1971) *Better services for the mentally handicapped*, London: HMSO

Despres C (1991) The meaning of home: Literature review and directions for future research and theoretical development, *Journal of Architectural Research* 8, 96–155

Doling J and Ronald R (2010) Home ownership and asset based welfare, *Journal of Housing and the Built Environment* 25, 165–73

Dolowitz D with Holme R, Nellis M and O'Neill F (2000) *Policy transfer and British social policy: Learning from the USA?* Buckingham: Open University Press

Donnison D (1967) *The government of housing*, Harmondsworth: Penguin

Duff C, Jacobs K, Loo S and Murray S (2012) *The role of informal community resources in supporting stable housing for young people recovering from mental illness: Key issues for housing policy-makers and practitioners,* AHURI Final Report No.199, Melbourne: Australian Housing and Urban Research Institute.

Dunleavy P (1981) *The politics of mass housing in Britain 1945–1975,* Oxford: Clarendon Press

Dunn J (2006) The meaning of dwellings: Digging deeper, *Housing, Theory and Society* 23(4), 214–15

Easthope H (2004) A place called home, *Housing, Theory and Society* 21(3), 128–38

Elstad J. (1998) The psycho-social perspective on social inequalities in health, in Bartley M, Blanc D. and Davey-Smith G. (eds) *The sociology of health inequalities.* Oxford: Blackwell, 39–58

Emerson, E. (2004). Deinstitutionalisation in England, *Journal of Intellectual and Developmental Disability* 29(1), 79–84.

Emerson E, Robertson J, Gregory N, Hatton C, Kessissoglou S, Hallam A et al (2001) Quality and costs of supported living residences and group homes in the UK, *American Journal on Mental Retardation* 106, 401–15

Emerson E, Davies I, Spencer K, and Malam S (2005) *Adults with learning difficulties in England 2003/4, Full Report,* Leeds: NHS Health and Social Care Information Centre

Esping-Andersen G (1990) *The three worlds of welfare capitalism,* Cambridge: Polity Press

Eurobarometer (2007) *Health and long-term care in the European Union,* Special Eurobarometer 283, Brussels: European Commission.

Evans S (2009) *Community and ageing: Maintaining quality of life in housing with care settings,* Bristol: Policy Press

Evans S and Means R (2007) *Balanced retirement communities? A case study of Westbury Fields,* Bristol: St Monica Trust

Farrington A and Robinson WP (1999) Homelessness and strategies of identity maintenance: A participant observation study, *Journal of Community and Applied Social Psychology* 9, 175–94

Fitzpatrick S (2000) *Young homeless people,* Basingstoke: Macmillan

Fitzpatrick S (2005) Explaining homelessness: A critical realist perspective, *Housing, Theory and Society* 22(1), 1–17

Fitzpatrick S, Bretherton J, Jones A, Pleace N and Quilgars D (2010) *The Glasgow hostel closure and reprovisioning programme: Final report on the findings from a longitudinal evaluation,* York: University of York

Fitzpatrick S, Pawson H, Bramley G and Wilcox S (2012) *The homelessness monitor: Scotland 2012,* London: Crisis

Foresight Mental Capital and Wellbeing Project (2008) *Final project report*, London: Government Office for Science

Forrest R and Kearns A (2001) Social cohesion, social capital and the neighbourhood, *Urban Studies* 38(12), 2125–43

Foucault M (1980) Body/power, in C Gordon (ed.) *Michel Foucault: Power/knowledge*, Brighton: Harvester

Foucault M (2002) The subject and power, in *Essential Works of Foucault 1954–1984*, vol. 3, edited by J Faubion, Harmondsworth: Penguin, 236–328

Franklin B (1998) Discourses and dilemmas in the housing and support debate, in I Shaw, S Lambert and D Clapham (eds) *Social care and housing*, London: Jessica Kingsley

Galster G (2012) Neighbourhoods and their role in creating and changing housing, in D Clapham, W Clark and K Gibb (eds) *The Sage handbook of housing studies*, London: Sage, 84–106

Gibson J (1975) Affordances and behaviour, in E Reed and R Jones (eds) *Reasons for realism: Selected essays of James J. Gibson*, Hillsdale, NJ: Erlbaum, 410–11

Gibson J (1986) *The ecological approach to visual perception*. Hillsdale, NJ: Erlbaum

Giddens A (1984) *The constitution of society*, Cambridge: Polity Press

Giddens A (1990) *The consequences of modernity*, Cambridge: Polity Press

Giddens A (1991) *Modernity and self-identity: self and society in the late modern age*, Cambridge: Polity Press

Gieryn T (2002) What buildings do, *Theory and Society* 31, 35–74

Gilleard C and Higgs P (2000) *Cultures of ageing: Self, citizen and the body*, Harlow: Prentice Hall

Glasby J (2012) *Understanding health and social care*, Bristol: Policy Press

Glasby J and Littlechild R (2009) *Direct payments and personal budgets: Putting personalisation into practice*, Bristol: Policy Press

Goffman E (1968) *Asylums: Essays on the social situation of mental patients and other inmates*, Harmondsworth: Penguin

Granovetter M (1973) The strength of weak ties, *American Journal of Sociology* 78, 1360–80

Gunnarsson E (2009) The welfare state, the individual and the need for care: Older people's views, *International Journal of Social Welfare* 18, 252–9

Gurney C (1999) Pride and prejudice: Discourses of normalisation in public and private accounts of home ownership, *Housing Studies* 14(2), 163–83

Gurney C (2000) Transgressing public/private boundaries in the home: A sociological analysis of the coital noise taboo, *Venereology* 13, 39–46

Hajighasemi A (2004) *The transformation of the Swedish welfare system: Fact or fiction?* Stockholm: Almquiest and Wiksell International

Harrison M, with Davis C (2001) *Housing, social policy and difference*, Bristol: Policy Press

Harré R (2002) Material objects in social worlds, *Theory, Culture & Society* 19(5–6), 23–33

Health and Social Care Information Centre (2009) *Community care statistics, home help and care services for adults: England 2008*, www.hscic.gov.uk/pubs/commcarestats08home

Health and Social Care Information Centre (2014) *Community care statistics: Social services activity, England*, www.hscic.gov.uk/catalogue/PUB16133/comm-care-stat-act-eng-2013-14-fin-rep.pdf

Heft H (1988) Affordances of children's environments: A functional approach to environmental description, *Children's Environments Quarterly* 5, 29–37

Heft H. (1989) Affordances and the body: An intentional analysis of Gibson's ecological approach to visual perception, *Journal for the Theory of Social Behaviour* 19, 1–30

Heft H (1997) The relevance of Gibson's ecological approach for environment–behaviour studies, in GT Moore and RW Marans (eds) *Advances in environment, behaviour and design*, vol 4, New York: Plenum, 71–108

Heft H (1998) Essay review: The elusive environment in environmental psychology, *British Journal of Psychology* 89, 519–523

Heft H and Kytta M (2006) A psychologically meaningful description of environments requires a relational approach, *Housing, Theory and Society* 23(4), 210–13

Hemingway L (2011) *Disabled people and housing: Choices, opportunities and barriers*, Bristol: Policy Press

Henning C and Lieberg M (1996) Strong ties or weak ties? Neighbourhood networks in a new perspective, *Scandinavian Housing and Planning Research* 13, 3–26

Henwood M (1986) Community care: Policy practice and prognosis, in Brenton M and Ungerson C (eds) *Yearbook of Social Policy 1986/7*. Longman: Harlow

Henwood B, Cabassa L, Craig C and Padgett D (2013) Permanent supportive housing: Addressing homelessness and health disparities? *American Journal of Public Health* December (suppl. 2), 188–92.

Heywood F (2001) *Money well spent: The effectiveness and value of housing adaptations*. Bristol: Policy Press

Heywood F (2005) Adaptation: Altering the house to restore the home, *Housing Studies* 20, 531–47

Heywood F, Means R and Oldman C (2002) *Housing and home in later life*. Buckingham: Open University Press

Hillcoat-Nallétamby S and Ogg J (2014) Moving beyond 'ageing in place': Older people's dislikes about their home and neighbourhood environments as a motive for wishing to move. *Ageing and Society* 34(10), 1771–96

Hills P and Argyle M (2002) The Oxford happiness questionnaire: A compact scale for the measurement of psychological well-being, *Personality and Individual Differences* 33(7), 1073–82

Hirsch F (1977) *Social limits to growth*, London: Routledge

Hoekstra J (2003) Housing and the welfare state in the Netherlands: An application of Esping-Andersen's typology, *Housing, Theory and Society* 20(2), 58–71

Holtermann S (1975) Areas of urban deprivation in Great Britain: An analysis of 1971 census data, *Social Trends* 6, 37–47

Hulse K, Jacobs K, Arthurson K and Spinney A (2011) *At home and in place? The role of housing in social inclusion*, AHURI Positioning Paper 177, Melbourne: AHURI Ltd

Hutson S (1999) The experience of homeless accommodation and support, in S Hutson and D Clapham (eds) *Homelessness: Public policies and private troubles*, London: Continuum, 208–25

Imrie R (1996) *Disability and the city*, London: Paul Chapman

Jacobs K, Kemeny J and Manzi A (1999) The struggle to define homelessness: A social constructionist approach, in S Hutson and D Clapham (eds) *Homelessness: Public policies and private troubles*, London: Cassell, 11–28

Johansson K, Josephson S and Lilja M (2009) Creating possibilities for action in the presence of environmental barriers in the process of ageing in place, *Ageing and Society* 29(1),49–70

Johansson L (1997) Decentralisation from acute to home care settings in Sweden, *Health Policy* 41(suppl.), 131–43

Johns H and Ormerod P (2007) *Happiness, economics and public policy*, London: Institute of Economic Affairs

Johnsen S and Quilgars D (2009) Youth homelessness, in S Fitzpatrick, D Quilgars and N Pleace (eds) *Homelessness in the UK: Problems and solutions*, Coventry: Chartered Institute of Housing, 53–72

Johnson RJ, Poulsen MF and Forrest J (2007) Ethnic and racial segregation in US metropolitan areas 1980–2000: The dimensions of segregation revisited, *Urban Affairs Review* 42(4), 479–504

Jones A and Pleace N (2010) *A review of single homelessness in the UK 2000–2010*, London: Crisis.

Judt T (2010) *Ill fares the land*, London: Penguin

Jupp B (1999) Living together: Community life on mixed tenure estates, London: Demos

Katz J, Holland C, Peace S and Taylor E (2011) *A better life: What older people with high support needs value*, York: Joseph Rowntree Foundation

Kearns A, Whitley E, Bond L and Tannahill C (2012) The residential psychosocial environment and mental wellbeing in deprived areas, *International Journal of Housing Policy* 12(4), 413–38

Kemeny J (1992) *Housing and social theory*, London: Routledge

Kemp P (2009) The transformation of private renting, in P Malpass and R Rowlands (eds) *Housing markets and ...* London: Routledge

King P (1996) *The limits of housing policy: A philosophical investigation*, London: Middlesex University Press

King P (2004) *Private dwelling*, London: Routledge

King P (2005) *The common place*, London: Routledge

Knutagård M and Boustedt Hedvall M (2013) *Peer review in Denmark: Sustainable ways of preventing homelessness*, Brussels, European Commission http://ec.europa.eu/social/main.jsp?catId=89&langId=en&newsId=1884&moreDocuments=yes&tableName=news

Knutagård M and Kristiansen A (2013) Not by the book: The emergence and translation of housing first in Sweden, *European Journal of Homelessness* 7(1), 93–115

Knutagård M and Nordfeldt M (2007) The emergency shelter as a recurrent solution, *Sociologisk forskning* 4, 30–58

Korpi W (1978) *The working class in welfare capitalism: Work, unions and politics in Sweden*, London: Routledge and Kegan Paul

Laing R (1969) *The divided self*, Harmondsworth: Penguin

Larsson K (2006) Care needs and home-help services for older people in Sweden: Does improved functioning account for the reduction in public care? *Ageing & Society* 26, 413–29

Larsson K (2007) The social situation of older people, *International Journal of Social Welfare* 16, S203– S218

Laslett P (1989) *A fresh map of life*, London: Weidenfeld and Nicolson

Layard R (2005) *Happiness: Lessons from a new science*, London: Allen Lane

Layder D (2004) *Social and personal identity*, London: Sage

Lee M (2006) *Promoting mental health and wellbeing in later life: A first report from the UK inquiry into mental health and wellbeing*, London: Mental Health Foundation and Age Concern

Lees L (2001) Towards critical geography of architecture: The case of an ersatz coliseum, *Ecumene* 8(1), 51–86

Leibfried S (1992) Towards a European welfare state? On integrating poverty regimes into the European community, in Z Ferge and J Kolberg (eds) *Social policy in a changing Europe*, Frankfurt/Main: Campus, 245–79

Lilja M, Mansson I, Jahlenius L and Sacco-Peterson M (2003) Disability policy in Sweden: Policies concerning assistive technology and home modification services, *Journal of Disability Studies* 14, 130–35

Lindbom A (2001) Dismantling the social democratic welfare model? Has the Swedish welfare state lost its defining characteristics? *Scandinavian Political Studies* 24(3), 171–93

Lipton F, Siegel C, Hannigan A, Samuels J and Baker S (2000) Tenure in supportive housing for homeless persons with severe mental illness, *Psychiatric Services* 51(4): 479–86

Lofstrand CH (2010) Reforming the work to combat long-term homelessness in Sweden, *Acta Sociologica* 53(1): 19–34

Lofstrand CH (2012) On the translation of the pathways housing first model, *European Journal of Homelessness* 6(2), 175–82

Lorimer H (2005) Cultural geography: The busyness of being 'more than representational', *Progress in Human Geography* 29, 83–94

Malpass P (2011) Path dependence and the measurement of change in housing policy, *Housing, Theory and Society* 28(4), 305–19

Mansell J (2006) Deinstitutionalisation and community living: Progress, problems and priorities, *Journal of Intellectual & Developmental Disability* 31(2), 65–76

Maslow A (1954) *Motivation and personality*, New York: Harper and Row

Matznetter W and Mundt A (2012) Housing and welfare regimes, in D Clapham, W Clark and K Gibb (eds) *The Sage handbook of housing studies*, London: Sage, 274–94

Means R, Richards S and Smith R (2008) *Community care*, Basingstoke: Palgrave Macmillan

Mencap (2012) *Housing for people with a learning disability*, London: Mencap

Miller D (2001) *Home possessions*, Oxford: Berg

Moore J (2000) Placing home in context, *Journal of Environmental Psychology* 20, 207–217

Morris J. (1993) *Independent lives: Community care and disabled people*, Basingstoke: Palgrave Macmillan

Musterd S (2012) Ethnic residential segregation: Reflections on concepts, levels and effects, in D Clapham, W Clark and K Gibb (eds) *Sage handbook of housing research*, London: Sage, 419–38

Musterd S and Ostendorf W (eds) (1998) *Urban segregation and the welfare state: Inequality and exclusion in western cities*, London: Routledge

Nash C (2000) Performativity in practice: Some recent work in cultural geography, *Progress in Human Geography* 24, 653–64

Nelson G, Sylvestre J, Aubry T, George L and Trainor J (2007) Housing choice and control: Housing quality, and control over professional support as contributors to the subjective quality of life and community adaptation of people with severe mental illness, *Administration and Policy in Mental Health and Mental Health Services Research* 34, 89–100

Nettle D (2005) *Happiness: The science behind your smile*, Oxford: Oxford University Press

New Economics Foundation (2009) *National accounts of well-being: Bringing real wealth onto the balance sheet*, London: New Economics Foundation

Nirje B (1969) The normalization principle and its human management implications, in R Kugel and W Wolfensberger (eds) *Changing patterns in residential services for the mentally retarded*, Washington, DC: Presidential Committee on Mental Retardation

Nord C. (2011) Architectural space as moulding factor of care practices and resident privacy in assisted living. *Ageing & Society* 31(6), 934–52

Nordfeldt M (2012) A dynamic perspective on homelessness: homeless families in Stockholm, *European Journal of Homelessness* 6(1), 105–23

OECD (2009) *Health at a glance 2009: OECD Indicators*, Paris, OECD Publishing

Olin E and Ringsby Jansson B (2008) Common areas in group homes: Arenas for different interests? *European Journal of Social Work* 11(3), 251–65

Olin E, Nordstrom M and Wijk H (2011) Privacy, meetings and rejections: A qualitative study among young persons with psychiatric disabilities, *Scandinavian Journal of Disability Research* 13(2), 135–50

Oliver M (1990) *The politics of disablement*, Basingstoke: Palgrave Macmillan

Oliver M and Barnes C (1998) *Disabled people and social policy: From exclusion to inclusion*, London: Longman

Olsson L and Nordfeldt M (2008) Homelessness and the tertiary welfare system in Sweden: The role of the welfare state and non-profit sector, *European Journal of Homelessness* 2, 157–73

Pannell J and Blood I (2012) *Supported housing for older people in the UK: An evidence review*, York: Joseph Rowntree Foundation

Pattison B, Diacon D and Vine J (2010) *Tenure trends in the UK housing system: Will the private rented sector continue to grow*, Coalville: British Social Housing Foundation

Pearlin LI, Liebermann MA, Menghan EG and Mullan JT (1981) The satress process, *Journal of Health and Social Behaviour* 22(4), 337–56

Pebley A and Vaiana M (2002) *In Our Backyard*, Santa Monica, CA: Rand Corp.

Peng I (2008) Welfare policy reforms in Japan and Korea: Cultural and institutional factors, in W van OOrschot, M Opielka and B Pfau-Effinger (eds) *Culture and welfare state*, Cheltenham: Edward Elgar,162–82

Percival J (2001) Self-esteem and social motivation in age segregated settings, *Housing Studies* 16(6), 827–40

Percival J (2002) Domestic spaces: Uses and meanings in the daily lives of older people, *Ageing and Society* 22, 729–49

Perrin B and Nirje B (1985) Setting the record straight: A critique of some misconceptions of the normalization principle, *Australian and New Zealand Journal of Developmental Disabilities* 11, 69–74

Petersson I, Lilja M and Borell L (2012) To feel safe in everyday life at home: A study of older adults after home modifications, *Ageing and Society* 32(5), 791–811

Pleace N, Fitzpatrick S, Johnsen S, Quilgars D and Sanderson D (2008) *Statutory homelessness in England : The experiences of families and 16–17-year-olds*, London: CLG

Porteous J (1976) Home the territorial core, *Geographic Review* 64, 383–90

Purkis A and Hodson P (1982) *Housing and community care*, London: Bedford Square Press/NCVO

Quilgars D and Bretherton J (2009) *Evaluation of the experiences of single people presenting as homeless in Glasgow*, York: Centre for Housing Policy, University of York

Rapoport A (1982) *The meaning of the built environment*, London: Sage

Ravetz A (2001) *Council housing and culture: The history of a social experiment*, London: Routledge

Renshon S (1974) *Psychological needs and political behaviour*, New York: The Free Press

Rodaway P (1994) *Sensuous geographies: Body, sense and place*, London: Routledge

Rose N and Miller P (2008) *Governing the present: Administering economic, social and personal life*, Cambridge: Polity

Rowles GD (1983) Place and personal identity in old age: Observations from Appalachia, *Journal of Environmental Psychology* 3(4), 299–313

Ryff CD and Keyes CLM (1995) The structure of psychological well-being revisited, *Journal of personality and Social Psychology* 69(4), 719–27

Sahlin I (1999) *European Observatory on homelessness: National report on Sweden. Supported Accommodation*, Brussels: Feantsa

Sahlin I (2005) The staircase of transition: Survival through failure, *Innovation: the European Journal of Social Science Research* 18, 115–36

Sahlin I (2006) Homelessness and the secondary housing market in Sweden. Paper presented at the ENHR (European Network for Housing Research) conference in Ljubljana, July 2006

Sahlin I (2010) Central state and homelessness policies in Sweden: New ways of governing, *International Journal of Housing Policy* 4(3), 345–67

Sandel M (2012) *What money can't buy: The moral limits of markets*, London: Penguin

Sassen S (1991) *The global city: New York, London, Tokyo*, Princeton, NJ: Princeton University Press

Saunders P and Williams P (1988) The constitution of the home: Towards a research agenda, *Housing Studies* 3(2), 81–93

Savage M, Bagnall G and Longhurst B (2005) *Globalization and belonging*, London: Sage

Scase R (1999) *Britain towards 2010: The changing business environment*, London: DTI

Scheff TJ (1988) Shame and conformity: The defense-emotion system, *American Sociological Review* 53, 395–406

Searle B (2008) *Well-being: In search of a good life*, Bristol: Policy Press

Sherman SR (1975) Patterns of contacts for residents of age-segregated and age-integrated housing, *Journal of Gerontology* 30(1), 103–7

Shilling C (1993) *The body and social theory*, London: Sage

Sixsmith J (1986) The meaning of home: an exploratory study of environmental experience, *Journal of Environmental Psychology* 6, 281–98

Skifter Anderson H (2002) Excluded places: The interaction between segregation, urban decay and deprived neighbourhoods, *Housing, Theory and Society* 19, 153–69

Smith M, Albanese F and Trude J (2014) *A roof over my head: The final report of the Sustain project*, London: Crisis and Shelter

Social Exclusion Unit (2000) *National strategy for neighbourhood renewal: A framework for consultation*, London: Cabinet Office

Somerville P (1992) Homelessness and the meaning of home: Rooflessness or rootlessness, *Journal of Urban and Regional Research* 16(4), 529–39

Somerville P (1997) The social construction of home, *Journal of Architecture and Planning Research* 14(3), 226–45

Standing G (2011) *The precariat: The new dangerous class*, London: Bloomsbury

Socialstyrelsen (2012) *Homelessness in Sweden 2011*, Stockholm: Socialstyrelsen

Suttles G (1972) *The social construction of communities*, Chicago: University of Chicago Press

Swedish Association for Local Authorities (Svenska Kommunförbundet) (2002) *Kommunernas Marknadsanvändning år*, Stockholm: Swedish Association for Local Authorities

Swenarton M (1981) *Homes fit for heroes*, London: Heinemann

Szebehely M and Trydegard G (2012) Home care for older people in Sweden: A universal model in transition, *Health and Social Care in the Community* 20(3), 300–9

Taylor R and Ford G (1981) Lifestyle and ageing, *Ageing and Society* 1, 329–45

Thompson S and Marks N (2008) *Measuring well-being in policy: Issues and applications*, London: New Economics Foundation

Thrift NJ (1997) The still point: Resistance, expressive embodiment and dance, in S Pile and M Keith (eds) *Geographies of resistance*, London: Routledge, 124–51

Thrift N (2004) Intensities of feeling: Towards a spatial politics of affect, *Geografiska Annaler* 86(1), 57–78

Tinker A, Wright F, McCreadie C, Askham J, Hancock R and Holmans A (1999) *With respect to old age: Long term care – rights and responsibilities. Alternative models of care for older people*, Research vol. 2, report for the Royal Commission on the Funding of Long Term Care, Cm 4192-II/2, London: The Stationery Office

Torgerson U (1987) Housing: The wobbly pillar under the welfare state, in Turner B, Kemeny J and Lunqvist L (eds) *Between state and market: Housing in the post-industrial era*, Stockholm: Almqvist and Wicksell International, 116–26

Townsend P (1962) *The last refuge*, London: Routledge and Kegan Paul

Townsend P (1979) *Poverty in the United Kingdom*, Harmondsworth: Penguin

Triangle Consulting (2014) Outcomes star, outcomes star.org.uk

Tsemberis S, Gulcur L and Nakae M (2004) Housing first, consumer choice, and harm reduction for homeless individuals with a dual diagnosis, *American Journal of Public Health* 94: 651–6

Turner B and Whitehead C (2002) Reducing housing subsidy: Swedish housing policy in an international context, *Urban Studies* 39, 201–17

Tyne A (1982) Community care and mentally handicapped people, in A Walker (ed.) *Community care*, Oxford: Blackwell and Robertson

Van Kempen R and Bolt G (2012) Social consequences of residential segregation and mixed neighbourhoods, in D Clapham, W Clark and K Gibb (eds) *The Sage handbook of housing studies*, 439–60

Wacquant L (2008) *Urban outcasts: A comparative sociology of advanced marginality*, Cambridge: Polity Press

Wahl H, Iwarsson S and Oswald F (2012) Aging well and the environment: Toward an integrative model and research agenda for the future, *The Geronologist* 52(3), 306–16

Walsh PN, Emerson E, Lobb C, Hatton C, Bradley V, Schalock RL et al (2010) Supported accommodation for people with intellectual disabilities and quality of life: an overview, *Journal of Policy and Practice in Intellectual Disabilities* 17(2),137–42

Wilcox S and Perry J (2014) *UK housing review*, Coventry: Chartered Institute of Housing

Wilkinson R (2005) *The impact of inequality: How to make sick societies healthier*, London: The New Press

Wilkinson R and Pickett K (2009) *The spirit level: Why more equal societies almost always do better*, London: Allen Lane

Willcocks D, Peace S and Kellehar L (1987) *The residential life of older people*, London: Polytechnic of North London

Williams V (2013) *Learning disability policy and practice: Changing lives*, Basingstoke: Palgrave Macmillan

Willmott P (1986) *Social networks, informal care and public policy*, London: Policy Studies Institute

Wolfensberger W (1972) *The principle of normalization in human services*, Toronto: National Institution of Mental Retardation

Young M and Willmott P (1957) *Family and kinship in East London*, London: Routledge and Kegan Paul

Index

Page spans may indicate repeated mentions rather than continuous discussion.